The Quest for Sanity

The Quest for Sanity

REFLECTIONS ON SEPTEMBER 11 AND THE AFTERMATH

A PUBLICATION OF

MCB
The Muslim Council of Britain
September 2002

In the name of God, the Most Gracious, the Ever Merciful

"Verily, God commands justice and
the doing of good, and liberality to kin, and
He forbids all shameful and evil deeds, and oppression.
He instructs you, that perchance you may take heed."

(THE QUR'AN, 16: 90)

"O you who believe!
Be of those who stand firmly before God as witnesses of justice.
And let not (even) the hatred of a people make you swerve from justice.
Be just - that is closer to piety.
And be conscious of God
For indeed God is well-acquainted with all that you do."

(THE QUR'AN, 5: 8)

O human beings!
We have indeed created you
from a single pair of a male and a female and have
made you into nations and tribes that you may know one another.
Indeed, the most honourable of you in the sight of God
is the one who is most deeply conscious of Him.

(THE QUR'AN, 49: 13)

Published by
The Muslim Council of Britain
P O Box 52, Wembley
Middlesex HA9 0XW
United Kingdom

Tel: 020 8903 9024
Fax: 020 9803 9026
Email: media@mcb.org.uk
Website: http://www.mcb.org.uk
Orders: http://www.mcb.org.uk/books

Published September 2002
ISBN 0-9543652-0-8

Design Zafar Abbas Malik

Printed and bound by
The Cromwell Press
Trowbridge
Wiltshire, UK

The Quest for Sanity CONTENTS

8 ISLAMIC VALUES

FOREWORD

All praise and gratitude is due to God, the Sustainer of all creation.
We praise Him and seek His help, guidance and forgiveness.

For the three thousand innocent people from twenty-eight nations who lost their lives on September 11, 2001 and the several thousand others who have subsequently lost their lives elsewhere, our prayers are for them – may God grant them eternal peace. For their surviving loved ones, we pray that God Most Gracious will bless them and grant them succour and strength and enable them to triumph over evil.

What happened on September 11, 2001 was simply evil and criminal. Regrettably, it has been used to set a global course of action with little respect for human life, national sovereignty and the rule of law.

In the process, Muslims the world over and the cherished religion of Islam – a religion for all humanity – have been made the focus of irrational anger and hate. Fortunately, however, there are many voices clamouring for sanity and justice. We expect that these voices will grow and that they shall eventually prevail.

Terrorism has no religion. Its aim is to spread enmity and destruction throughout civilised societies. In combating terrorism we must ensure that we ourselves do not terrorise others and dehumanise ourselves. It is time that the international community freed itself from the calculus of terror and direct all its energy towards building a just and terror-free world.

The Quest for Sanity is an attempt to reflect on the many and varied challenges that the world now faces in the wake of that fateful day.

In response to these challenges, we are deeply conscious of the fact that Islam places a unilateral obligation on Muslims towards the welfare of their fellow human beings and the societies in which they live and to work for the common good of all. The need to protect and preserve social order is a supreme value in Islam.

We should always be careful not to be provoked or to act in anger lest we be distracted from our fundamental commitment to Islam and humanity. We need to play our full and equal part in the life of our nation if society is to overcome its prejudices and phobias about Islam. In this, we acknowledge the efforts of all our affiliates in The Muslim Council of Britain as well as others in the community and the wider society who are working for the welfare and stability of our society.

We are grateful to all those who have contributed to this publication as writers and sponsors. I would also like to record my appreciation for the support of the office bearers and my other MCB colleagues and in particular the effort of AbdulWahid Hamid, Jamil Sherif, Inayat Bunglawala and Zahra Williams in putting together this book.

May Almighty God reward them abundantly and guide us all.

Iqbal AKM Sacranie OBE
Secretary General
The Muslim Council of Britain

INTRODUCTION

All people – the world over – who respect the sanctity of human life and who have a sense of justice and what is right were horrified as they watched planes ploughing into the twin towers in New York and the Pentagon in Washington. That fateful day remains etched in the consciousness of the world. What madness, what cold, pre-meditated madness could ever contemplate, let alone execute, such a horrendous crime in which thousands of innocent people were bound to, and did perish?

As we recall that fateful day, we register again the abhorrence that we feel towards such inhuman atrocities and acts of wanton destruction. We pray for all those who were murdered on that day. And we pray that God in His infinite grace will give strength and succour to the loved ones – the parents, the spouses, the children – the friends and colleagues of those whose lives and hopes ended in such a horrible way. We know - just as we know that there must be the final Judgement to come - that in the fullness of time, the planners and perpetrators of these atrocities will get their just recompense.

The purpose of this book is to reflect on that day of horror and anguish. The first piece in Section One evokes some of the range of emotions displayed then and two other pieces draw attention to some of the finest human qualities that such appalling events can produce. Simultaneously, across the world from New York, in London, a young mother realises she has cause to be anxious. But Sarah Joseph's piece is much more than dealing with anxiety. Here also, up front, is a record of the swift and unanimous condemnation by Muslim leaders and scholars throughout the world of these atrocities. Their responses clearly set out Islamic teachings while getting rid of the canard put out by some in high places that Muslims were tardy or even hypocritical in their condemnations.

Section Two focuses on how British Muslims as a community responded to September 11. The Muslim Council of Britain as a national umbrella body, found itself in the eye of the storm and sought to discharge its responsibilities with faithfulness to the noble teachings of Islam which stress the honour our Creator has bestowed on the children of Adam, and the sanctity of human life.

In the face of potential and actual harm, the MCB sought as best as it could, and hopefully with wisdom, to protect the well-being of the community. It articulated and circulated widely the nature and the implications of 'Our Social Contract' with the state and society in which we live. 'As citizens of Britain,' it declared, 'we have a social contract to maintain the peace and stability of this country', to 'uphold the rule of law and follow ethical policies both at home and abroad'.

Office-bearers of the MCB, chairpersons of the various committees and others met with Government ministers, leaders of faith communities, the Commissioner of the Metropolitan Police, the Greater London Authority, local education authorities, school teachers and others to discuss how best to safeguard the community and promote harmony in society. A number of positive and practical initiatives came from these meetings such as the standing consultation between the police and representatives of the Muslim community to discuss and deal with problems as they arise on a regular basis.

Again and again, the MCB and its affiliates found that it had support from many individuals and institutions in the wider society. The forces for good are not always silent. It is the voices of hate and bigotry that are often louder and bolder. We quote some memorable samples of both in our Section Three which includes the cautionary words of the Bishop of London in 'Careless words cost lives'. His call for the 'common defence of the values and laws which make civilised co-existence possible' must be heeded. Such voices of honesty and compassion have sustained, and continue to sustain many a vulnerable individual and community in times of anxiety and fear.

As Inayat Bunglawala's account here shows, sections of the British media fuelled the fear of Islam and worked to demonise Muslims, sometimes with help from other Muslims on the fringe - the people whom they love to hate. Moreover, there are politicians and even members of the Government who have singled out the Muslim community as being 'integration-resistant'. Again, as always, there have been sane voices bucking the negative trend and people who are prepared to stand up for truth and justice and human dignity. Inayat concludes that the Muslim community is an integral part of pluralist Britain and that the British character of this community should be recognised in order for Muslims to assume their rightful place in the nation's future.

Brian Whitaker, the Middle East Editor of *The Guardian*, refreshingly argues that in spite of the negative effects, 'September 11 has also created an opportunity for British Muslims'. While far more readers of newspapers come across Islam and Muslims more frequently than before – and this he shows by statistical data, it is now up to Muslims to ensure that the coverage of Islam and Muslims is 'both fair and accurate'. He encourages The Muslim Council of Britain to provide 'a simple, factual guide to the things journalists should know about Islam'. This needs to be done bearing in mind, of course, that in the matter of winning minds and hearts there can be no quick fixes.

Other pieces deal with media coverage and the stereotyping of Muslims in a negative way. This evidently is now a global sport. Professor Mohamed Elmasry, national president of the Canadian Islamic Congress, points out in his piece on Muslims and the media in Canada that 'Some Canadian media have taken pains to restate their anti-Islam and anti-Muslim biases often enough to convince the vulnerable and uninformed among their readers and listeners that the worst possible things are probably true of *all* Canadian Muslims – including their next-door neighbours, co-workers, colleagues, medical professionals and others'.

In a comment that has powerful resonance for us here in Britain, Elmasry states: 'But anti-Islam in the media is not our sole concern. Canadian Muslims are also very disturbed about the increasing pressure to link patriotism, the idea of being a "good citizen", with unqualified support for enormous government increases in military spending, the passing of multiple anti-terrorism laws, and the economic and cultural Americanization of Canada at the expense of all other priorities, particularly those that our country traditionally valued, such as the elimination of homelessness and child poverty.'

There is thus plainly a growing awareness of the extent to which this 'war on terrorism' is helping to destroy the fabric of normal civic society, causing fear, distress and hardship throughout the world and dehumanising us all.

In Britain, the events of September 11 continue to have grave repercussions. Mahmud Al Rashid shows how in October 2001, the UN Human Rights Committee expressed concerns about the UK government's plans to extend anti-terrorist legislation in the wake of September 11. And he argues that 'combating terrorism should not become an aim in itself, but rather the achievement of a just, humane and free society should be our goal'.

The distressing stories are recounted of two individuals and their families who have suffered, one through over-zealousness or sheer bloody-mindedness on the part of the law and the other through blind hate.

The cases against alleged suspects like Lotfi Raissi have been found wanting in courts of law because of lack of evidence. There is alarm that the Home Office's sweeping powers for detention post-September 11 are affecting the due process for checking evidence. This can only damage the integrity of the criminal justice system in the long term. The consequences of secret unaccountable government should surely have been learned after the Scott Inquiry into the arms-for-Iraq affair that held its public hearings in 1993-94 and which dramatically highlighted the victimisation of innocent people by covert agencies pursuing their own agendas.

'It is not a war against Islam and Muslims,' the British Prime Minister and others kept on saying. Yet, it is almost exclusively Muslim individuals, groups and institutions that are bearing the brunt of harassment, the erosion of civil liberties, financial hardship and ruin.

Section Four and parts of section Six consider the consequences of the climate of fear that is fuelled by a manic media and its awesome power to demonise. There has been a rise in Islamophobia as the EU Monitoring Commission report has shown. Christopher Allen, one of the co-authors of the Report together with Professor Jorgen Nielson, describes the context and the climate in which the report was prepared. Much in the same vein, we include a significant piece of the academic research of Dr Lorraine Sheridan of the University of Leicester. These document the rise of religious discrimination against Muslims in parts of Britain and throughout Europe in the wake of the September 11 atrocities. In Britain, Muslims do not have any protection under the law for discrimination against them on religious grounds.

We do not in any way try to make out that Muslims are the salt of the earth and deserve special treatment and consideration. But there are certain improvements that can be made in the legislative provisions of the country that would give Muslims the same protection that other communities in Britain enjoy and make them less vulnerable. While a Jew or a Sikh has protection against discrimination under the Race Relations Act, Muslims – since they do not belong to a particular race or ethnic group – do not have any legal protection against discrimination on religious grounds not only in the field of employment but in other areas such as the social services, health and public services. The research of Dr Lorraine provides further evidence – if evidence is needed – for the need to have laws introduced in Britain to afford protection against discrimination on religious grounds. We urge the

Home Secretary to act to meet this long standing need and cogently argued case for a reform of the law in this regard.

Side by side with this of course is the need for education and better community relations. In this Muslims themselves need to play a more active role. The experience of the Muslim community of Exeter is a wonderful example of good practice in this field. No doubt such examples of openness, trust and mutual support are to be found in various parts of the country. These examples need to be replicated.

Acts of human rights abuses in Britain, serious as they are, appear much less so when looked at in the context of the horrifying global war on terror. This book would be of no moral worth if it did not deal with the terrible aftermath and the continuing fallout of the bold and unchallenged responses on the part of the most powerful nation on earth.

Sadly and almost immediately after September 11, the United States unleashed its 'war on terrorism'. Dutifully, the British government and others joined this 'war' that really has no frontiers, no laws, and no scruples. The manner in which this 'war' has been and is being prosecuted remains profoundly disturbing. The primary declared target of this war has been an individual and a group (once funded and supported by the United States) who have been held responsible for the September 11 attacks, and against the government of a country that provided them a safe haven. The spokesman for this government kept on insisting on the need to be shown 'the evidence' that the alleged perpetrators were involved the atrocities in the US, and stressed their willingness to extradite them if this evidence was produced. Surely, that was fair and civilised.

That government has been smashed. The innocent poor, battered, hungry and starving people of Afghanistan have paid with their lives, and the awesome natural beauty of that land has been further pulverized by tons of ordnance from the skies. There seems to be no respite for this wretched country, stricken by years of drought and famine, devastated by foreign invasion, super power machinations and the ferocious rivalry of Afghan warlords.

The atrocities committed on September 11 were base deeds. The aftermath of September 11 has seen further baseness. It is as if a stage had been set awaiting an event, once transpired, would allow the wheels of a plot to continue their well-oiled course. There has been the most cynical and opportunistic power-play after September 11. Thus the United States has extended its hegemony in resource-rich Central Asia and numerous tyrannies from Israel to China have been able to act with even greater ruthlessness under the convenient cover of 'fighting terrorism'. Racists and anti-Muslim ideologues have also been emboldened and Islam, derived from the word meaning 'peace' and which literally means devotion to God, stands much maligned.

Yet, in spite of the devastation that has been unleashed against Afghanistan, the world has still not been shown any evidence and no evidence has been produced, let alone subjected to any judicial scrutiny. All the conventions of international law have been set aside to wage this war. These are some of the themes explored and the questions raised in the critical piece by Professor Khurshid Ahmad. Questions refuse to go away. Is this the basis of conducting international relations? Are there hidden agendas (recall the book by the courageous writer and journalist John Pilger) behind the 'war against terrorism'? These are questions that ordinary people in the world are asking more and more. Will we ever get satisfactory answers? Will the truth ever be out?

There is now a sinister agenda based on 'pre-emptive strike' against any real or concocted threat, and 'regime change'. The very parties that supplied and condoned the use of chemical weapons against the Kurds of Iran and Iraq are now clamouring to justify the invasion of Iraq, citing possession and possible use of weapons of mass destruction as their reason! Even as they advance their arguments, they continue to tolerate the weapons of mass destruction held by preferred regional allies like Israel. The war on terror is increasingly emerging as a pretext for wars to gain strategic control of oil resources and the possible redrawing of regional maps without any concern for people's lives and the pain and suffering they leave behind for decades. The statement by Mo Mowlam quoted in the 'Sane Voices' section is instructive.

The war on terror has spread and has already claimed more innocent lives than the terrorist attacks on New York and Washington. While everyone across the globe has been affected in varying ways by these events, it is true to say that the primary focus of world attention has fallen on Muslims and Islam.

While governments and many institutions in the West and elsewhere have been keen to say that the 'War on Terror' is 'not a war against Islam and Muslims' measures being taken in the US and other parts of the world are almost solely targeted at Islam and Muslims. Dr Daud Abdullah in his piece shows how this war is being used as a cover to create mayhem and erode human rights and civil liberties on a massive scale in many countries of the world. In this context, it may be interesting to note that the late Israeli chemistry professor, Dr Israel Shahak of the Peace Now movement and known for his courageous defence of Palestinian human rights, warned of what he called the mounting of a 'cosmic war against Islam and Muslims'. Not just a 'global' but a 'cosmic' war. Such a war he said was conceived as part of Israeli Zionist strategy. Section Six of this book highlights some aspects of the global impact of the war on terrorism.

The piece by a young American writer Tavis Adibuddeen describes what is happening in the USA where individuals have been locked up without charges or the need to produce any evidence and where the funds of all the major Muslim charities have been frozen. Many sane Americans, including courageous academics and public figures (see *The Guardian*, June 14, 2002 for details of the 'Not in Our Name' campaign) have protested and continue to protest against the oppressive measures of their government.

War propaganda sets out to demonise and cast the perceived enemy or the 'other' in gruesome caricatures. At the turn of the last century, British rivalry with the Ottomans created a genre of black propaganda in which Sultan Abdul Hamid was depicted on posters with blood dripping from his mouth. In the same vein the propagandists during the Great War put out the story that the Kaiser ate babies. The Germans responded by spreading the rumour that the King-Emperor had taken flight from London and had been seen in Lucknow! In the Vietnam war, Ho Chi Minh was portrayed as a 'mad man' by the Nixon entourage.

Daily, throughout many countries of the world, Muslims are being called upon to defend themselves and the religion of Islam from scurrilous attacks. It is not just ill-informed hacks who are guilty (we do of course pay tribute to the fine and courageous journalists and feature writers to whom the world owes a continuing debt of gratitude).

The venomous falsehood also and often comes from academics in prestigious universities. It sometimes appears that this is their sole raison d'etre, whether they are located in London, Princeton or Montreal. They say that the evil in the world does not just come from extremist groups of fanatics and fundamentalists who are out to destroy the West and civilization itself. The evil that is perpetrated by Muslims, they say, is not simply part of the aberrant behaviour of misguided individuals or hate-filled groups.

And there are, it is sad and painful to say, such individuals and groups in some Muslim communities and society. And we are not just talking of the usual range of criminals. We are talking of people who in the name of Islam have torched churches and murdered worshippers, who have attacked and killed visitors to their country and who have even turned their murderous hate on their fellow Muslims. Such acts, we know, have absolutely no justification in Islam. However, we need to be careful in attributing responsibility when such crimes are committed. Just one recent spectacular example: the bombings in early 2000 that blew up residential blocks in Moscow and caused massive destruction and carnage. They were blamed on Chechen Muslim 'terrorists' but turned out to be the work of Putin himself and elements in the GRU (the Russian military intelligence service) and were used as the pretext for unleashing more terrorism on an already pitiful and ruined Chechnya. What cold, pre-meditated madness could ever contemplate, let alone execute, such murderous crimes against one's own fellow citizens? In a letter to Prime Minister Tony Blair on the eve of his visit to Moscow in March 2000, The Muslim Council of Britain drew his attention to Putin's 'dirty tricks'. The same Putin, can one imagine, is now shoulder to shoulder with the USA and Britain in their war on terror.

So, the evil that besets the world, it is now often said, comes not from misguided individuals and vicious groups, but from the religion of Islam itself and from its principal sources, the Qur'an and the precedents of the Prophet Muhammad (may God bless him and grant him peace). We hear glib statements backed by spurious scholarship that Islam is fundamentally illiberal and cannot fit in with modernity – whatever this is, that it is inherently violent and misogynous, that it is oppressive in its treatment of minorities. We thus find veteran academics like Professor Bernard Lewis and his proteges calling for the 'reformation' of Islam while others work to bring it in line with secular universalism, and so on.

The 'war on terror' is not being waged by military means alone, but by economic strangulation, the introduction of draconian laws that allow people to be held, detained and even 'disappeared' without the need for any evidence let alone proof of guilt being shown. It is also a propaganda war and a total war on all fronts for dismantling the cultural heritage, demonising the values and subverting the way of life of more than a billion people on earth. Recall President Bush enlisting the popular entertainment skills of the moguls of the Hollywood film industry after 9/11 in the war against terror. And a new music and news radio station has been launched in Arabic to target youth listeners in the Middle East. It is nothing but terror in the name of civilization; it is falsehood in the name of civilization; it is greed in the name of civilization.

This war is against all the fundamental values that Americans proclaim: 'We hold these truths to be self-evident that all men are created equal, that they are endowed by their Creator with certain inalienable rights, that among these are life, liberty and the pursuit of happiness.' These glorious words are known and repeated by all Americans. The sane people of America need to distance themselves from the power-driven 'segment of

US society' (see the quote in 'Sane Voices') and reclaim these self-evident truths, so that others may regain their inalienable rights to life, liberty and the pursuit of happiness. To deny these to others is to deny them to ourselves. For no oppressor and no tyrant can ever be free.

Now, as part of the war on terror, we thus hear calls and measures to close down Qur'anic schools or madrasahs, often the only providers of literacy in some of the poorest parts of the world. These measures strike at the very foundations of Islamic education and Muslim societies, and even of enlightened human society itself. Those who have any understanding of history would know that the Qur'anic legacy has had a positive and critical mark on European development. There is of course no doubt that the content of curricula and educational methods in Muslim institutions need urgent and wide-ranging improvement. But this does not mean that they should be rooted out. This is nothing but arrogant imperialism and it is reasonable to expect that it will be resolutely resisted.

Conscious Muslims are the first to recognise that the Muslim ummah throughout the world is in a right old mess and much needs to be done – on all fronts and at all levels – to make this ummah both as a whole and as individuals reflect in a genuine way the ideals and values of Islam. There is the propensity on the part of Muslims to blame others constantly for all that is wrong in themselves and in their societies. While there are indeed historical and continuing efforts to destabilize Muslim societies – and this is undoubtedly a major, if not the major, purpose of the war against terror – Muslims need to recognize that their regeneration can only come from within the authentic and broad worldview of Islam and through their own efforts.

Section Seven focuses again on Britain and examines the unique unfolding of the British Muslim identity with pieces on aspects of community and citizenship and the challenge of connecting to the wider world. Work needs to be done to engender a positive sense of belonging and responsible citizenship amongst Muslim youth. The Muslim family and community have their important role to play, though much can be done at school through improved curricula and other institutional initiatives. The British Isles is now home to 1.8 million Muslims. They form part of the future of the country – 50% are under the age of 30. The section shows that the British Isles has long-standing connections with Islam going back a millennium. Muslims and Islam are inherent in the social fabric. Muslims are not a minority community, but Britons whose way of life is Islam.

Our final section on Islamic Values seeks to show that Islam with its firm points of reference is in accord with the best of human nature and seeks to protect and promote the finest values of human freedom and responsibility.

Two pieces by Professor Muhammed Abdel Haleem, a scholar who has a rare appreciation of the richness and subtleties of Qur'anic Arabic, show how the lofty, tolerant and humane religion of Islam has been misunderstood and misinterpreted by some scholars, including some Muslims themselves. These pieces are excerpts from his recent 'Understanding the Qur'an – Themes and Style' which is one book no current writer on Islam and Muslims can ignore.

Other pieces give a glimpse of the noble character of the Prophet Muhammad and his unchallenged reputation for truthfulness, trustworthiness and integrity. We believe that the world will be a dark and spiritually impoverished place without the clarity, the intellectual soundness, and the stable moral underpinning of Islam properly understood.

This of course does not make Muslims any the less committed to pluralism and the respect for the right of people to nurture their multiple cultures. This commitment is not something that springs from convenience and opportunism but is derived from the Qur'an itself and the precedents of the noble Prophet Muhammad as he drew up what has been described as the first written constitution of the world (see the piece by the Sudanese scholar, Professor Zakaria Bashier). These are the sort of binding precedents that make The Muslim Council of Britain genuinely committed to pluralism and participation in the public life of our country.

Muslims wish and are required to live in peace and harmony with their neighbours whatever their faiths, ethnicities and mother tongues. It may be considered remarkable that the Prophet Muhammad instructed a group of his persecuted companions in the early days of his mission to seek asylum in a Christian country. But this wonderful story shows, among other things, that the virtues of compassion and justice are not the preserve of any one people, religion or civilization but are universal human values which we all need to internalise and uphold.

The world, however, now stands at a crossroads – the descent to a jungle where might is right and xenophobia prevails, or the ascent to civilised values and mutual respect – surely the saner way.

This book was put together in a very short space of time. We wish to thank all those who responded, some with amazing speed, to requests for contributions and expertise. We pray that it will be of some benefit in these perilous times.

AbdulWahid Hamid

1

A Morning of Horror,
Days of Anguish

Yours, Faithfully

KAAMILEH HAMID

Despair does not tread a lonely path. He gathers people to his bosom in a cold embrace and feeds them panic in doses some are unable to withstand - some, that is, caught firmly in his clutches. Others reach out a hand to Courage and are set free. They warmly link arms and hold their heads up high, together, with valour and dignity.

It is all too easy to say 'I know how you feel' but is true empathy merely a fallacy?

Picture yourself in the shoes of those who were victims that fateful September 11 – a day where calling 911 would have been too little too late. Picture yourself standing and watching a wave of rubble, blasting splinters of glass and life-choking dust, surge forwards towards you, engulfing you and knowing there was nothing you could do, knowing that your screams would only be stifled and not heard.

Try to chase away the images that fly in swarms in your mind as a plague, and fail you will. The world was advised that the scenes broadcast on the television might be unsuitable for those less able to handle such horror. Watching person after person hurl themselves from the imploding buildings to the cement streets below in the hope that they would be safe only begs the question – who could be prepared for scenes such as this?

Picture yourself in a plane staring with wide-eyed helplessness out of a cubby hole of a window, knowing that you have nowhere to go. Picture yourself knowing that you will not see the light of days to come or the shining faces of those you love.

Imagine the scenes of carnage, the endless searching, the endless hoping. And then the reality of it all for you, that the miracle of finding your mother, your father, your brother or sister, those you love, would never be. Imagine the scores of people running, standing and kneeling with blood and tears flowing freely together down raw cheeks. Picture the anguish of those frantically pacing hospital corridors in search of someone special to them.

Look. Remember. That is what you will see.

In those pictures, you would only have glimpsed the shadow of Despair and not stared him in the face, as did those that terror-stricken day. Yes, they stared but they did not bond intimately. No, they stood apart, far apart, preparing for a duel. Despair has a place but not beside Courage. Despair has a place but not beside Faith and Trust in God and Belief in a life, yet unseen, a source of boundless Hope.

Look. Remember. You shall see a difference.

You will see emerging from the swirling dust, a fireman cradling your loved one, you will see a hand held out to another in common humanity, common love of life.

Look again and you will see a man carrying in his arms a disabled lady down flight after flight of stairs, doctors and nurses working tirelessly to relieve the pain of the overflowing stream of ailing. Those in cities far, far away giving what they could – giving blood, giving money and prayer after prayer, tear after tear.

Look again and you will see food being donated to keep the hunger of the rescue workers at bay, to keep them strong, and fearless. You'll see the smoldering ashes illuminated by the ever glowing, bright searchlights, illuminating too the dirt-streaked faces full of determination to find every last living soul and to put to rest others in dignity.

Never will you see humanity work together so well except when Tragedy knocks loudly on the door. On September 11 he was certainly beating vehemently.

Those horror filled minutes, those hours, those days will forever be etched in the minds and hearts of many. In them pain and sorrow is found in abundance. Bittersweet memories of times of old will flitter with saddening continuity - the magnificence of the twin towers, the apple of New York's eye, the Pentagon and all in it, and the many brave on the plane which crashed in the fields of Pennsylvania will not be forgotten. All of these places were filled with bustling activity. People laughed and talked, life was ever present and destruction was far from the thoughts of all.

That was then but what of now? The past has a strange way of becoming the present and the present of becoming the future. Many will look into the eyes of a youth and see the reflection of the child's father – now gone. To all those left behind in a tide of angst and misery it is easy to say that the pain will begin to subside – easy to say but not an easy thing to live with. To all of those who exist with the visions, the smells and the feeling of being trapped, of wanting to escape, it is easy to say live and learn – but it's not so easy to move on.

Those who visit Ground Zero today, speak of a silence of such magnitude that you are left in awe. It is a cavern, a void in a city that never sleeps. Buildings rise up to the heavens above, towering over you and you know with certainty that nothing, nothing on this earth would be able to replace what was lost – not the buildings, not the lives, not the love and not the memories that some hoped would have been made.

It is difficult to see how the world will emerge and grow in the wake of such enormity. Years from now, when the young are older and the older have seen too much, we shall ask each other where we were on September 11 and we shall trade stories of hardship and of lessons learned and Faith will gather us to his bosom in a warm embrace feeding us doses of compassion all can imbibe.

A Tribute to
Mohammed Salman Hamdani

NATASHA RAFI

New York recently bestowed its highest honours on a young Pakistani-American who gave his life saving others on September 11, 2001.

In a home on a quiet street in Bayside, Queens, a Pakistani-American family and a dog named Ulysses mourn the loss of a son, brother, and best friend, an unusual victim of 9/11.

Twenty-three year old Mohammed Salman Hamdani lived here and worked far from the Twin Towers in the relatively secluded Upper East Side of Manhattan. He had no known reason to be near Ground Zero that day, but apparently rushed toward the burning towers to help. His selfless act was completely misunderstood at first and his disappearance that morning fed rumours that he was in some way linked to the attacks. Later it became clear that Sal, as he was known by his friends, gave his life at the World Trade Centre in a courageous attempt to save others.

Now, after six long months, Hamdani's reputation finally has been cleared and he has been eulogised as an American hero and martyr. At his funeral service on 5 April, 2002 New York Mayor Michael Bloomberg, Police Commissioner Raymond Kelly and dozens of his fellow police cadets sat barefoot on the carpeted floor of the Islamic Centre mosque in Manhattan, as family members and others paid their tributes to a young man who was a Star Wars fan and whose license plate read 'Yung Jedi'. Congressman Gary Ackerman presented the family with a US flag that had flown over the Capitol building, noting that Hamdani was "a hero and a real martyr in the finest sense".

"We have an example of how one can make the world better," said Bloomberg. "Salman stood up when most people would have gone in the other direction. He went in and helped people."

For his parents, Saleem and Talat Hamdani, there was never any question; they knew Sal would have gone to help. Still, they hoped he was alive, even hoped he was one of those detained for questioning by authorities, as dozens of Muslim men were at the time.

That fragile hope came to an end on the night of 20 March this year, when two police officers from the local precinct drove up to the Hamdani home to deliver the news that Sal's remains had been identified and he had indeed perished in lower Manhattan on that infamous day. At Hamdani's long-delayed funeral, attended by several hundred mourners, his mother addressed her firstborn in a heartfelt tribute. "The day you were born I came to know the joy of motherhood," she said. "Today I understand its pain. Salman, you wouldn't let me celebrate your graduations. 'This is nothing to be proud of, Mama. I will tell you when to celebrate.' So you did. You told the world loud and clear when to celebrate today."

Hamdani was born in Karachi and was just 13 months old when his family moved to the US in 1979. He was a trained medical technician and member of the police cadet corps. Last year, he graduated from Queens College with a major in chemistry and was applying to medical school while he worked full time at Rockefeller University as a lab analyst. Just the weekend before September 11, Hamdani was writing his application essays.

On the night of 10 September, 2001 his father recalls, "I was not feeling very well so Salman checked my blood pressure and told me to call him if I needed him." That was the last time Mr. Hamdani saw his son. The next morning Mrs. Hamdani left home at 7:30 a.m. for her job as a seventh-grade English teacher.

Salman usually left for work at around 8:15 a.m. No one knows for sure when he left that fateful morning of 9/11, or how he managed to get to ground zero, since traffic in Manhattan had been halted shortly after the disaster. The best guess is that Hamdani may have seen the Towers burning from the elevated tracks of the Number 7 train he used to take from Queens to his job in Manhattan. As fate would have it, he did not bring his cell phone with him that morning, having left it at work the previous day. Police say that it is likely he was able to hitch a ride on a police car or ambulance, since he carried police ID.

Later that afternoon Hamdani's uncle went to Rockefeller University and found out that his nephew had never shown up for work. Three days later his parents officially reported him missing and discovered something about their son which they had never known before. Hamdani was a registered bone marrow donor, a fact that eventually helped in identifying his remains through DNA analysis.

A month later, on 11 October, a US Senate bill was passed that mentioned Hamdani as an example of patriotism under section 102 (6). "Many Arab-Americans and Muslim Americans have acted heroically during the attacks on the United States, including Mohammed Salman Hamdani, a 23-year-old New Yorker of Pakistani descent, who is believed to have gone to the World Trade Centre to offer rescue assistance and is now missing."

Mrs. Hamdani has established a memorial fund in her son's name at Rockefeller University to provide scholarships to Pakistani-American students who wish to pursue medicine.

Immigrant Muslims are painfully aware that the attacks on September 11 have affected their image in their adopted homeland. "My son's actions that day are a glimmer of hope for the community," says Mr. Hamdani, who owns a general store in Brooklyn. "His example is now a part of US history."

From *The Friday Times* of Pakistan, 31 May, 2002

Brother, If You Don't Mind...

USMAN FARMAN

My name is Usman Farman and I graduated from Bentley with a Finance degree last May. I am 21 years old, turning 22 in October; I am Pakistani, and I am Muslim. Until 10 September 2001, I used to work at the World Trade Centre in Building 7. I had friends and acquaintances who worked in Tower 1 right across from me. Some made it out, and some are still unaccounted for. I survived this horrible event.

I'd like to share with you what I went through that awful day, with the hope that we can all stay strong together through this tragedy of yet untold proportions. As I found out, regardless of who we are, and where we come from, we only have each other.

I commute into the city every morning on the train from New Jersey. Rather, I used to. I still can't believe what is happening. That morning I woke up and crawled out of bed. I was thinking about flaking out on the train and catching the late one, I remember telling myself that I just had to get to work on time. I ended up catching the 7:48 train, which put me in Hoboken at 8:20 am. When I got there I thought about getting something to eat, I decided against it and took the PATH train to the World Trade Centre. I arrived there at 8:40 in the morning. I walked into the lobby of building 7 at 8:45 - that's when the first plane hit.

Had I taken the late train, or gotten a bite to eat, I would have been five minutes late and walking over the crosswalk. Had that happened, I would have been caught under a rain of fire and debris. I wouldn't be here talking to you. I'd be dead.

I was in the lobby, and I heard the first explosion; it didn't register. They were doing construction outside and I thought some scaffolding had fallen. I took the elevators up to my office on the 27th floor. When I walked

9

in, the whole place was empty. There were no alarms, no sprinklers, nothing. Our offices are, or rather, were on the south side of building seven. We were close enough to the North and South Towers, that I could literally throw a stone from my window and hit the North tower with it.

My phone rang and I spoke with my mother and told her that I was leaving. At that moment I saw an explosion rip out of the second building. I called my friend in Boston, waking her up and told her to tell everyone I'm okay, and that I was leaving. I looked down one last time and saw the square and fountain that I eat lunch in covered in smouldering debris. Apparently, I was one of the last to leave my building. When I was on the way up in the elevators. My co-workers from the office were in the stairwells coming down. When I evacuated, there was no panic. People were calm and helping each other; a pregnant woman was being carried down the stairwell.

I'll spare the more gruesome details of what I saw, those are things that no one should ever have to see, and beyond human decency to describe. Those are things which will haunt me for the rest of my life. My heart goes out to everyone who lost their lives that day, and those who survived with the painful reminders of what once was. Acquaintances of mine who made it out of the towers, only got out because 1000 people formed a human chain to find their way out of the smoke. Everyone was a hero that day.

We were evacuated to the north side of Building 7, still only one block from the towers. The security people told us to go north and not to look back. Five city blocks later I stopped and turned around to watch. With a thousand people staring, we saw in shock as the first tower collapsed. No one could believe it was happening. It is still all too surreal to imagine. The next thing I remember is that a dark cloud of glass and debris about 50 stories high came tumbling towards us. I turned around and ran as fast as possible. I didn't realize until yesterday that the reason I'm still feeling so sore was that I fell down trying to get away.

I was on my back, facing this massive cloud that was approaching, it must have been 600 feet off, everything was already dark. I normally wear a pendant around my neck, inscribed with an Arabic prayer for safety; similar to the cross. A Hasidic Jewish man came up to me and held the pendant in his hand, and looked at it. He read the Arabic out loud for a second. What he said next, I will never forget. With a deep Brooklyn accent he said, "Brother, if you don't mind, there is a cloud of glass coming at us, grab my hand, let's get the hell out of here." He helped me stand up, and we ran for what seemed like forever without looking back. He was the last person I would ever have thought, who would help me. If it weren't for him, I probably would have been engulfed in shattered glass and debris.

I finally stopped about 20 blocks away, and looked in horror as Tower 2 came crashing down. Fear came over me as I realized that some people were evacuated to the streets below the towers. Like I said before, no one could have thought those buildings could collapse. We turned around and in shock and disbelief began the trek to midtown. It took me three hours to get to my sister's office at 3rd Avenue and 47th Street. Some streets were completely deserted, completely quiet, no cars, no nothing… just the distant wail of sirens. I managed to call home and say I was okay, and get in touch with co-workers and friends whom I feared were lost.

We managed to get a ride to New Jersey. Looking back as I crossed the George Washington Bridge, I could not see the towers. It had really happened.

As the world continues to reel from this tragedy, people in the streets are lashing out. Not far from my home, a Pakistani woman was run over on purpose as she was crossing the parking lot to put groceries in her car. Her only fault? That she had her head covered and was wearing the traditional clothing of my homeland. I am afraid for my family's well being within our community. My older sister is too scared to take the subway into work now. My 8-year-old sister's school is under lockdown and armed watch by police.

Violence only begets violence, and by lashing out at each other in fear and hatred, we will become no better than the faceless cowards who committed this atrocity. If it weren't for that man who helped me get up, I would most likely be in the hospital right now, if not dead. Help came from the least expected place, and goes only to show, that we are all in this together … regardless of race, religion, or ethnicity. Those are principles that this country was founded on.

Please take a moment to look at the people around you. Friends or strangers, in a time of crisis, you would want the nearest person to help you if you needed it. My help came from a man who I would never have thought would normally even speak to me. The one thing that won't help is if we fight amongst ourselves, because it is then that we are doing exactly what they want us to do.

My name is Usman Farman and I graduated from Bentley with a Finance degree last May. I am 21 years old, turning 22 in October; I am Pakistani, and I am Muslim, and I too have been victimized by this awful tragedy. The next time you feel angry about this, and perhaps want to retaliate in your own way, please remember these words: "Brother, if you don't mind, there is a cloud of glass coming at us, grab my hand, let's get the hell out of here."

I have questioned my faith, and have had my faith questioned. I have not found it wanting

SARAH JOSEPH

"Two aeroplanes have gone into the World Trade Centre."
It's my mother's voice. It takes a moment for the words to register,
I can hear them but I can't understand their meaning.

"What?" She repeats the words. Slowly they began to sink in,
"Oh God, I hope it's not Muslims."

Me, a Muslim yet this is my first thought. I am programmed to have this as my first thought. Me - who knows Islam, who lives amongst Muslims. Me - who loves Islam, who loves Muslims, who is a Muslim. O God! What hope the rest.

My second thought? "We're going to get it."

My Mum too thinks it's Muslims, "who else would commit suicide" - her, who knows Muslims, who loves Muslims – she too is programmed. If her – O God! What hope the rest.

With no access to a television I log onto to the BBC's website. I read the words - it is still not registering.

I turn on the radio, Radio 5 Live, "and next we have Anjem Choudhury from the Al-Muhajiroun, a group that wants World domination". And some people believe we are going to be invaded by little green men from Mars – but we don't take them seriously. The words sound like something out of a 1950's alien B-movie. In any other circumstance you would laugh. I reach for my address book and call the show. "We don't know who is responsible yet. Remember Oklahoma. You have to behave responsibly. We have to go out tomorrow in our hijabs. Our children have

to go to school. We have to lead normal lives. You can't have cues like this."
He apologises and promises that all reporting will be balanced.

I call the MCB office, it seems that I'm the first one to break the news
– well I am not going to be their last call.

Still my mind has not taken in the actual events.

A whirlwind day of constant phone calls, finally we eat dinner, or at
least push it around our plates. Mum calls and she speaks to my husband:
"tell Sarah not to wear her scarf tomorrow." He relays the message. What do
you say?

My mum is the first to call the next morning: "How can I take my
scarf off?" I begin to sob down the phone. My tears fall on my three-week-
old baby as she feeds from me. "Should I pretend I am not a Muslim?
Should I tell myself I don't believe in God? Should I lie to the world and to
myself? Should I bring the children up as nothing? Should they change their
names? Should I reverse my son's circumcision? Where does it begin and
where does it end?"

If those that say that "religion is a lifestyle-choice" and refuse us anti-
discrimination legislation could understand how I feel at that moment. If I
could choose another way I would, but to believe in God is as natural to me
as breathing. I can't imagine living any other way. Leading any other life –
other than a life which is conscious of God - would be a lie.

She understands, she agrees with me, she just fears for me. She
remembers the Gulf war when people spat at me in central London, when
they raised their arms in 'Heil Hitler' salutes. She's just a mother and she
fears for her daughter.

I'm just a mother and I fear for my daughter - at three weeks old she
sleeps the sleep of the innocent. If I am to bring up this baby as a Muslim,
then I must make it safe to be one.

And so began a whirl wind few months of interviews and speaking
engagements. So many people were sympathetic, so many people genuinely
wanted to understand - yet still so much uncovered ground, so much
ignorance, so many misconceptions. People wanted to know so I spoke
from the heart. I told an audience at the launch of Islam Awareness Week
which took place in the first week of November:

"Thirteen years ago I became drawn to the simple faith of Islam:
"believe in God and thereafter be upright". Little did I know then that that
decision would lead me to the life it has. A life, where for at least ten of
those years, I have been asked to explain my faith and articulate its message
of peace and justice.

I have never ever felt that there is a conflict with me as a Briton and me as a Muslim. God made me English, and I don't question His motives for doing so. As an English woman, I grew up knowing my rights and my duties, and I feel an intense sense of social obligation towards my community and my society, which my faith enhances and increases.

Yet so easily, my loyalty to my country and my fellow countrymen are called into question. Indeed my very "right" to be here is called into question. The less well educated offer the suggestion that I "bleep off back to my own country"; some broadsheet columnists and commentators politely suggest I abandon any emotional feelings to people of my shared faith for to do otherwise makes me a fifth columnist, then they witter on about Britain as my "host" country.

Britain does not "host" me – this is my home. I am no guest. My family have been here for generations, fought in our wars on land and sea, have dressed the ladies at Victoria's Diamond Jubilee and survived the sinking of the Titanic. The daffodils and tulips of Spring; the roses and lavender of Summer, the very shade of light and the crispness of the air are embedded in my subliminal consciousness so that England is the only place I can ever imagine calling home. I have travelled the world and cannot imagine living anywhere else, indeed nowhere am I more English than when I am abroad! Although I know God created the whole world, He chose that I will always be an English woman wherever I may roam.

But my religious faith is Islam, and Islam is perceived as foreign and a thing apart. It is not foreign – well, only as foreign to these shores as Christianity once was – for both faiths emanate from the same part of the world, come from the same God and hold to the same Prophets.

Many of my fellow countrymen have chosen the same path as I, both now and in the past. I think of William Henry Abdullah Quilliam a Liverpudlian solicitor who embraced Islam in 1887. He headed a fine and active Muslim community in Liverpool – mainly of converts. I think of Lord Headley Al Faruq, not the first, but the *third* peer to embrace Islam; however his was the most public conversion, and caused quite a sensation in 1913!

I mention these gentlemen because they were English Muslims from 100 years ago. They were not quiet wall flowers, indeed they did not always agree with the decisions of the day and spoke out when they felt they had to, but their dignity and position as Englishmen were never brought into question.

Islam Awareness Week has been going for 7 years now, the activities of groups such as the Islamic Society of Britain have been going still longer. It is not the type of work that grabs headlines: it's not aggressive enough!

But it involves hundreds of ordinary Muslims giving up time and energy to tell ordinary people about their faith. This work goes on in local libraries, town halls and school halls, people's homes and the High Street, and never before has this work seemed more urgent, more pressing, more important.

The recent events have drawn Islam once again into the spotlight. Our papers and our televisions show us pictures of angry men with placards, angry men with beards, angry men with turbans, angry men with guns, oppressed women in burkhas, oppressed women - silent. The current crisis is being billed as Islam versus Christianity.

These images and this billing are so far removed from the message of Islam which I know and love that sometimes it is hard to bear.

This whole mess – it is not Islam versus Judaism. Moses went to Pharaoh and asked him to set his people free. He demanded of the powerful Pharaoh that his civilisation not be built on the backs of slaves. He spoke for the poor, the weak, the disposed and the oppressed. His message is in the Qur'an.

This is not Islam versus Christianity. Jesus Christ came to the lost sheep of the children of the house of Israel. He spoke for the poor, the weak, the dispossessed and the oppressed. His message is in the Qur'an.

This is the message of Islam. Islam and consequently Muslims will always speak for the poor, the weak, the dispossessed and the oppressed. A quality I find in my fellow Englishmen who are renowned for speaking up for the under-dog!

Whoever oppresses, even if they claim to be a Muslim, the Qur'anic message stands against them. Islam is versus those who oppress, who spread tyranny, who dispossess, who misuse power - in the name of freedom or in the name of God.

Islam is versus any who act only out of self-interest, whoever they may be.

The Qur'an demands "be just: even if it be against yourself, for justice is closest to God consciousness."

This would seem to be a powerful message for all human beings – as we face the issues of the present crisis, and as a principle for the future. We all want peace, and if we are to attain it, be sure that peace has to be built on the foundation of justice."

"Peace has to be built on the foundation of justice" - how I meant those words.

Isn't that what we all want - peace and a just society? Do we have either?

I was reared to believe that Britain is a just society. That there are basic principles and values which make it so. I was reared on the principle that people are innocent until proven guilty and that we must live by the Rule of Law. These were two of the foundation principles of my upbringing.

I was brought up to believe in British justice - justice based upon a set of rules. I was brought up to believe that if you stuck to the rules then you would never go far astray. I was brought up also to believe that rules applied to individuals, to communities and to countries. As a Muslim those beliefs were enhanced not diminished.

After September 11 I had to examine my faith. My faith in Islam was not shaken to its core, even though those who asked me: "do you feel ashamed to be a Muslim?" thought that it should be.

If Muslims carried out the attack on the World Trade Centre, then those events are so highly unconnected to Islam and on being a Muslim they have no bearing on me or my faith.

However, my faith that we as a nation hold to the principles that we are innocent until proven guilty and that we hold to the Rule of Law - that has been shaken.

We rounded up people and have detained them without trial. We presumed guilt for the attacks even before the buildings collapsed. We ostracised a whole community within our midst - "guilty by shared faith".

We charged, and found guilty, without trial or adherence to law, a man, an organisation and a country. As a consequence there is room for doubt and fantastic conspiracy theories, the gulf of distrust ever widening.

Yet still we bombed a country. Yet still we killed as many Afghan civilians as civilians who were killed in the World Trade Centre.

We want freedom so we lock ourselves in chains.

There was a brief moment when I thought that September 11 would change the world. America had, for the first time in a very long while, the moral high ground. But it was squandered on the altar of "national security." That great monster which swallows up all reason and principle – even the principles we say we are protecting.

The Rule of Law – the foundation of a just and civil society. It is what raises us above the rule of the mob and vigilantism.

"Bobby-Jo is a nigger who looks at white women the wrong way – he must be guilty of Mary-Ann's rape. So Bobby-Jo is strung up on the rope of the Lynch Mob."

"Muslims are fanatics and they hate the West. They must be guilty. So Muslims get lynched."

The attack on Afghanistan seems like State Vigilantism, an International Lynch Mob. Instead of rope however, we had daisy cutters and cluster bombs.

Worse still it gave every regime with a "problem Muslim population" the excuse to deal with it using brutality and violence. It gave every regime an excuse to discard the Rule of Law, if it knew what it was in the first place.

There is no doubt in my mind that Islam speaks for peace and justice. That as a Muslim I am commanded to be just even if it be against myself. I have questioned my faith and have had my faith questioned. I have NOT found it wanting.

However, do we as a nation speak for peace and justice? Would we as Britons be just, even if it be against our own interests? I am questioning my country and I hope I do not find it wanting.

Being a Muslim... Being a Briton... I can't stop being either. Being loyal however doesn't mean silence; loyalty means that I will always try to "be just, even if it be against myself".

Condemnation of September 11 atrocities Statements of Muslim Scholars Worldwide

From the very outset, Muslim scholars and religious leaders of standing across the world have expressed their shock and sorrow at the loss of thousands of lives in New York, Washington and Pennsylvania on September 11. To them, regardless of who was responsible, the events bore absolutely no relation to the teachings of Islam and the exemplary conduct of the noble Prophet Muhammad, may God bless him and grant him peace.

Britain
The Muslim Council of Britain convened a meeting of scholars, imams (mosque leaders) and ulama (religious scholars) on 29 September 2001 at the London Islamic Cultural Centre. The conclusions were then circulated for wider endorsement. The resulting document therefore had the support of the heads of the leading ulama associations in the UK, such as the Jamiat-e-Ulama, Jamiat Ahle Sunnat, the World Islamic Mission, the Jamiat Ahle-Hadith, as well as of heads, directors and imams of the main organisations, mosques and communities in the country, including the UK Islamic Mission, the London Central Mosque, the East London Mosque and the Khoja Shia Ithna 'Asheri Community in Britain. Scholars involved included Rachid Ghannouchi, an intellectual activist, and the Qur'an scholar Saleem Kayani.

In their written statement, the assembly declared that it was a criminal act to take the life of a human being without due process of law. The killing of innocent people whether done by individuals, groups, organisations or state institutions, was condemned in Islam. On this basis the meeting absolutely condemned the atrocities in America on September 11.

The statement was translated into Urdu and Gujarati and circulated to all mosques in the UK. It received wide publicity, and the MCB was contacted by Muslims and the wider community for further information. One respondent was Mr Napier, who tragically lost his brother in the World Trade Centre. He wrote to the MCB: "I have read the statement following the meeting on 29 September of British imams and scholars on this matter and take great comfort from the clarity with which the events of that day have been condemned as, essentially, unIslamic." For the full statement and list of participants and endorsements see the MCB web site.

United States of America
On 12 September Muslim scholars in North America unanimously condemned the attacks on the World Trade Centre and Pentagon. These included Shaikh Muhammad Hanooti, member of the Fiqh Council of North America who stated: "Islam tells us that murdering one person is equal to murdering all humanity. We fear that a great many innocent lives have been lost in this barbaric attack." He added, "We pray to God to enable the people of the United States of America to have peace, stability, security and prosperity."

The Detroit-based Shari'a Scholars Association of North America (SSANA) said that there was no cause that could justify "this type of an immoral and inhumane act that has affected so many innocent American lives". The Association's statement added, "Certainly, there is no justification for these acts from either an Islamic perspective or, in truth, from the perspective of any other moral and freedom-loving people. These acts diminish the freedom of all Americans, including American Muslims. Our condolences go out to all of the victims of these inhumane acts." For further details see http://www.islamonline.net/English/News/2001-09/13/article1.shtml

Saudi Arabia
On 14 September 2001 the head of Saudi Arabia's Islamic judiciary, Shaikh Salih al-Lahidan, described the attacks on New York and Washington as despicable acts. In response to a media question he responded:

> "Attacks upon those who have not attacked you and to kill innocent people who have committed no crime against you are among those things forbidden in Islam ...[Islam] does not allow the shedding of blood except for a legally justified reason ... to kill a person who has not perpetrated any crime, nor done anything deserving of being killed, is considered one of the

major sins and the most heinous of crimes. Accordingly, the crimes that occurred in America are no doubt among the most dangerous criminal acts which Islam in no way agrees with and it is not permissible for anyone to condone. It is an abomination." For the full text of the judge's statement see http://www.thetruereligion.org/lahidan.htm

Another eminent voice from Saudi Arabia has been that of Muhammad Aal ash-Shaikh, the country's Grand Mufti and also head of its 'Committee of Major Scholars'. He declared:

"Due to abundant questions and enquiries that have been brought to us concerning what has happened in the United States of America a few days ago, I say, seeking aid and assistance from God, the Unique; what has happened in the United States of America, in which thousands of souls have passed away, on account of actions that Islamic Law does not sanction, and which are not from this religion - these actions do not agree with the spirit and foundations of the moral and legal code of Islam from numerous angles:

Verily, God commands with justice and benevolence, and the giving (of charity) to kin, and He forbids obscene and evil deeds, and oppression. He cautions you, that perchance you may remember.

God, free is He from all imperfections, says: "O you who believe, be of those who stand up to God as witnesses of justice. And let not the hatred of a people make you swerve away from justice towards them. Verily, be just and that is closer to piety." Hence, even hatred and dislike do not allow the commission of injustice and oppression...

These atrocities that have taken place in the United States – and whatever else of their nature such as plane hijackings and taking people hostage or killing innocent people without a just cause – this is nothing but a manifestation of injustice, oppression and tyranny, which Islamic Law does not sanction or accept. Instead, all this is expressly forbidden and it is among the gravest of sins.

The Muslim who learns the details of his religion, and who

acts on the Book of God and the example of His Prophet (peace be on him) does not allow himself to fall into such actions as these." For full text see http://www.thetruereligion.org/ashshaikh.htm

Iran

On 17 September 2001, Iran's leader Ayatullah Ali Khamenei left no doubt about his strong condemnation of the outrages in New York and in Washington. "Mass killings of human beings are catastrophic acts that are condemned wherever they may happen and whoever the perpetrators and the victims may be," he said. And he warned strongly against a large-scale military assault on Afghanistan.

Source: http://news.bbc.co.uk/1/hi/world/middle_east/1549573.stm

In November 2001, President Khatami, a religious scholar in his own right, visited New York on the occasion of an inter-faith conference. In an address in the Cathedral of St. John the Divine. he began with the following words, "In the name of God, the Merciful, the Compassionate. In this holy place of such a distinguished gathering, I begin in the name of and with the remembrance of God in this time of distress and anguish. More than before, we need to remember His name and seek peace and solace in so doing. My deepest sympathies go to the American people." Referring to the September 11 atrocities he added:

"What we are witnessing in the world today is an active form of nihilism in social and political realms threatening the very fabric of human existence. This new form of active nihilism assumes various names and it is so tragic and unfortunate that some of those names bear a semblance of religiosity and some proclaim spirituality....vicious terrorists who concoct weapons out of religion are superficial literalists clinging to simplistic ideas. They are utterly incapable of understanding that perhaps inadvertently they are turning religion into the handmaiden of the most decadent ideologies."

For full text of the speech see http://www.wcrp.org/RforP/Press%20Releases /KHATAMI_TRANSCRIPT.html

Pakistan

In October 2001, Pakistan's Jamaat-e-Islami, a leading Islamic organisation, through its Vice-President, Professor Khurshid Ahmad, issued a response on behalf of Islamic movements:

Protection of human life and respect for it are among the basic teachings of Islam, and there is no distinction in this regard between Muslim and non-Muslim, man and woman, friend and foe. The value of life is equal for all and to take one's life without justification is in violation of the commands of God and His Prophet. God says in the Qur'an, 'We made Adam and his progeny respectable and dignified.' This refers to all human beings not just Muslims or People of the Scriptures.

Also the Qur'an states:

Do not kill any soul whose killing has been forbidden by Allah, except by right. (17:33)

He who killed any person, unless it be a person guilty of manslaughter, or of spreading chaos in the land, should be looked upon as though he had slain all mankind, and he who saved one life should be regarded as though he had saved the lives of all mankind. (5:32)

How can a religion that imparts such teachings tolerate the killing of innocent people in an act of terrorism? This is why Muslims not only in America and Europe but from all over the world, their movements and the governments of all Muslim countries have felt shock over the death of thousands of people in the terrorist acts of September 11. They have felt it deeply in the core of their hearts and have condemned it without any reservation and have called for bringing the perpetrators to book. To us, this is not an American loss, but the loss of all humanity. The sorrow is not restricted to America; it is shared by all humanity.

For full text see http://www.jamaat.org/Isharat/2001/ish1001.html

Dr Tahir ul Qadri, founder of the Minhaj-ul-Quran movement of Pakistan, on 18 September declared on Pakistan TV, "Terrorism is not allowed in Islam. [Even] in war it is not allowed to destroy buildings, burn or destroy trees or crops so that the earth does not become deserted. It is totally against Islam to kill non-combatants, women, minors, the blind, monks, elderly, those physically incapable of fighting and the insane or delirious. Just killing people (indiscriminately) is not jihad and is against the spirit of Islam. So people must understand that terrorism and jihad are two different things."

Source http://www.therevival.co.uk/news/qadri_ptv.htm

Egypt

At a press conference on Monday 24 September, Shaikh Mohamed Sayed Tantawi, the Grand Imam of Cairo's al-Azhar mosque at the world-famous Al-Azhar University, denounced the "mean and hideous act" of September 11: "Attacking innocent people is not courageous... and will be punished on the Day of Judgment... It's not courageous to attack innocent children, women and civilians."

Source: http://www.ahram.org.eg/weekly/2001/552/p4fall3.htm

OTHER RESPONSES

Joint Declaration of Islamic movements

On 18 September, over 100 prominent Islamic political leaders drawn from across the Muslim world issued a statement expressing their horror on the events of the preceding week. An extract is presented below:

> "We unequivocally condemn the dastardly terrorist attack on establishments in New York and Washington, whose victims belong to some forty countries and major religions of the world. Islam upholds the sanctity of human life as the Qur'an declares that killing one innocent human being is like killing the entire human race. The tragedy of the September 11 is a crime against humanity and Muslims all over the world mourn all victims of this aggression as a common loss of America and the whole world.
>
> We also affirm that victims of terrorism in all parts of the world deserve equal sympathy and concern and all those who stand for the equality of humankind must condemn and fight terrorism in all parts of the world.
>
> We also uphold and affirm the principle that whoever is responsible for acts of terrorism against human beings - individual, group or government - must be brought to book and punished for that without let or discrimination.
>
> But any attempt to arbitrarily punish people in the name of a 'war against terrorism' without establishing through an impartial process the guilt of the suspected would also constitute an act of terrorism and cannot be allowed or condoned. Independent proof of guilt is a minimum demand of principles and justice and natural and international law.

We therefore appeal to all Governments of the world, particularly the US Government, not to resort to any arbitrary or unilateral use of force only on the basis of suspicion nor try to become the accuser, the prosecutor, the judge, and the executor rolled into one. We also beseech the Secretary General of the UN and the leaders of all Arab, Muslim and European countries to play their role in saving the world from wanton bloodshed and escalation of violence leading to greater conflicts and confrontations between the states and the people of the world.

Terrorism can be fought only by resort to means that are just, judicious and conducive to peace and tranquillity in the world. We must not be a party to or even passive spectators of steps that smack of vendetta, vengeance, arrogance and international intimidation. Let all people stand for justice and make a concerted effort to fight terrorism by punishing its perpetrators through due process of law and also strive for the elimination of all the injustices, exploitations and hegemonistic policies that lie at the root of many a terrorism in the world."

Signatories included Mustafa Mashhur, Muslim Brotherhood, Egypt; Qazi Hussain Ahmed, Jamaat-e-Islami, Pakistan; Matiur Rahman Nizami, Jamaat-e-Islami, Bangladesh; Rachid Ghannouchi, Nahda Renaissance Movement, Tunisia; Fadil Noor, Parti Islam, Malaysia; Hedayat Nur Wahid, Parti Keadilan, Indonesia. For the Arabic original see *al-Quds al-Arabi* (London), September 14, 2001, p. 2

Statement of Shaikh Yusuf Al-Qaradawi
The day after September 11, the renowned Muslim scholar Shaikh Yusuf al-Qaradawi denounced the attacks and encouraged Muslims to donate blood to the victims of the attack. He issued a statement stating that:

"Our hearts bleed for the attacks that has targeted the World Trade Centre, as well as other institutions in the United States despite our strong opposition to the American biased policy towards Israel on the military, political and economic fronts. Islam, the religion of tolerance, holds the human soul in high esteem, and considers the attack against innocent human beings a grave sin...

The Prophet, peace and blessings be upon him, is reported

to have said, 'A believer remains within the scope of his religion as long as he doesn't kill another person illegally.' Even in times of war, Muslims are not allowed to kill anybody save the one who is involved in face-to-face confrontation with them. They are not allowed to kill women, old persons, children, or even a monk in his religious seclusion.

Islam never allows a Muslim to kill the innocent and the helpless. If such attacks were carried out by a Muslim, in the name of our religion, I condemn the act and indict the perpetrator. We do confirm that the aggressor deserves the deterrent punishment irrespective of his religion, race or gender. What we warn against, even if this becomes a reality, is to hold a whole nation accountable for a crime carried out by a limited number of people or to characterise a certain religion as a faith that gives support to violence and terrorism."

For an English translation of the interview see http://www.islam-online.net/English/News/2001-09/13/article25.shtml

Statement of Ayatullah Sayyed Muhammed Hussein Fadlallah
On September 14 Ayatullah Fadlallah from Lebanon issued a statement describing the World Trade Centre and Pentagon attacks as "acts of suicide which are not rewarded [by Islam] because they are crimes." He added: "Islamists who live according to the human values of Islam could not commit such horrible crimes

Source: *Agence France Presse*, September 14, 2001

In October 2001 Baroness Thatcher, former British Prime Minister, famously suggested that Muslim religious leaders had not done enough about September 11 and that she "had not heard enough condemnation from Muslim priests (sic)". The facts belie her remarks.

All web site addresses (URLs) referred to above are listed in the MCB web site (www.mcb.org.uk/bookref) as hyperlinks.

2

What the MCB has Done

In the Eye of the Storm
The MCB – Fulfilling Its Responsibilities
◆ ◆ ◆

British Muslim Youth Survey
◆ ◆ ◆

In the Eye of the Storm

The MCB – Fulfilling Its Responsibilities

From September 11 and the critical days and weeks that followed, British Muslims were thrust in the limelight like never before. The Muslim Council of Britain was soon made aware that British Muslims were likely to become targets – whether from sections of the public wanting to vent their anger at whomever they associated with those responsible or from racist groups seeking to exploit the situation.

From the dark hours of that Tuesday, the MCB struggled to correct the dangerous misrepresentations of Islam and Muslims that were beginning to be aired in some sections of the world, and to alert the authorities to unjustified attacks on the life and property of British Muslims. Though the sanctity of life is one of the paramount values of Islam, the power of the media was such that by Tuesday 7.30 pm the MCB had received its first hate mails with bizarre references to 'Islamic terrorism' and 'Islamic violence' (see article by Inayat Bunglawala for examples).

The MCB issued a press statement on the same day with an unequivocal condemnation of the atrocities. Shocked and anguished at the killing of innocents, the MCB grasped every opportunity to convey its abhorrence of the atrocities that claimed thousands of lives from every part of the world, including British Muslims. For those who equated Islam with terrorism, the MCB could but quote from the Qur'an on the sanctity of life in Islam: "Whoever takes an innocent life, it is as if he has killed the whole of humanity, and whoever saves one life, it is as if he has saved the whole of humanity" (5: 32).

Fourteen Days of High Drama

The next day, Mr Blair himself acknowledged the previous day's 'very strong statement of condemnation from The Muslim Council of Britain, echoing that of the American Muslim Council'. The Prime Minister also declared that the act of terrorism had nothing to do with Islam or Muslims, and government took up his lead. From the outset the MCB urged the Prime Minister to use his influence so that the crisis was not worsened through reactions and presumptions of guilt.

The Home Office shared concerns about the physical well-being of the Muslim community. As reports of attacks on Muslim individuals and institutions started to come in, the Home Office and police forces throughout the country were asked by Muslim organisations, including the MCB, to make arrangements to ensure that incidents of hate crimes against Muslims were minimised. Police guards were posted outside mosques and Islamic centres and people were urged to take care and report any incidents. On 12 September, Mr David Westwood, Chairman of the Race and Community Business Group of the Association of Chief Police Officers, sent a message to the MCB, "I assure you that the British Police service is sensitive to the potential of victimisation or even demonisation of the Muslim community."

By 12 September most other Islamic organisations had also released public statements condemning the atrocities. On major issues there is usually co-operation and co-ordination. The MCB therefore convened a meeting inviting all the major national Islamic organisations in Britain. This would provide the first opportunity for Muslims in leadership positions from different organisations to come together and talk about what had happened the previous day and decide how to proceed.

As attendees arrived at Regent's Park Mosque that evening, the police guards at the entrance provided a visual reminder of the changed landscape they now inhabited. The media were not too far away either. Inside the mosque camera crews from TV stations were in place to ask for views.

As they sat round the oval table on the first floor of one of Britain's most famous institutions facing one another, there was a palpable air of concern amongst the leaders and representatives of the organisations invited. Collectively the burden of responsibility upon them was immense. Even though they represented different strands of thought and opinion amongst the Muslim community, there was total agreement on the main points. This was a barbaric act of terrorism that has no place in Islam. It needed to be condemned totally. A joint statement was then released.

The Qur'an equates the murder of one innocent person with the murder of the whole of humanity.

We, the Muslims of Britain, wish to offer our deepest sympathies to the families of those who have been killed or injured following the atrocities committed in the United States. We utterly condemn these indiscriminate terrorist attacks against innocent lives. The perpetrators of these atrocities, regardless of their religious, ideological or political beliefs, stand outside the pale of civilised values.

Terror affects us all. Terror of this enormity must not be compounded by knee-jerk reactions that would make victims of other innocent people. We would remind the government and the media that the consequences of unsubstantiated speculation in the past, such as the case of the Oklahoma bombing, produced a climate of fear among Muslims that should not be repeated.

There exists a heightened sense of insecurity amongst Muslims in Britain though we warmly welcome our Prime Minister's comments yesterday when he emphasised that Muslims in this country clearly condemn this atrocity. The Prime Minister warned against speculation that can endanger the lives of the entire community. Our thoughts and heartfelt concerns are with all those affected at this mournful moment.

The MCB, in conjunction with the Islamic Cultural Centre, Association of Muslim Schools, Al Khoei Foundation, the Muslim College and the Forum Against Islamophobia and Racism (FAIR), organised a press conference in London on 13 September. It was another opportunity to reinforce the MCB's message and express condolences. Yousuf Bhailok and Iqbal Sacranie asked that the media exercise "responsible journalism" and not unwittingly fuel religious and social anxieties in the aftermath of the attacks. Michele Messaoudi of FAIR mentioned recent incidents involving Muslim schoolchildren and women in headscarves. She said that the Muslim community was being targeted and singled out for abuse and harassment. The conference was well attended with representation from *The Guardian*,

Associated Press, BBC Breakfast News, Radio 5 Live, ARY Digital, Zee TV, and other media bodies.

On the occasion of the special debate in Parliament on 14 September the MCB prepared a statement that was sent individually to each MP. With the aim of ensuring that one tragedy did not lead to more innocent lives being lost, it noted that "a historic burden of responsibility lies with our elected representatives to demonstrate the supremacy of the rule of law by seeking just means to counter the great injustice that is terrorism. There must be no more innocent victims to add to the toll of suffering caused by those guilty of this terror".

It also alerted the House of Commons to the worry of the British Muslim community that a climate of intolerance and revenge was emerging, directed at them. The father of the House, Tam Dalyell MP, and MEPs, including John Bowis, the MEP for London, responded with words of support. The Foreign Secretary, Rt Hon Jack Straw, also took the initiative to improve community relations. In a newspaper article he recognised how the Muslims viewed the US tragedy: "It's a sense of shock and loss which, I know, is strongly shared by the Muslim communities here in Bradford and across our country...blaming Islam for what has happened would be as wrong as blaming Christianity for sectarian attacks in Northern Ireland." Gradually the tide of vitriolic emails received by the MCB grew smaller and was replaced by a greater number of positive messages of support and encouragement. The full record was published on the MCB web site for all to view.

The MCB in a meeting with Ken Livingstone, Mayor of London, on 19 September, requested guidelines to be issued to head teachers. At a separate meeting with David Blunkett, the Home Secretary, the need for the introduction of legislation to deal with incitement to religious hatred was stressed, as well as the need to expedite the enacting of the law against discrimination on religious grounds. The MCB itself issued a letter of guidance on 19 September to over a thousand community organisations and mosques on issues of personal safety and mosque protection.

The MCB convened a special meeting of its Central Working Committee on 22 September, attended by the Director General of the Islamic Cultural Centre, Dr Ahmad Al-Dubayan, and other distinguished Muslims, including religious scholars. At the meeting, Khurshid Drabu, barrister and human rights expert stressed that "Muslims are and must be seen to be firm upholders of justice and the rule of law, and so must governments and coalitions who have declared a war on terrorism." On behalf of Muslim imams and ulama, Dr Suhayb Hassan also quoted the

Qur'an to highlight the uncompromising Islamic concern for justice: "O ye who believe! stand out firmly for Allah, as witnesses to fair dealing, and let not the hatred of others to you make you swerve to wrong and depart from justice. Be just, that is next to piety, and fear God. For God is well-acquainted with all that you do." The economist Iqbal Asaria reminded the meeting that more than half of British Muslims were born in this country and Britain was their only home. "We must all realise that citizenship carries rights as well as obligations," he said. "We must adopt the principled stance that the rule of law is inviolable. Muslims have a duty to participate in the society and they have a responsibility to add value to society as a whole. Otherwise, Muslims are in danger of being ghettoised communities and run the risk of being put in concentration camps." He also noted that such camps were not unknown in recent European history.

One participant at the MCB meeting recounted how he felt a shiver running down his back when he heard President Bush talking about 'If you are not with us, you are against us.' This was the language of the repressive regime in the Middle East under which he lived and which stifled not only all dissent but also all discussion and made everyone guilty of suspected treason.

The extra work generated by September 11, not least the unprecedented media attention upon the MCB, meant that work on other areas came to a virtual halt as nearly everyone's attention was diverted to helping out on this issue. Volunteers were drafted into the office, people took time off work to help out, a system for logging hate incidents was set up and the phones never stopped ringing. People worked more or less round the clock. An emergency committee was established to co-ordinate work across the various committees. It met weekly and was open to people from different community organisations that wanted to be kept abreast of the latest developments and contribute ideas.

In the meantime, more hate mail streamed into the MCB office. However Muslims were not the only victims of hostility. There were instances of Sikhs being mistaken for Muslims and being subject to intimidation and harassment. Dr Fatma Amer represented the MCB at a meeting of the Sikh community on 20 September.

Community Representation and Work

There was a growing sense of anxiety within the Muslim community. Women wearing the hijab were particularly vulnerable as they were easily identifiable as Muslims. Some women restricted their movements as a precaution. Muslims, both men and women who were identifiable as such, were urged to exercise care when using public transport and some Muslim schools closed temporarily. A number of incidents of verbal and physical abuse and mosque desecration occurred, that were centrally logged. The MCB also set up a help-line at its office as a contact point for anyone in distress. The MCB established contact with a variety of public bodies and government departments to raise the community's concerns and ensure some action was taken.

Prime Minister Tony Blair invited members of the British Muslim community to a meeting at 10 Downing Street on 28 September. Representing the MCB were Yousuf Bhailok, Iqbal Sacranie, Tanzeem Wasti and Dr Fatma Amer. Mr Blair denounced abusive behaviour against Muslims as "acts and attitudes [that] have no proper place in our country". The meeting was an opportunity for a frank and robust exchange of views, in which was highlighted the massive problem of the emerging refugee crisis in Afghanistan and the need to secure justice, and not vengeance, in the capturing of those accused of having carried out the terrorist attack. A delegation from the MCB also subsequently met Conservative Party Leader Iain Duncan Smith a few days later.

On 29 September, The Muslim Council of Britain convened a unique meeting of scholars, imams and ulama to discuss world events and their impact on British Muslims. They were asked to provide advice and guidance to the community. A detailed statement prepared by the Ulama was then translated into Urdu, Bengali and Gujrati and circulated by the MCB to all mosques and Muslim community organisations. The full text was made available on the MCB web site.

The MCB's regular newsletter, 'The Common Good' at the end of September also provided information that might be useful to the community, including examples of good practice projects adopted by mosques and Islamic associations to dispel stereotypes and communicate with neighbours and other faith groups. The newsletter included a 'social contract', calling on British Muslims to be "faithful to the Islamic values of truth, justice, care and compassion".

Faithful to the Islamic values of truth, justice, care and compassion, Muslims should have nothing to hide and fear and remain open and transparent as we go about our daily lives. While further upheaval and devastation is being visited on Muslim communities, and the fires of civil war are being stoked up in Muslim lands, it is natural to feel pain and anguish especially when injustice is being done and the misery of starving and destitute populations is compounded over and over again.

As British Muslims we have the right and the duty to use wise counsel and all our powers of argument and persuasion to impress on our government the duty to uphold the rule of law and follow ethical policies both at home and abroad. As citizens of Britain, we have a social contract to maintain the peace and stability of this country. No one must be tempted to commit any criminal or subversive activity.

One of the immediate results of the atrocities of September 11 is that the phenomenon of 'Islamophobia' has been released anew on an unprecedented scale. Terms such as Islamic terrorists are being bandied about not only by the media but by security agencies and people in government. Much of this may be quite deliberate. Islam as a religion has nothing to do with terrorism. However, there is a lot of confusion and ignorance about Islam and Muslims and a dominant image of Muslims is often that they are extremists. We have a duty to set the record straight.

At these times especially, everyone including Muslims should be especially vigilant for their own safety and that of their neighbours. People must be careful how they respond to acts of provocation, misinformation and disinformation which tend to proliferate especially in times of war. We must not act on the basis of hearsay. The instructions of the Qur'an are clear: "When a mischief-maker comes to you with some news, check it out lest you cause injury to someone out of ignorance." "When ignorant people address them, worshippers of God Most Gracious reply, 'Peace!'."

A remarkable meeting at The Methodist Central Hall in Westminster held on 3 October endorsed a statement bringing together London's faith communities. Attended by the Bishop of London and representatives from other faiths, the meeting concluded with a signed statement from religious leaders that condemned indiscriminate acts of violence against innocent people. A number of speakers, including Atma Singh of the Greater London Authority, called for the pursuit of justice without vengeance. The Bishop of London observed that 'terror makes victim of us all' and said that he was appalled by the use of terms such as 'crusade' in the aftermath of the tragedy. Dr Anas Abu Shadi, Deputy Director of the Islamic Cultural Centre, participated in the public reading of the statement, and Mahmud Al-Rashid spoke on behalf of the MCB. He called for the planners and perpetrators of the September 11 atrocity to be brought to trial in an international court. The MCB was against the intimidation and threats of war in Afghanistan, and the impact of these actions had been to force hundreds of thousands to flee their homes in terror. Ajmal Masroor of the London Civic Forum Executive provided a rousing concluding address.

On 9 October, reflecting the community's anger with US-led strikes against Afghanistan, the MCB issued a press release noting, "British Muslims want justice to be done for the horrifying events of September 11. These day and night strikes – which are already leading to innocent civilians deaths amongst the long-suffering Afghan population – will not achieve this purpose. In Islam, all innocent human life is precious. These attacks will only lead to further polarisation in the world. This will not be a fitting memorial to those who died in the September 11 atrocities. We are now hearing talk of 'widening the war' to encompass other Muslim countries. We fear that these events could spiral out of control. We urge world leaders to react with reason and awareness of the long-term consequences of their actions." The statement underlined the belief that the phenomena of mass terrorism could only be resolved through examining and addressing the root causes of terrorism.

Positive Outcomes

Throughout this initial period there were many distressing instances ranging from irresponsible and sometimes malicious comments in the media through to physical attacks on Muslims. But there have been many positive outcomes too.

In an important issue of policy the MCB took a public stand to confront groups within the community that not only misrepresent the values of Islam but also cause ill will through foolish statements and quixotic behaviour. The MCB now urges TV producers and newspaper editors not to offer a high profile to such people, who not only do not represent the mainstream community views and feelings, but indirectly inflame passions and spread hatred.

A reception organised by the MCB in November 2001 at the London Islamic Cultural Centre provided an opportunity to thank some of the Muslim community's well-wishers who had sent in messages of support. The renowned photographer Peter Sanders presented a slide show based on his travels in the Muslim world, providing guests with a flavour of the expanse and cultural richness of the world of Islam. The atmosphere of the meeting was warm and open, with guests using the opportunity to enquire about Islam and exchange points of view. Many other Muslim organisations hosted such events, and such efforts have created new bridges and friends.

The MCB has encouraged its affiliates - especially mosques - to open their doors to members of the public who wanted to know about what Islam really stands for. There is a greater move at the grass-roots level to seek out a dialogue with other faith groups and build trust and understanding at the local level.

Interspersed amongst the e-mail messages of hostility received by the MCB there were also messages of care and concern – from which a great deal of strength and encouragement was drawn. For example, a Muslim community leader, A K Gheewala of Leicester, found something of personal significance in the catalogue of emails available on the MCB web site: "I have spent more than five hours in reading emails posted on this subject. Fortunately, letters with positive views outnumber the letters projecting total ignorance towards Islam and Muslims. As a chair of Muslim welfare trust and a member of many other voluntary and community groups, on behalf of the entire Muslim community, I wish to thank all those who have either been sympathetic to us or have written against the racist/prejudiced remarks. I would request other friends to become familiar with Islam, its philosophy and teaching before arriving at any conclusion. On reflection I consider it a shortcoming that we are failing to convey the correct message of Islam."

The initiatives taken by the MCB in establishing contact with public bodies and government departments have also borne fruit, for example leading to the standing consultation between the police and representatives of the Muslim community to discuss and deal with problems as they arise on a regular basis.

September 11 and its aftermath has been a searing experience, in which representative bodies serving the Muslim community have endeavoured to keep a steady ship in a period of continuing agitation and turmoil. They would need to demonstrate the same qualities and commitment in the days ahead.

British Muslim Youth Survey

In December 2001, the Youth and Research & Documentation committees of the MCB launched an online youth survey with the aim of collecting data on attitudes to the September 11 attacks, the aftermath, and life as a young British Muslim. The survey preserved the anonymity of respondents and the findings were used by the MCB to better understand the concerns and perceptions of young persons in the community. About 100 British Muslim teenagers, roughly equal numbers of boys and girls, participated. No claims are made for the statistical validity of the survey results because the sample size was limited.

The survey was administered through a network of 'survey managers' responsible for allocating usernames and passwords to young persons to allow them access to the questionnaire on the web site. The web based survey collected data automatically, capturing it in a database. The survey form was also available in hard-copy format. Teachers, madrasah instructors and youth organisations were encouraged to participate.

From those surveyed, the dominant feelings concerning the September 11 attacks were ones of sadness and shock on first hearing of the attacks. These feelings were followed by outrage and shock on first hearing of the involvement of Muslims in the attacks although boys were noticeably more guarded in disclosing their feelings. The majority of respondents believed that Islam either prohibited or discouraged such attacks. When questioned about the bombing of Afghanistan, many responded again with sadness and outrage concerning the attacks.

Questions posed regarding the best aspects of life in Britain showed that for boys, freedom and tolerance were the most important. The boys showed they appreciated the freedom to practice Islam. The good standard of living was highlighted along with the educational facilities available. They praised the availability of mosques with good prayer facilities and the option to learn at Islamic lectures.

For girls, freedom in Britain was also highly rated, along with the multicultural climate and education. They were appreciative of non-Muslims showing tolerance. They voiced their appreciation of the potential for positive input into society, interacting with other Muslims and their families within mosques as well as being active by talking to people about Islam and learning more about it in Islamic circles.

Perhaps reflecting the number of young persons who were children of refugees or asylum seekers in the survey, their observations on the 'best aspects of living in Britain' included comments such as: 'you can get more security', 'living in a cleaner area, 'we have food and water', 'there isn't much fighting' and 'we have better health care'.

The worst aspects of living in Britain for boys included experiences of racism and the moral climate. They displayed feelings of alienation, questioning why people thought of them as different and why their status as British Muslims was not accepted by many non-Muslims.

The boys also spoke of the many distractions that surrounded their lives as British Muslims: "I think (it is difficult) being able to live a Muslim life. As a teenager I have been and still get distracted, and see many Muslims do things that Islam does not permit simply because it's becoming more accepted." Many express the fear of keeping to the tenets of Islam in a western non-Muslim world with the prevalence of drugs, clubs, violence, unlawful sex and corruption, and wished for a proper Muslim environment to live in. However, there were a few that found no difficulty at all to life in Britain as a young Muslim.

For girls, along with the issue of racism, the worst aspects of life in Britain were the lack of respect and being made to feel like an outsider. Wearing of the headscarf was very hard, because of comments and criticism. Some found it difficult to get people to understand the reasons behind acts of worship.

In a similar way to the boys, the girls felt that they were constantly viewed as foreigners and had difficulties fitting in as they feel they are not accepted. They too felt that there were too many distractions around, which weakened their faith and traditions. They found that many people have an irrational fear of Muslims, blaming them for any number of crimes.

Other observations about the worst aspects of life in Britain included 'bad weather' and 'constant darkness' and 'Non Halal Food in parties'.

Based on the experience of this pilot survey, the MCB is planning more extensive youth attitude social surveys.

3

The Media

British Muslims and the Media
INAYAT BUNGLAWALA
◆ ◆ ◆

Islam and the British Press
BRIAN WHITAKER
◆ ◆ ◆

Muslims and the Media in Canada
MOHAMMED ELMASRY
◆ ◆ ◆

Of Sane and Other Voices
◆ ◆ ◆

British Muslims and the Media

INAYAT BUNGLAWALA

The Muslim Council of Britain issued a press release condemning the attacks of September 11 within three hours of the attacks occurring, saying:

> "Whoever is responsible for these dreadful, wanton attacks, we condemn them utterly...No cause can justify this carnage. We hope those responsible will swiftly be brought to justice for their unconscionable deeds."[1]

Within 48 hours the MCB had organised a well-attended press conference where all the main Muslim leaders from around the UK signed a statement stating that the attacks were morally indefensible and called on those who had planned them to be brought to justice. On 12 September the Prime Minister himself made reference to the MCB's unequivocal position of outright condemnation in his press conference outside 10 Downing Street.[2]

By the early evening of September 11, however, the MCB had already started receiving from some members of the public, the first of what proved to be a very long stream of hate-mail via its web site. These have been collated and put on display on the MCB's web site. The following are a few typical examples:

> Tuesday 11 September 2001 at 19:37 anonymous
> Are you happy now? Salman Rushdie was right your religion is a joke! Long live Israel! The US will soon kill many Muslim

women and children! You are all subhuman freaks!

Tuesday 11 September 2001 at 20:43 Roland Taylor
I am sorry but I don't believe you at all. You will slaughter
anyone and everyone to gain world domination. You can never
be trusted ever again. I may now even begin to have sympathy
with the National Front. [expletive] YOU and GO TO A
MUSLIM HOME COUNTRY.

Wednesday 12 September 2001 at 18:30 anonymous
The rest of the world will now join to smash your filthy disease
infested Islam. You must be removed from great [sic] Britain in
body bags

Media fuelled the fear of Islam
In the meantime, large sections of the media, instead of designating columns
and inches to the mainstream Muslim voice, irresponsibly went to a tiny
fringe element with minuscule support within the British Muslim
community to allow them to widely air their unrepresentative views[3]. Of the
over 800 mosques in the UK, only one was run by a known 'radical'. Yet this
one mosque (Finsbury Park, London) received more media coverage than all
the rest put together. Very little attempt was made to explain that these
'radicals' had no standing in the wider Muslim community[4]. The situation
was akin to taking a member of the racist British National Party and saying
his views were representative of ordinary Britons.

After deliberately seeking out and courting fringe figures and printing
their reckless and inflammatory comments, the newspapers would then
publish outraged follow-up pieces by their leading columnists and writers[5]
who were given free rein to demonise the Islamic faith and its followers.

Indeed, there appeared to be a symbiotic relationship between large
sections of the media and these 'radical' figures with both sides feeding off
each other. This has no doubt contributed to the pervasive feelings of
suspicion towards the media in the Muslim community. Ordinary Muslims
were caught in a no-win situation.

The distinguished defence editor of the Daily Telegraph, Sir John
Keegan, mused over the way Western and Muslim 'Oriental' people
conducted war. Whereas Westerners fought according to 'rules of honour',
said Keegan:

"Orientals, by contrast, shrink from pitched battle, which they often deride as a sort of game, preferring ambush, surprise, treachery and deceit as the best way to overcome an enemy…This war [in Afghanistan] belongs within the much larger spectrum of a far older conflict between settled, creative productive Westerners and predatory, destructive Orientals."[6]

The Christian polemicist Patrick Sookhdeo was given a platform to allege that:

> "Unlike Islam, Christianity does not justify the use of all forms of violence. Islam does."[7]

This type of disparaging journalism only led to inflaming the prejudice of Islamophobia against British Muslims. The MCB began to receive report after report of mosques being despoiled; one Bolton mosque was even fire-bombed while there were still children inside performing their prayers[8]. Muslim cemeteries were vandalised and desecrated. By the end of the week of September 11, there emerged the first confirmed reports of grievous bodily assaults on Muslims. In Swindon, a nineteen year-old Muslim woman wearing a headscarf was left hospitalised after being chased and hit hard on the head with a baseball bat[9]. In London, an Afghan cab driver was left paralysed from the neck down after being savagely beaten with a bottle and then punched and kicked repeatedly by three men[10]. In Exeter, two days after the September 11 attacks, eight pigs' heads were thrown into the car park of the local mosque and a banner was erected saying, "The blood of the American people is on the hands of every Muslim. Nuke 'em, George[11]."

From all over the country, from Dover, Birmingham, Oldham, Southend, Glasgow and Edinburgh, the story was the same[12]: ordinary British Muslims, with their persons and their property, were paying the price for a terrorist crime in which they were in no way involved and for which they were not responsible.

BNP enters the fray

Into this combustible mix now stepped the British National Party advocating a new "Campaign To Keep Britain Free of Islam". Its web site encouraged visitors to download BNP leaflets which stated that Islam stood for Intolerance, Slaughter, Looting, Arson and Molestation of women.

The BNP's anti-Muslim campaign involved the distribution of thousands of CDs, tapes and leaflets claiming that Islam posed a threat to Britain. According to a report in *The Observer*[13], some Sikh activists in

Southall, west London, had passed hundreds of addresses of Sikh and Hindu community leaders to BNP activists who wanted their support. In a widely distributed cassette labelled as a joint statement from the BNP and the Sikh and Hindu communities, Nick Griffin, the BNP leader, read and commented on the Qur'an, followed by a discussion with a Midlands-based Sikh activist. The language used can only be described as inflammatory. The tape quoted Griffin as saying 'Islam is the biggest threat Britain has ever faced,' and an unnamed BNP member said on the tape: 'This is our country and you [Muslims] will never take it from us.' Griffin also went on to describe Islam as a religion that brings 'communal conflict, civil war and death to every country in which it gets a foothold'.

Unlike Jews and Sikhs, British Muslims – the UK's biggest minority community - are not classified as a 'race' and hence, are not protected by the 1976 Race Relations Act. Twenty years on, the British National Party recognising this gap in the law has abandoned its crude racist rhetoric of yester year and has reformulated it into a more socially acceptable and wholly lawful anti-Muslim diatribe.

Newspapers and broadcasters urged to show responsibility
By the end of September 2001, in an effort to try and redress the imbalance in reporting about the Muslim community, The Muslim Council of Britain had written to the main broadcasters, the BBC, ITN and Sky, urging them to give greater coverage to mainstream Muslim voices. The MCB also visited the offices of the *Daily Mail*, *The Times*, *The Independent* and the popular London paper, the *Evening Standard*, meeting with their editors and senior staff to convey the same message.

The bombing of Afghanistan
By this time it was evident that the United States was determined to start its bombing campaign of Afghanistan at the earliest opportunity. Various newspaper polls had found that around 80% of the British Muslim community was opposed to a war with Afghanistan. Most Muslims were deeply concerned that a war would lead to very heavy losses amongst Afghan civilians who were entirely blameless for the events of September 11. The MCB sought to reflect this grassroots feeling and called on the government to avoid joining an American-led war which would be certain to inflict enormous suffering on the innocent people of Afghanistan. The MCB issued a statement urging that:

"As grief gives way to anger the challenge lies in holding true to our democratic and civilised principles which places justice ahead of retribution…a historic burden of responsibility lies with our elected representatives to demonstrate the supremacy of the rule of law by seeking just means to counter the great injustice that is terrorism. There must be no more innocent victims to add to the toll of suffering caused by those guilty of this terror."[14]

Subsequent events demonstrated that the fears of many British Muslims were well founded. The US strategy of sustained high-altitude bombing, together with the use of the cluster and 'daisy-cutter' bombs, resulted in fatal and devastating errors. It is notable that with the exception of *The Guardian*[15], to the best of our knowledge, no other British newspaper reported on the estimated number of deaths and heavy injuries amongst Afghan civilians. This telling omission served to underline a widespread cause of concern amongst British Muslims that the lives of the Americans who were killed on September 11 seemed to be judged as being of greater worth than those of destitute Afghan Muslims.

Media coverage incites hatred against British Muslims

Enormous media exposure was given to the news that a handful of British Muslims had decided to make their way to Afghanistan to help resist the expected US invasion. Instead of contextualising this news by pointing out that the vast majority of British Muslims had chosen to express their opposition to the war through peaceful means, letters to MPs and other forms of political lobbying, the press coverage in some quarters seemed almost designed to stir up violence against British Muslims. Large sections of the media engaged in a deliberate and incendiary policy of exaggeration and scaremongering that was certain to contribute towards inciting a hatred of mainstream British Muslims.

The columnist, Melanie Phillips led the pack:

> "The attitude of many British Muslims should cause the greatest possible alarm that we have a fifth column in our midst… Thousands of alienated young Muslims, most of them born and bred here but who regard themselves as an army within, are waiting for an opportunity to help to destroy the society that sustains them. We now stare into the abyss, aghast."[16]

The well-known TV personality Robert Kilroy-Silk wrote:

> "The 'Moslem problem' is an important one. How we deal with the 'enemy within' will have momentous and long-term consequences for race relations in this country for years."[17]

The columnist Carol Sarler regretted that British Muslims had been treated with 'tolerance':

> "It is this tolerance that, I fear, is going to bite us. It is the same tolerance that allows an indigenous population to host another that hates us and says so, in loud, haranguing, roving gangs that terrorise our inner cities in the name of Allah."[18]

In an ITN news bulletin, the reporter Terry Lloyd described the Muslim cities of Islamabad, Cairo and Istanbul as the "terrorist capitals of the world".[19] ITN later apologised to the Muslim community for the use of this offensive phrase when asked to clarify its exact meaning.[20]

The Palestinian academic Edward Said once observed that:

> "Malicious generalizations about Islam have become the last acceptable form of denigration of foreign culture in the West; what is said about the Muslim mind, or character, or religion, or culture as a whole cannot now be said in mainstream discussion about Africans, Jews, other Orientals, or Asians."[21]

The cancer of Islamophobia

Since the Runnymede Trust's report on Islamophobia was first published in 1997 there has been no shortage of evidence concerning the widespread extent of discrimination that British Muslims now face every day. In 2000, the Home Office-commissioned Derby report on *Religious Discrimination in England and Wales* which interviewed members of all the major faith communities in the UK found that British Muslims suffer "a consistently higher level of unfair treatment' than most other religious groups".[22]

On 23 May 2002, the European Union Centre on Racism and Xenophobia published a detailed report on anti-Islamic incidents throughout the UK for the period September 11 till December 31 2001 (see article by Christopher Allen).

Yet, despite this overwhelming evidence to the contrary, we still find commentators eager to belittle the claims of Islamophobia and even question the motives of the Muslims who reported such attacks to the police:

> Ten months on [from September 11], there is little sign of the predicted wave of bile, beatings and hate mail… Indeed, it is probably all the hype about Islamophobia after 11 September that encouraged many Muslims to report such minor incidents in the first place.[23]

Islam Awareness Week

The annual national Islam Awareness Week held this time on 4-10 November 2001 assumed a greater poignancy. Organised by the Islamic Society of Britain – an affiliate of the MCB – its main aim was to dispel common misconceptions about the Islamic faith. Public events were held throughout the country and mosque doors were opened up to the public to invite them to exchange views and learn more about their Muslim neighbours. The ISB also invited thirty leading public figures to sign a pledge card calling for tolerance and mutual respect between members of faith and non-faith groups. The pledge card was immediately signed by the Prime Minister, the leader of the Liberal Democrats, the Head of the Civil Service, some editors of national newspapers and other prominent figures.

Amidst a huge amount of rather mixed media coverage, *The Times* welcomed this "assertive initiative" by British Muslims[24], while *The Mirror* criticised the leader of the Conservative Party, Iain Duncan Smith for conspicuously failing to sign the Pledge Card[25]. David Mellor, the former Conservative Cabinet Minister, blasted the pledge card and strikingly called on the organisers to "stick their petition where the sun doesn't shine".[26]

Government interventions

The Prime Minister Tony Blair's high-profile call on Britons not to make scapegoats of its Muslim community in the wake of the September 11 attacks was heartening and served to strengthen nerves at a very tense time. Unfortunately, the responses of some of his Ministers were far from reassuring.

Evidently worried about the rise in support for the far right in the UK and Europe due largely to its exploitation of the sensitive issues of immigration and asylum seekers – many of whom were from Muslim countries, the Home Secretary David Blunkett, in trying to reclaim ground lost to the far right, crassly warned of schools being 'swamped' by the children of asylum seekers. It is perhaps indicative of the measure of hostility now being engendered towards asylum seekers that the word 'bogus' was no longer even thought necessary to be prefixed to them, it was simply assumed that they had no legitimate claim to seek safety in the UK.

In May 2002, the Minister for Europe, Peter Hain, caused deep unease in the Muslim community when, in a widely quoted interview[27], he singled out the Muslim community as containing elements who were "very isolationist". Bearing in mind that there is probably no faith community in the country that does not contain individuals to whom this description could also be accurately applied, this was seen as being an unnecessarily provocative remark given the circumstances. No recognition was given to the fact that every year record numbers of British Muslims were graduating from British universities and entering all the mainstream professions. Muslims can now be found in all fields of public life, including the medical sector, teaching, the unions, the media, sports and politics. Indeed, within the space of just one generation, the vast majority of the Muslim community have made remarkable progress in the process of integration.

This is not to suggest that the process is by any means complete. That some measure of work is still needed to facilitate the integration of sections of the community on the periphery of British life, and to protect those that do seek integration against forms of discrimination based on religious affiliation, is uncontested. The point being made here is that remarks by members of the Government that single out the Muslim community as being 'integration-resistant' are both false and unhelpful.

Bucking the trend

Still, there were some hopeful signs. In a supportive two-page editorial spread, the UK's biggest selling tabloid[28] declared that, "Islam is not an evil religion" and urged Britons to be more sensitive to Muslim concerns about stereotyping. *The Daily Telegraph* published a special 16-page colour supplement to inform its readers about basic Islamic beliefs and teachings, while *The Guardian* ran a week long Muslim Britain series which was perhaps the most extensive and positive look at the British Muslim community that had yet appeared in a national newspaper in the UK[29]. *The Daily Mirror*, under the editorship of Piers Morgan, underwent a remarkable transformation after September 11 and began a move away from celebrity/trivia-driven features towards more serious journalism. This proved to be quite beneficial in relation to its coverage pertaining to Islam and Muslims in general. A further welcome step has been the move by the *Daily Express* to use the spelling 'Muslim' rather than 'Moslem', after representations from The Muslim Council of Britain in July 2002. The latter perverse spelling – as Brian Whitaker notes in his contribution - is prevalent in a number of newspapers and the MCB intends to pursue the matter.

Channel 4's short season of programmes on British Muslims in March 2002 did not receive the enthusiastic welcome given to the BBC's British Islam season aired in August 2001. This was perhaps because the BBC, unlike Channel 4, had done its groundwork and taken time to establish links with the Muslim community to organise complementary off-air activities that accompanied the British Islam season.

The British Muslim community has attracted an enormous amount of attention since September 11. It has had to come to terms with media and political scrutiny placing it firmly in the limelight and under the microscope. But the Muslim community is a resilient one and has fared pretty well in coping with the pressure that has come to bear upon it this last year. It has taken important steps in correcting misconceptions of Islam and the assumption that Islam in Britain is something of a 'perennial outsider'.

That the Muslim community is an integral part of pluralist Britain should by now be recognised. The British character of this community should also be recognised. Our government, by outlawing incitement to religious hatred and religious discrimination, would help to ensure that Muslims, together with other communities, assume their rightful place in the nation's future.

Notes

1. MCB press release, 11 September 2001
2. The Times, 13 September 2001
3. *The Guardian*, 12 Sept 2001; *Scottish Daily Record*, 12 Sept 2001; *The Times*, 12 Sept 2001; *Daily Telegraph*, 13 Sept 2001; *The Independent*, 13 Sept 2001; *Daily Star*, 13 Sept 2001; *Financial Times*, 13 Sept 2001
4. There were a few exceptions. "There is an enemy but it is neither Islam nor the Arab world (which is probably too diverse to permit characterisation as a single unit). Each religion has its zealots. Those on Islam's fanatical fringes are the enemies of freedom and tolerance. Tony Blair said yesterday that the vast majority of the world's Muslims were decent, upright people who had been equally appalled by what had happened. It is their voice that must be heard.", *The Herald*, 13 September 2001.
5. See for example: "Evil 'Enemy Within' May Hit Britain", *The People*, 16 Sept 2001; "British Extremists Urge Young Muslims To Fight US", *Daily Telegraph*, 17 Sept.
6. *Daily Telegraph*, 8 October 2001
7. *Daily Telegraph*, 17 September 2001
8. *The Times*, 19 September 2001
9. Reuters, 18 September 2001
10. *The Mirror*, 19 September 2001 11. *The Independent*, 7 August 2002
12. UK Report Sept 11 – Dec 31st 2001, EU Monitoring Centre on Xenophobia and Racism, May 2002
13. 23 December 2001

14. MCB press release, 14 September 2001
15. 20 December 2001
16. *Sunday Times*, 4 November 2001
17. *The Express on Sunday*, 28 October 2001
18. *Daily Express*, 15 November 2001
19. ITN news broadcast, 28 December 2001
20. Letter to the MCB on 10 January 2002
21. *Covering Islam*, Edward Said, 1997, page xii
22. Religious Discrimination in England and Wales, p vii
23. Josie Appleton, Spiked Online, 2 July 2002
24. 7 November 2001
25. 6 November 2001
26. *The People*, 11 November 2001
27. *Sunday Times*, 12 May 2001
28. *The Sun*, 13 Sept 2001
29. *The Guardian*, 17 –22nd June 2002

Islam and the British Press

BRIAN WHITAKER

It is difficult to talk about the coverage of Islam in the British press without also discussing the effects of September 11. I have spoken to many people who feel that September 11 has had a very negative effect on the Muslim community in Britain, and I know that many hold the media at least partly responsible for this.

We could spend a lot of time discussing the negative effects, but rather than dwell on that, I want to suggest that September 11 has also created an opportunity for British Muslims.

I will begin with some figures. Below are the results of a computer search for articles containing the word "Muslim" that appeared in the national dailies during a 12-month period which ended in early last September - in other words, before the attacks in the United States - some papers use the spelling "Moslem", and this is included in the totals:

Guardian........................ 817
Independent................... 681
Times.............................535
Telegraph...................... 417
Mail...............................202
Mirror............................164
Express..........................139
Sun.................................80
Star................................40

How Can We Explain These Differences?

First, references to Muslims in the newspapers appear in an international context rather than a British one. The broadsheet newspapers at the top of the list contain more international news, and therefore more references to Muslims.

A survey a couple of years ago found that 85% of mentions in *The Guardian* and *The Times* were in a non-British context. My own rather hasty research, covering a single week, found that about 55% of references were in an international context. Obviously the level varies according to what is happening at a particular time.

Second, *The Guardian* and *The Independent* appear at the top of the list. I suggest this is because they tend to take more interest than *The Times* and *The Telegraph* in minority groups generally – not just Muslims.

Third, there also seems to be a perception among the popular tabloid papers that Islam is not a subject which interests their readers. But there are also some big differences among the tabloids: *The Mirror* talks about Muslims twice and much as *The Sun*, while *The Sun* talks about them twice as much as *The Daily Star*.

Now consider how this has changed as a result of September 11. Here are the counts for a 12-month period ending 19 June 2002:

	Total	Increase
Guardian	2,043	250%
Independent	1,556	228%
Times	1,486	278%
Telegraph	1,176	282%
Mail	650	322%
Mirror	920	561%
Express	305	219%
Sun	526	658%
Star	144	360%

These changes are very dramatic. Typically, the increase in references to Muslims among the broadsheet papers is around 250-280 per cent. But in the case of *The Mirror* it's 561% and for *The Sun* 658%.

One conclusion from this is that newspaper readers are far more aware of Islam now than they were a few months ago (though, of course, these particular figures do not tell us anything about the quality of the information they have been getting). Furthermore, journalists are writing about Islam far more than they were a few months ago. To do this, they have largely had to educate themselves. I remember one period towards the end of last year when just about everybody in our office who had anything to do with the coverage of Afghanistan was reading Ahmed Rashid's book on the Taliban.

Because of my own job writing about the Middle East, I now get two or three other journalists coming to me each week with queries about Islam. Sometimes they want to check facts for a story. Sometimes they come with complaints from readers and want to know if there's any substance in the complaint. I have certainly noticed a big increase in this sort of thing since September 11.

When I said earlier that there is an opportunity here, what I meant is that there is more interest in Islam among non-Muslims in Britain than ever before. Depending on how this is handled, it can either work to the detriment of Muslims or to their advantage.

If it is to work to their advantage, then Muslims must play a part in helping to educate journalists about Islam and in ensuring that the coverage is both fair and accurate.

What are the Areas for Improvement?

My own personal observation is that problems occur less often with ordinary news reporters than with feature writers and columnists who tend to be strong on opinions but pay less attention to the facts.

There are at least four very persistent stereotypes that crop up time and again in different articles. These tell us that Muslims are intolerant, misogynistic, violent or cruel, and finally, strange or different. Under the "intolerant" heading we find words such as stern, severe, harsh, puritanical. The last thing you would expect Muslims to do is laugh, enjoy themselves or tell jokes.

The image of violence and cruelty is not just related to terrorism:

....

RSPCA HONOURS EXPRESS REPORTING

The Daily Express will today scoop a top award for its campaigns against animal cruelty.
The Royal Society for the Prevention of Cruelty to Animals is to give us its National Media award for 2000.

The citation describes the award as for "an outstanding and sustained contribution to the field of animal welfare".

The RSPCA cites a string of articles and campaigns in the

Daily Express including the suffering of exotic pets such as iguanas through the ignorance of their owners, the need to protect Britain's porpoises and dolphins, and a graphic account of the cruel slaughter of British sheep in Paris to celebrate the Moslem festival of Eid el Kebir.
Daily Express, 30 June, 2001

The idea that Muslims are strange or different crops up in all sorts of places. For example, you find travel articles describing some exotic place where the sound of "wailing" can be heard coming from the mosque. In travel articles about Muslim countries you'll find many of the attitudes and cliches that were condemned many years ago in Edward Said's book ' Orientalism'.

We tend to write about Muslims mainly when they cause trouble. The negative stories often come from other countries but obviously they have some effect on readers' perception of Muslims in Britain. We can do our best to handle these stories sensitively, but we can't stop writing them. What we can do is balance the negative coverage with what the Americans would call "affirmative action". In other words, we can make a point of writing about Muslims, at least some of the time, in a non-violent, non-threatening context.

There is a lot of ignorance about basic facts regarding Islam, and I will give you two examples that cropped up in the Guardian. One - in the education section of all places – described the Ka'bah in Makkah as the Prophet's tomb. Another, in a reader's letter, explained the hadith as "the sayings of the Prophet in the Koran" – which to anyone who knows anything about the Qur'an is an obvious contradiction.

The Mail and *Express* spell Muslim as "Moslem", and several others spell Qur'an as K-O-R-A-N. *The Express* has now adopted the spelling 'Muslim' following MCB representation. This may seem a relatively trivial issue, but there's no good reason for these perverse spellings and it's a sign of disrespect if you don't try to spell them properly.

What Can be Done?

1. COMPLAINING

- Stereotypes are self-perpetuating unless people challenge them. Once they are challenged, writers start to back off, or at least start to qualify them a bit.
- Demand correction of factual errors. If complaining about the use of words, be prepared to suggest alternative terminology.

- Don't try to censor opinions, but engage in debate - through letters to the editor or directly with the writers concerned - if you think this will be productive. Some people respond to that, but in some cases it's a waste of time.
- Effective complaining requires organisation, both to monitor what is published and to ensure that complaints are formulated in the best way.

2. EMPLOYMENT

There are clearly not enough Muslims working in journalism. There are all sorts of possible explanations for this apart from discrimination – for example, the tendency of sons in Asian families to follow in their father's business, or the perception of journalism as a somewhat alcoholic profession. (That is probably not true any more, because it's quite difficult to drink and operate a computer at the same time!)

Whatever the reasons, we must do something about it. Over the last few years, most newspapers have made serious efforts to recruit black journalists, and we should do the same for Muslims. We should also learn from the mistakes made when papers first started employing black journalists – in particular, we should avoid the "ghetto effect" of asking Muslims to write mainly about Islam.

3. EDUCATION

Finally, as I mentioned earlier, many journalist have had to take a crash course in Islam since September 11. For the most part, it's been a hit-and-miss affair, and we need something better.

This is one area where the Muslim community can work with the media. What we need as a simple, factual guide to the things journalists should know about Islam, together with a list of the most common mistakes. We also need some guidelines for best practice, similar to those that were developed for reporting racial issues a few years ago. I know that the Muslim Council of Britain is already looking into this, but the sooner it is ready, the better for all of us.

Based on a presentation delivered at the symposium 'The West and Islam in the media', 20-21 June 2002, Islamic Cultural Centre, London

Muslims and the Media
in Canada

MOHAMMED ELMASRY

"We have to fear our (Muslim) neighbours down the street...
They provide the culture in which fifth columns grow..."
wrote a Canadian columnist shortly after September 11, 2001.

Less than two weeks later, the same columnist wrote, "From the beginning, Western attempts to draw a distinction between Islamist terrorists and Islam resulted in a lopsided effort." And then in March of this year, he recycled his argument, saying, "The terrorist enemy has no armies to send against us; it has to penetrate our perimeter through fifth-columnists."

Unfortunately, such statements are not exceptions to the rule – they are one small sample of many similar arguments that have been prolifically emblazoned across Canadian editorial pages since the 9/11 atrocities in America.

Even before 9/11, the Canadian Muslim community including the Canadian Islamic Congress and some interested academics have believed that the media's frequent demonic portrayal and mis-representation of Islam and Muslims has been one of the most persistent, virulent, and socially significant sources of anti-Islam in Canada.

While some media sources, both print and broadcast, have realized the implications of such discrimination and have tried to act responsibly, certain specific and often predictable others have been actively incorporating the most explicit expressions of anti-Islam into their coverage, resulting in prejudicial, inciteful, and extremely dangerous biases against all Muslims.

Such irresponsible journalism serves to reinforce the gross

misconception that Islam is entirely unidimensional, monolithic and singular, without any internal differentiation or opinion. Through indiscriminately saddling Canadian Muslims with the weight of conflicts in Afghanistan, Kashmir, India, Palestine and elsewhere, the media have deliberately attributed a full spectrum of negative anti-Islam characteristics to the entire global Muslim community.

Some in the media have traditionally and too freely coupled their understanding of Islam or Muslim with inappropriate terms such as "extremist," "fundamentalist," "fanatic," or "terrorist," but the increase in negative repetitious usage since 9/11 has underlined a new and disturbing development.

Whilst the intention of such descriptions has always been that Islam is the inherent "other enemy" of the West, recent usage of these terms now infers, as my introductory quotation suggests, that these same "extremists", "fundamentalists", "fanatics" and "terrorists" are rampant among us in Canada and are willing to do the same to Canadians as they did to thousands of unsuspecting Americans. Some Canadian media have taken pains to restate their anti-Islam and anti-Muslim biases often enough to convince the vulnerable and uninformed among their readers and listeners that the worst possible things are probably true of *all* Canadian Muslims – including their next-door neighbours, co-workers, colleagues, medical professionals and others.

If Usama bin Laden and his supporters indisputably planned and executed the 9/11 terrorist acts then, yes, certain individual Muslims are guilty. But Islam is not Muslims. Even if 1,500 Muslims were to commit similar acts every year – an unimaginable scenario – they would represent only one criminal per million.

Thus, as a living faith with nearly 1.2 billion global adherents that has survived as a world religion for more than 1400 years, Islam needs no defence – but our children here in Canada do. As young and vulnerable human beings, they need to be protected against the lifelong social and psychological damage inflicted by hate-mongering, negative stereotyping, and smear campaigns against their self-identity, self-esteem and human dignity.

We are gratified that many Canadians have been drawn to explore Islamic teachings, that many have found them attractive, and have embraced them in a spirit of love and compassion. But Canadian Muslims and their children still must be protected against discriminating bigotry, harassment, and mental and physical abuse.

Analogies are being made to the representation of the Jews in such early twentieth century literature as 'Mein Kampf,' where gross exaggeration and dehumanisation proved to be fatally dangerous for more than six million of them. What, then, could be the parallel consequences for Muslims? German academic Gunther Grass states that such beliefs about Islam in the West and the current climate of hate against it bring us very close to a situation not unlike that which prompted Germany's infamous "Kristallnacht" in 1938. Once "the enemy" has been so dehumanised and portrayed as demonic and parasitical, what further justification is needed to persecute and finally exterminate it?

But anti-Islam in the media is not our sole concern. Canadian Muslims are also very disturbed about the increasing pressure to link patriotism, the idea of being a "good citizen," with unqualified support for enormous government increases in military spending, the passing of multiple anti-terrorism laws, and the economic and cultural Americanisation of Canada at the expense of all other priorities, particularly those that our country traditionally valued, such as the elimination of homelessness and child poverty.

Anti-Islam is most dangerous because it does not respect the individual. It is an indiscriminate prejudice that tarnishes everything and everyone it touches, not only the 650,000 Muslims who call this great country home, but also the motives and attitudes of more than 30 million Canadians, in turn determining their behaviour toward, and beliefs about, Islam and Muslims.

We have seen this prejudice become so socially significant that the actions of a small group of Muslims on September 11, 2001 were enough to influence and mobilize many misguided people to attack the innocent Muslims in our midst – women harassed for wearing the hijab, bearded young men abused because of their appearance, places of worship and learning firebombed and vandalized. It is the time to differentiate between the real "them" and the real "us," and apportion blame for the horrors of terrorism where it belongs.

Of Sane and Other Voices

Richard Chartres, Bishop of London

The precise identity of those responsible (for the atrocities in Washington and New York) remains unclear but a connection with Middle Eastern terrorist groups has been assumed. It is at this point that the old wartime adage, "Careless talk costs lives" has a fresh relevance. Any language which demonises the whole Islamic world and drives a wedge between Muslims and their neighbours makes a tragic and dangerous situation, infinitely worse…

The Muslim Council of Britain has issued a strong statement to the effect that "terror makes victims of us all". The Council is right in branding this as an attack on the whole civilised world. As Bishop of a city which has been the victim of terrorist attacks in the past, it is good to stand shoulder to shoulder with British Muslim leaders in an unequivocal condemnation of these crimes.

If Europe is to find the moral courage to defeat terrorism, then it has to rekindle conviction about the things that are worth dying and living for. An indiscriminate tolerance for all views, which lacks clarity about what is good and true, undermines the will to resist the terrorist. At the same time it opens up a vacuum which can easily be filled with irrational calls for violence against scapegoats.

Christians will not make their proper contribution to the struggle that is in progress unless they are robust about their own faith and convictions. But they also need to be urgent about finding allies in other faith communities for a common defense of the values and laws which make civilised co-existence possible.

The Times, 14 September 2001

Naom Chomsky

What is the "new war on terrorism"? The goal of the civilised world has been announced very clearly in high places. We must "eradicate the evil scourge of terrorism," a plague spread by "depraved opponents of civilisation itself" in a "return to barbarism in the modern age," and so on. Surely a noble enterprise! So the "New War on Terrorism" is, in fact, led by the only state in the world that has been condemned by the International Court of Justice for international terrorism and has vetoed a resolution calling on states to observe international law, which is perhaps appropriate.

Public Lecture at the Music Academy, Chennai (Madras), India, November 10, 2001

The new millennium quickly produced two terrible new crimes, added to the gloomy record of persisting ones. The first was the terrorist attacks of September 11; the second, the response to them.

Writing in 'Shattered Illusions', July 2002

John Pilger

Since September 11, the war on terrorism has provided a pretext for the rich countries, led by the United States, to further their dominance over world affairs. By spreading fear and respect, as a Washington Post reporter put it, America intends to see off challenges to its uncertain ability to control and manage the global economy, a euphemism for the progressive seizure of markets and resources by the G8 rich nations.

Znet Magazine, 5 January 2002

Amnesty International

The current US-led "war against terrorism" is being accompanied by massive transfers of military aid to governments that have shown little regard for human rights protection. The US has maintained, or even increased, existing military aid to countries such as Israel (US$2.04 billion), Egypt (US$1.3 billion), Jordan, Tunisia and Colombia. Military sales to countries such as Saudi Arabia and Turkey have been maintained. In addition, the US Congress has been considering an emergency supplemental spending law allowing a further US$1.3 billion. This would enable US arms purchases, military combat training, advisers and military bases for Afghanistan, Pakistan, India, Tajikistan, Uzbekistan, Kyrgyzstan, Azerbaijan, Armenia, Georgia, Turkey, Somalia, Yemen, Kenya, Indonesia and the Philippines - all countries where serious and systematic human rights violations have been committed.

http://web.amnesty.org/802568F7005C4453/0/80256AB9000584F680256BDD005D494B?Open &Highlight=2,G8

George Monbiot

"If any government sponsors the outlaws and killers of innocents," George Bush announced on the day he began bombing Afghanistan, "they have become outlaws and murderers themselves. And they will take that lonely path at their own peril." I'm glad he said "any government", as there's one which, though it has yet to be identified as a sponsor of terrorism, requires his urgent attention. For the past 55 years it has been running a terrorist training camp, whose victims massively outnumber the people killed by the attack on New York, the embassy bombings and the other atrocities laid, rightly or wrongly, at al-Qaida's door. The camp is called the Western Hemisphere Institute for Security and Cooperation, or WHISC. It is based in Fort Benning, Georgia, and it is funded by Mr Bush's government.

The Guardian, 30 October 2001
http://www.guardian.co.uk/comment/story/0,3604,583192,00.html

Professor Robert Jensen, University of Texas

Let me say up front that I believe that in light of what is happening in Afghanistan at the moment, the topic of free speech seems, in some sense, trivial. I do not mean that speech does not matter. I believe free speech is a good thing in and of itself. But my main concern at the moment is not the intrinsic value of free speech, the way it fosters the growth and development of individuals, which is one powerful argument for protecting free speech. Right now, free speech is on my mind because I live in the nation that has the most destructive military capacity in the history of the world. I live in a nation that has repeatedly demonstrated its willingness to use that capacity to kill, and kill civilians. And I live in the nation that at this moment is using that capacity again to kill civilians in a conflict that is being sold to us as a war on terrorism that will keep us safe, but is, I believe, primarily a war to extend the power of a particular segment of US society.

From a talk to University of Texas teach-in on war and civil liberties, November 1 2001 – for full text see http://uts.cc.utexas.edu/%7Erjensen/freelance/attack15.htm

Arundhati Roy

The US government, and no doubt governments all over the world, will use the climate of war as an excuse to curtail civil liberties, deny free speech, lay off workers, harass ethnic and religious minorities, cut back on public spending and divert huge amounts of money to the defence industry. To what purpose? President Bush can no more "rid the world of evil-doers" than he can stock it with saints. It's absurd for the US government to even toy with the notion that it can stamp out terrorism with more violence and oppression. Terrorism is the symptom, not the disease. Terrorism has no country. It's transnational, as global an enterprise as Coke or Pepsi or Nike. At the first sight of trouble, terrorists can pull up stakes and move their 'factories' from country to country in search of a better deal. Just like the multi-nationals.

The Guardian, 29 September 2001

John Berger

Now that the number of innocent civilian victims killed collaterally in Afghanistan by the US bombardments is equal to the number killed in the attack on the Twin Towers, we can perhaps place the events in a larger, but not less tragic perspective, and face a new question: is it more evil or reprehensible to kill deliberately than to systematically kill blindly? (Systematically because the same logic of US armed strategy began with the Gulf war.) I don't know the answer to the question. On the ground, among the cluster bombs dropped by B52s or the stifling smoke in Church Street, Manhattan, perhaps ethical judgments cannot be comparative.

The Guardian, 29 June 2002
http://www.guardian.co.uk/comment/story/0,3604,746253,00.html

Robert Fisk

If the US attacks were an assault on "civilisation", why shouldn't Muslims regard the Afghanistan attack as a war on Islam?

The Independent, 8 November 2001

George Monbiot

Dear President Bush,

In commemorating the victims of the attacks on New York and Washington last week, you called for disputes to be "settled within the bounds of reason". You insisted that "every nation in our coalition must take seriously the growing threat" of biological and chemical weapons. You assured us that on this issue "there is no margin for error, and no chance to learn from mistakes... inaction is not an option". These are sentiments with which most of the world's people would agree. While many of us believe that attacking Iraq would enhance rather than reduce the possibility that weapons of mass destruction will be used, few would dispute that chemical and biological agents present a grave danger to the world. So those of us in other nations who have followed this issue are puzzled. Why should you, who claim to want to build "a peaceful world beyond the war on terror" have done all you can to undermine efforts to control these deadly weapons? Why should the congressmen in your party have repeatedly sabotaged attempts to ensure that biological and chemical agents are eliminated?

The Guardian, 19 March 2002

http://www.guardian.co.uk/comment/story/0,3604,669896,00.html

Gore Vidal

President Bush's June graduation address to the cadets at West Point is the fullest articulation, so far, of the new strategic doctrine of pre-emption. The radical idea being touted by the White House and Pentagon is that the United States has the right to use military force against any state that is seen as hostile or makes moves to acquire weapons of mass destruction--nuclear, biological or chemical.... It is a doctrine without limits, without accountability to the UN or international law, without any dependence on a collective judgement of responsible governments and, what is worse, without any convincing demonstration of practical necessity.... To propose abandoning the core legal restraint on international force in relations among states is to misread the challenge of September 11. It permits states to use force nondefensively against their enemies, thereby creating a terrible precedent.

The Nation, 15 July 2002

http://www.thenation.com/doc.mhtml?i=20020715&c=2&s=falk

Rahul Mahajan

The United States seeks nothing less than the establishment of complete control over all significant sources of oil, especially of the Middle East, which holds roughly two thirds of the world's proven reserves. The twin requirements of U.S. imperial control and the constant feeding of an industrial system based on ever-increasing levels of fossil fuel consumption dovetail with the systematic attempts of the United States to keep Middle Eastern countries from developing independent economies to set the stage for large-scale re-colonisation, through war, "covert" action, and economic coercion. This war is not about minor domestic squabbles between Democrats and Republicans, but about a very ugly New World Order, in which innocents in the Middle East, Central Asia, and in the United States pay for the imperial dreams of an increasingly detached American elite.

http://commondreams.org/views02/0805-08.htm

Edward Said

... so remorseless has been the focus on it [Palestinian struggle] as a phenomenon apart, a pure, gratuitous evil which Israel, supposedly acting on behalf of pure good, has been virtuously battling in its variously appalling acts of disproportionate violence against a population of three million Palestinian civilians. I am not speaking only about Israel's manipulation of opinion, but its exploitation of the American equivalent of the campaign against terrorism without which Israel could not have done what it has done... that this evil has been made consciously part of George W Bush's campaign against terrorism, irrationally magnifying American fantasies and fixations with extraordinary ease, is no small part of its blind destructiveness.

Al-Ahram Weekly Online, 8-14 August 2002
http://www.ahram.org.eg/weekly/2002/598/op2.htm

Faisal Bodi

Forgive me if this is getting tedious, but it would not be necessary had western commentators called this monster by its name - instead of exaggerating the extent of resurgent anti-semitism to evoke sympathy for Israel's irredentism in the Holy Land. In fact, the media has signally avoided giving due weight to the anti-Islamic face of the renascent right. The history of contemporary European Islamophobia starts with the fall of the iron curtain and the appearance of a new challenger to western capitalist hegemony. In a still self-consciously Christian Europe, this ideological competition has been grafted on to the legacies of the Crusades and Ottoman-Christian rivalries, and the perceived demographic and cultural threat posed by a growing Muslim population.

The Guardian, 14 May 2002
http://www.guardian.co.uk/comment/story/0,3604,715150,00.html

George Monbiot

But the US government has several pressing domestic reasons for going to war. The first is that attacking Iraq gives the impression that the flagging "war on terror" is going somewhere. The second is that the people of all super-dominant nations love war. As Bush found in Afghanistan, whacking foreigners wins votes. Allied to this concern is the need to distract attention from the financial scandals in which both the president and vice-president are enmeshed. Already, in this respect, the impending war seems to be working rather well.

The Guardian, 6 August 2002
http://www.guardian.co.uk/comment/story/0,3604,769699,00.html

John Lloyd

The respect Americans once accorded to Europeans' culture, wisdom and manners has not just disappeared, it has turned into an aggressive contempt. The US, at least at the elite level, and perhaps more widely, has become seized by the idea that we Europeans are weak, whinging and hopeless; ungrateful, mean and ignorant; guilty, cynical and exhausted.

Financial Times, 2 August 2002

Trevor Phillips, deputy chair of the Greater London Assembly

Imagine what it feels like to be a British Muslim today. Already in the shadow of September 11, you hear from a Labour cabinet minister that you have failed to seek a "sense of belonging". Parliament decides that we need draconian special measures to tackle a "handful" of potential terrorists; yet there's still no legal remedy for the religious discrimination experienced by Muslims every day.

The Guardian, 19 December 2001

Madeline Bunting

No one culture has evolved the perfect formulation of human values. Any good liberal must agree with that. The limitations are apparent of the liberal model of an individual pursuit of happiness. Can that guide us through an environmental crisis and grotesque economic inequality? What liberal hasn't pondered how to reinvigorate social solidarity, or revitalise concepts of the common good? These are familiar symptoms of the crisis in western thought. Because we are at war, we do not have to abandon our capacity for humility and self-criticism, nor the search in other cultures for the inspiration for new thinking.

The Guardian, 15 October 2001
http://www.guardian.co.uk/Columnists/Column/0,5673,574046,00.html

Professor Michael Sells

The media show repeated images of criminals ... surrounded by images of Islam, by Qur'anic calligraphy, with sounds of the Islamic call to prayer - often spliced with images of their crimes, such as Saddam with an American child hostage or pictures of the planes hitting the towers and the towers falling...Then, after showing repeatedly such images, the television newscasters make pronouncements on how Muslims should not be targeted or discriminated against. But as any advertising executive knows, images and symbolic associations are infinitely more powerful than words. Associations are as powerful as images: the term "Islamic terrorist" instead of "terrorist acting in the name of Islam," repeatedly used in contexts of emotion, anger, and stress, links the two terms in a way that makes it difficult for many to disassociate them in any context...It is vital that Americans come to know the Qur'an better and Islamic civilization more deeply.

http://www.haverford.edu/relg/sells/interlinkedfactors.htm

Peter Preston

When, long ago, Woodward and Bernstein found Deep Throat, they also found double trouble. A single source, according to the Washington Post house rules, wasn't enough. You had to have two separate ones to write the story that destroyed Richard Nixon. But that was politics, not war. And we live in more self-interested times.

This morning, there's Kerim Chatty, a Swede who was going to crash a plane into a US embassy, according to Swedish military intelligence sources. Or wasn't, according to Swedish police sources. Who had four accomplices, or worked alone (same sources). To this confusion, CIA, FBI and Scotland Yard sources added their bemused little codicils......

I am a reader - a mere reader - too, now. I wish to be informed reliably: because I have a right to know. And I'm sick of smudgy sources.

You can guess a bit of what's going on: the Pakistanis dumping on the Afghans and vice-versa; the Saudis briefing against Iran; the Kurds briefing against Saddam Hussein; and the Israelis briefing against everybody. You want "convincing proof"? We sell it by the rod, pole and perch, sir. Thus President Saddam, who wasn't in the frame after 9/11, is suddenly back as public enemy number one. Thus "western intelligence reports" begin to overflow with his al-Qaida links.

The Guardian, 2 September 2002
http://www.guardian.co.uk/comment/story/0,3604,784503,00.html

Mo Mowlam

Why is he [Bush] so determined to take the risk [of attacking Iraq]? The key country in the Middle East, as far as the Americans are concerned, is Saudi Arabia: the country with the largest oil reserves in the world, the country that has been prepared to calm the oil markets, producing more when prices are too high and less when there is a glut....Since September 11, however, it has become increasingly apparent to the US administration that the Saudi regime is vulnerable..The Americans know they cannot stop such a revolution. They must therefore hope that they can control the Saudi oil fields, if not the government. And what better way to do that than to have a large military force in the field at the time of such disruption. In the name of saving the west, these vital assets could be seized and controlled.....This whole affair has nothing to do with a threat from Iraq - there isn't one. It has nothing to do with the war against terrorism or with morality. Saddam Hussein is obviously an evil man, but when we were selling arms to him to keep the Iranians in check he was the same evil man he is today. He was a pawn then and is a pawn now. In the same way he served western interests then, he is now the distraction for the sleight of hand to protect the west's supply of oil. And where does this leave the British government? Are they in on the plan or just part of the smokescreen? The government speaks of morality and the threat posed by weapons of mass destruction, but can they really believe it?

The Guardian, 5 September 2002
http://www.guardian.co.uk/comment/story/0,3604,786180,00.html

Patrick Sookhdeo

Unlike Islam, Christianity does not justify the use of all forms of violence. Islam does.

The Daily Telegraph, 17 September 2001

Silvio Berlusconi

We should be conscious of the superiority of our civilisation, which consists of a value system that has given people widespread prosperity in those countries that embrace it, and guarantees respect for human rights and religion. This respect certainly does not exist in the Islamic countries.

26 September 2001

http://www.guardian.co.uk/waronterror/story/0,1361,558866,00.html

The Spectator

The truth is that there are elements of the Koran which do legitimate hostility towards us infidels. The Koran does give scriptural cover for judicial brutality and the ill-treatment of women. In the headiness of its poetry and rhetoric, it is easy to see how the Koran can help induce a divine rage and suicidal madness.

3 November 2001

http://www.spectator.co.uk/article.php3?table=old&section=current&issue=2001-11-03&id=1188

Daniel Pipes

Public opinion in the Muslim world is volatile, responding to developing events in an emotional, superficial, and changeable way.

http://www.danielpipes.org/article/417

There is no substitute for victory. If the U.S. government wishes to weaken its strategic enemy, militant Islam, it must take two steps. First, continue the war on terror globally, using appropriate means, starting with Afghanistan but going on to wherever militant Islam poses a threat, in Muslim-majority countries (such as Saudi Arabia), in Muslim-minority countries (such as the Philippines), and even in the United States itself. As this effort brings success, secondly Washington should promote moderate Muslims.

http://www.danielpipes.org/article/417

Sir John Keegan

Orientals, by contrast, shrink from pitched battle, which they often deride as a sort of game, preferring ambush, surprise, treachery and deceit as the best way to overcome an enemy...this war [in Afghanistan] belongs within the much larger spectrum of a far older conflict between settled, creative productive Westerners and predatory, destructive Orientals.

John Keegan is Defence Editor, *The Daily Telegraph*; 8 October 2001

Robert Kilroy-Silk

The 'Moslem problem' is an important one. How we deal with the 'enemy within' will have momentous and long-term consequences for race relations in this country for years.

The Express on Sunday, 28 October 2001

Melanie Phillips

The attitude of many British Muslims should cause the greatest possible alarm that we have a fifth column in our midst...thousands of alienated young Muslims, most of them born and bred here but who regard themselves as an army within, are waiting for an opportunity to help to destroy the society that sustains them. We now stare into the abyss, aghast.

Sunday Times, 4 November 2001

David Mellor

....Britain's Muslims should be making a commitment or two to us. Such as that they understand that being British imposes obligations of loyalty that some seem only too ready to abandon with talk of their religion being far more important than their nationality.

The People 11 November 2001

Carol Sarler

It is this tolerance that, I fear, is going to bite us. It is the same tolerance that allows an indigenous population to host another that hates us and says so, in loud, haranguing, roving gangs that terrorise our inner cities in the name of Allah.

Daily Express, 15 November 2001

Patricia Crone

Mohammad's God endorsed a policy of conquest, instructing his believers to fight against unbelievers wherever they might be found. In short, Mohammad had to conquer, his followers liked to conquer, and his deity told him to conquer.

Quoted in the article 'The Great Koran Con Trick', *The New Statesman*, 10 December 2001

Melanie Phillips

Having never had a 'reformation' which would have forced it [Islam] to make an accommodation with modernity, it is fundamentally intolerant and illiberal.

The Spectator, 11 May 2002
http://pws.prserv.net/mpjr/mp/sp110502.htm

Ian Buruma

Muslims have a harder time entering the mainstream of European societies. It is difficult to imagine a programme similar to Goodness, Gracious Me that treated Islam satirically. The enemies of Rushdie were somewhat lacking in the humour department, especially about themselves.

The Guardian, 21 May 2002
http://www.guardian.co.uk/g2/story/0,3604,719159,00.html

A US secret service agent
"ISLAM IS EVIL."

The graffiti left by after raiding the home of a Muslim in Dearborn, Michigan on 25 July 2002
http://www.cair-net.org/asp/article.asp?articleid=882&articletype=3

Ian Buruma

A Muslim priest who refuses to distinguish between spiritual and secular authority cannot be a democratic citizen. If he wishes to live in a democracy, however, he will have to give up all claims to temporal power...Anything the west can do to break such monopolies, through economic, diplomatic, or even, if necessary, military means, is surely a good thing. If that is globalisation or imperialism, I am for it.

The Guardian, 2 July 2002
http://www.guardian.co.uk/g2/story/0,3604,747601,00.html

Samuel Brittan
Islamist militancy is a self-confessed threat to the values not merely of the US but also of the European Enlightenment: to the preference for life over death, to peace, rationality, science and the humane treatment of our fellow men, not to mention fellow women. It is a reassertion of blind, cruel faith over reason. One does not have to be a scholar of Islam to say this.

The Financial Times, 31 July 2002
http://www.samuelbrittan.co.uk/text120_p.html

Mark Steyn
... the psychotic death-cultism of radical Islam.

The Daily Telegraph, 3 August 2002
http://www.portal.telegraph.co.uk/opinion/main.jhtml?xml=%2Fopinion%2F2002%2F08%2F0
3%2Fdo0302.xml

Franklin Graham
If you buy the Koran, read it for yourself, and it's in there. The violence that it preaches is there.

US evangelist on Fox News cable network's "Hannity & Colmes" program, 5 August 2002
http://www.cair-net.org/asp/article.asp?articleid=887&articletype=3

William Oddie
Just below the surface of the West's troubled collective unconscious, a killer anxiety is struggling to be born. It is that Islam - not just "Islamic fundamentalism" but Islam *tout court* – is going to become not merely one of the hazards we will have to negotiate from time to time, but something a great deal more dangerous.

The Daily Telegraph, 8 August 2002
http://www.telegraph.co.uk/news/main.jhtml?xml=%2Fnews%2F2001%2F11%2F08%2Fnodd
08.xml

All web site addresses (URLs) referred to in this book are listed in the MCB web site (www.mcb.org.uk/bookref) as hyperlinks

4

Impact on the UK

Legal Developments Since September 11: A Short Survey

MAHMUD AL RASHID

The signs were ominous even before September 11. The proscription, in February 2001, of 21 international organisations under the Terrorism Act 2000 caused great consternation. Sixteen of the 21 organisations are based in nine Muslim countries. There are large numbers of Muslims from these nine countries - who have no connection with these 16 organisations - living and working in the UK, and the proscription has been described as "criminalizing communities" by casting a slur and tainting Muslims as a whole. Of course, proscribing these organisations is not going to stop their activities in their respective countries, but it has led to the situation where any Muslim who does not look "right" is instantly suspected of some misdemeanour. Even in the work place there are increasing reports of jokes about Muslim colleagues being members or supporters of Al-Qaida. For many the situation became intolerable and they simply left their jobs.

The sense of hope given by the incorporation of the European Convention of Human Rights (ECHR) into British law was short lived. Article 9 of the ECHR, the freedom of religion provisions, was hailed as a positive development for the integration of faith communities into mainstream life. However, there still remains no comprehensive protection against religious discrimination (despite research from the University of Derby finding that British Muslims suffered a "consistently higher level of unfair treatment" than other religious groups) and at the first real test of the Human Rights Act 1998, the UK government balked and derogated from Article 5 of the ECHR. This happened when 11 Muslims were arrested under anti-terrorism legislation and detained in high security prisons under conditions so severe that leading medical experts had raised serious concerns about their health and complained of unprecedented Home Office interference. The men were not charged and not told why or for how long they would be detained. Such detention is contrary to Article 5, so the UK government decided to excuse itself from its obligations rather than recognise the rights of such individuals. Two of the detainees decided they would rather leave the UK than remain incarcerated indefinitely. The others challenged their detention in court and it was ruled (on 30 August 2002) that though the derogation was justified, it discriminated against foreign nationals. As of writing, both parties are appealing and the nine remain locked up.

There seems to be a post-September 11 fallout that has affected certain judges in British courts. Back in 1998 the Home Office decided to deport Shafiqur Rahman, an Imam from Oldham, who was living here with his British wife and children. The Home Secretary felt that because of Mr Rahman's support for an organisation in Pakistan his presence in the UK was contrary to the interests of national security. Mr Rahman won his appeal at first instance, even though some of the evidence against him was given in "closed" sessions where neither he nor his lawyers were permitted inside the court and so had no idea what that evidence was. The Commission found that Mr Rahman was not a threat to national security; that he was not recruiting British Muslims to undergo "militant training"; and that he had not raised any funds for the organisation he supported.

An interesting twist to this case was when members of MI6 and MI5 were giving evidence (from behind screens) they disclosed that they had been targeting Imams to become informers on the Muslim community. They became evasive when asked whether even during the height of IRA terrorism they had targeted Catholic priests for such roles.

Another interesting twist to this case was that Mr Rahman was refused legal aid before the Commission, despite the complexity and potentially serious consequence to him. The Lord Chancellor refused to authorise legal aid payment and when this decision was challenged in the High Court, Mr David Pannick QC said that the Immigration Advisory Service (IAS), which had absolutely no experience of such cases, could conduct Mr Rahman's appeal. On appeal the judges in the Court of Appeal said that they were certain the judge hearing Mr Rahman's appeal would "bend over backwards" to make sure he was adequately represented. So he had to be represented free of charge before the Commission and when the matter went to the House of Lords his QC was permitted £90 an hour and a maximum of 100 hours preparation and research. This contrasted with the vast resources of the Home Office (including the intelligence services) and no limitations were put on their lawyers' time. As for their fees, they were paid

- also out of public funds remember - a minimum rate of £250 an hour. "Equality of arms" and "level playing field" do not come rushing to mind.

The Home Office appealed the decision of the Commission and won both in the Court of Appeal and in the House of Lords. The case was heard by the Lords in May 2001 and judgment was handed down in October 2001. There was nothing in the Rahman case which had anything to do with September 11 yet Lord Hoffmann, when the case was being argued in May 2001, questioned Mr Rahman's counsel whether an attack on the World Trade Centre would be a threat to Britain's national security. In a postscript to his judgment he said "I wrote this speech some three months before the recent events in New York and Washington. They are a reminder that in matters of national security, the cost of failure can be high. This seems to me to underline the need for the judicial arm of government to respect the decisions of ministers on the question of whether support for terrorist activities in a foreign country constitutes a threat to national security."

Take the case of Iftikhar Ali. He is a member of Al-Muhajiroun (A-M) and used to work for London Underground. One Friday, outside a mosque in East London, he was giving out the usual A-M leaflets, which their members have been doing for years. At worst these unsolicited leaflets cause annoyance and many are simply thrown away. On this occasion the Attorney-General, Peter Goldsmith QC, decided to give his consent to Mr Ali being prosecuted under the Public Order Act 1986. He felt the leaflet was an incitement to racial hatred. The offending material, he thought, was a hadith which talks of a battle between Muslims and Jews before the end of the world. Of course, one can find alarming and apocalyptic stories in almost all religious texts, but this particular hadith caught the Attorney General's attention and he authorised prosecution. In court the judge, Jeremy McMullen, commented "words created 1,400 years ago are equally capable of containing race hate as words created today." Mr Ali was duly convicted and sentenced in May 2002.

One of the more interesting twists to this prosecution was that Muslim organisations, led by the MCB, had been campaigning for the outlawing of incitement to religious hatred. The government responded by adding a clause to its post-September 'tough on terrorism' legislation: the Anti-terrorism, Crime and Security Bill. Comedian Rowan Atkinson was discomfited enough to write to *The Times*, warning that people like him would be arrested for mocking religion. More serious objections were based around unjustified restrictions on freedom of expression. No one seemed to notice that incitement to racial hatred had been outlawed for many years without any lasting damage to freedom of expression. The government was defeated twice in the Lords and quickly dropped the incitement provisions. Many Muslims felt Mr Blunkett was, like the grand old Duke of York, merely marching them up the hill only to march them down again. It was clear that the incitement measures were "included as a sop to Muslims to compensate for the likelihood that they might be the main targets of the anti-terrorism measures in the Bill," wrote the Guardian on 10 December 2001. The irony of it all is that whereas Muslims were seeking new laws to protect them from incitement, the person to actually get prosecuted for incitement was a Muslim who distributed a leaflet that had done the rounds for many years and contained a hadith that had been in universal circulation for 1400 years! The whole incitement debacle sent a very discouraging message to Muslims asking for protection from inflammatory and aggressive language.

Then, of course, there is the prosecution of the rioters from last summer. Judge Gullick was enjoying passing draconian sentences on Muslims from the northern towns. In imprisoning Shazad Ashraf for five years, he said, "I am not concerned with [the origins of the riots.] It must be made clear to everyone that on such tumultuous and riotous occasions, each individual who takes an active part ... is guilty of an extremely grave offence simply by being in a public place and being engaged in a crime against the peace. It would be wholly unreal, therefore, for me to have regard to the specific acts which you committed." Judge Gullick was determined to establish his own sentencing principles. Ashraf had pleaded guilty and his five years was supposed to be a discounted sentence, but Judge Gullick warned him "I should make it plain that those who choose to run their not guilty pleas up to the wire until they can see the colour of the jury's eyes should know that the discount will be substantially and visibly reduced from that which they would otherwise have earned for an early guilty plea."

There was a marked difference between the sentences given to the Asians from Bradford and those handed down to white men jailed for their part in the Burnley riot. The average sentence given to the 26 white men in March was 26 months; this is less than half of what Asians from Bradford were sentenced to – 54 months imprisonment, even though the judge at the trial of the white rioters said the troubles began after a group of 20-30 white men chanted racist abuse outside a pub where they had been drinking.

In October 2001 the UN Human Rights Committee expressed concerns about the UK government's plans to extend anti-terrorist legislation in the wake of September 11. It was also concerned about the Terrorism Act 2000 and was disturbed by the outbreak of racist violence in the summer of 2001. The Committee was highly critical of various aspects of asylum law and policies including detention of asylum seekers, use of vouchers and dispersal.

No doubt terrorism is a scourge which needs eliminating. But the almost exclusive focus on Muslims is a gross distortion of reality and there is a failure to understand and tackle the causes of terrorism. Combating terrorism must not become an aim in itself, but rather the achievement of a just, humane and free society should be our goal. It appears much of recent anti-terrorism legislation echo the urgings of Benjamin Netanyahu in his book 'Fighting Terrorism'.

In 1977 Professor Paul Wilkinson, anti-terrorism expert from St. Andrews, wrote in 'Terrorism and the Liberal State' that "the primary objective of counter-terrorist strategy must be the protection and maintenance of liberal democracy and the rule of law. It cannot be sufficiently stressed that this aim overrides in importance even the objective of eliminating terrorism and political violence as such. Any bloody tyrant can 'solve' the problem of political violence if he is prepared to sacrifice all considerations of humanity, and to trample down all constitutional and judicial rights."

Professor Wilkinson repeated these sentiments in his paper for the Lloyd Committee on whose report the Terrorism Act 2000 was predicated. "It must be a cardinal principle of a liberal democracy," he insisted, "in dealing with problems of terrorism, however serious these may be, never to be tempted into using methods which are incompatible with the liberal values of humanity, liberty and justice. It is a dangerous illusion to believe one can 'protect' liberal democracy by suspending liberal rights and forms of government ... even in the most severe cases, the liberal democracy must seek to remain true to itself ... Another kind of betrayal is the deliberate suspension or limitation of civil liberty on grounds of expediency. However hard the going gets in coping with severe internal or international terrorism, or both, a liberal democratic government has a primary duty to preserve constitutional government."

Post- September 11 it is even more vital that the government heeds such advice, if we are to avoid an era of repression unmatched by anything seen in the last century. The high-profile arrest and detention of Lotfi Raissi, the acquittal of Suleyman Zain-ul-Abidin despite the best efforts of Labour MP Andrew Dismore, the internment of the un-named nine, the draconian anti-terrorism legislation are all betrayals of the values of liberal democracy. The laws passed and the messages sent by those enforcing it have done nothing to remove the anti-Muslim sentiment that is prevalent in society. Rather they have pandered to the wishes of the extremists.

A Sorry Farce:
The Story of Lotfi Raissi
'A web of circumstantial evidence.'

Lotfi Raissi, 27, an Algerian pilot, was arrested in London on 21 September 2001 at the request of the American FBI. Gun-toting police officers entered his flat in Colnbrooke near Slough, at three in the morning and pulled him from his bed. For one bizarre moment he thought that he was being kidnapped. Raissi should have known something terrible was up when one of the officers looked at the framed 737 pilot's certificate on the wall and turned to his colleague, smiled and said: "He's our man." With a gun placed against his head he was marched out into the street and bundled naked into the back of a police car. Leaving him shivering, officers then searched his home. Only later was a white boiler-suit passed into the car.

The charges initially brought against him by the Crown Prosecution Service was that he was the "lead trainer" of the September 11 hijackers. Raissi was accused of teaching the September 11 suicide hijackers to fly and of having close ties with Hani Hanjour, the alleged pilot of the plane that crashed into the Pentagon. The prosecution claimed that Lotfi Raissi had paid for Hanjour and other men to have sessions on flight simulators and regularly telephoned and travelled with Hanjour. He was held at the Belmarsh prison under a severe security regime that allowed only 15 minutes of exercise in a day. It was to be six weeks before he could see his wife again, behind a glass partition.

In December, prosecutors said there was "a web of circumstantial evidence" pointing to his involvement "in a terrorist conspiracy which culminated in the events of September 11", although no proof was forthcoming. Based on these charges, Raissi faced extradition to the United States. Lotfi Raissi was the first person to be accused of involvement in the attacks on the World Trade Centre and was originally told he could face the death sentence in the US. At his first brief appearance in court, Judge Timothy Workman denied Raissi's request for bail: I'm refusing bail on the grounds that I think there is a substantial risk you would fail to surrender,'' he said. However the judge also noted that on the occasions that Raissi had appeared before him, the US had said that these were simply holding charges and that "more serious charges linking him to September 11 would be proffered".

After five months in custody, the US authorities failed to come up with enough evidence to substantiate a single serious charge and Raissi eventually appeared in court accused of failing to declare a previous criminal conviction and an old tennis injury when he applied for a pilot's licence. The BBC's Gordon Corera said: "All they could muster was that he had lied about an injury and an old theft conviction on his application for a pilot's licence. Any evidence linking him to the attacks was wrong."

The court heard he had been convicted in 1993 of stealing a briefcase and its contents. He was fined £150 and £30 costs at Uxbridge Magistrates Court. Edward Fitzgerald QC, defending, said he was entitled under English law to treat the offence as a spent conviction. "There was no deception because it was as if there were no previous convictions." He said there was no evidence to suggest that if Mr Raissi had declared the conviction that it would have prevented him being granted a licence. Mr Fitzgerald told the court that the knee surgery had not been mentioned in the application for a medical certificate because it had been disclosed in an earlier application for a certificate.

Although the US government claimed that Lotfi Raissi should be denied bail because he was a suspect in their inquiries into the atrocities and was likely to abscond, the district judge at Bow Street Magistrates Court, Timothy Workman, decided that five months in custody as a category 'A' prisoner in the high security unit of Belmarsh prison on minor charges was enough. Judge Workman said: "I discharge the defendant on all eight charges...Several allegations involving terrorism have been made but I would like to make it clear that I have received no evidence to support that contention...On the representations made to me today to me on behalf of the American government and on behalf of the defendant, I am satisfied that there is no likelihood of terrorist charges being prefered against Mr Raissi in the near future...I am also satisfied that the links that the government had previously put before this court which was thought to connect the defendant to others in the terrorist organisation can no longer be substantiated."

But James Lewis QC, for the US government, said Raissi would "continue to be subject to ongoing investigations into those associated with the September 11 attacks". Hugo Keith, QC, defending, said the American authorities had refused to admit that they had pursued the wrong man in this case while his client had remained in custody in fear for his life. Every further day Raissi spent in custody was an affront to justice.

In April 2002, Raissi's case was thrown out entirely when a district judge, also sitting in Bow Street magistrates court, London, concluded there was not a shred of evidence to support the contention he was involved in terrorist activity.

Outside court, Mr Raissi's solicitor, Richard Egan, read a statement on behalf of his client:

> "Mr Raissi has been held for five months on the basis of wholly unsubstantiated allegations before being released on bail. Not only that but he and his family have had to endure the finger of suspicion being pointed at them. At the very least one would hope for an apology.
>
> Bearing in mind the length of time this case has already gone on it is absurd to suggest there is still an ongoing investigation into Mr Raissi. It is time the whole sorry farce came to an end. It is time his absolute innocence was recognised."

Lotfi speaking to Audrey Gillan of *The Guardian*, painted a graphic picture of his ordeal: "You cannot begin to consider what it is like to have the world's media along with the government of the United States believing that you are responsible for the most dreadful act of terrorism the world has ever seen. I was separated from my family and had to face this ordeal alone...I am totally sympathetic to the suffering of the American people caused by the appalling tragedy that occurred on September 11, but I would also like to add that I have become in turn a victim of that atrocity... I am not a terrorist – I abhor terrorism, and my family in Algeria has fought terrorism and been the victims of it for a decade. I understand that the FBI has to investigate that appalling criminal act to the full extent of their ability. I also understand that as a pilot and as an Algerian who had been in the United States that they would wish to scrutinise my background. What shocked me, however, was that it took five months before the United States Government informed the court that they were no longer seeking to extradite me on terrorist charges. Those five months have destroyed me and all those dear to me, and I do not believe that I will ever recover from the experience. I am a pilot, an Algerian, and a Muslim, and proud to be so, but this is not a crime.

They needed a scapegoat and the beauty of the scapegoat they created was that they knew I was innocent and they probably knew in the first seven days of the investigation that I had nothing to do with it. The beauty of this scapegoat is that he has to be a pilot, a Muslim, he has to be Arabic. So they have the jackpot, the scapegoat, bingo. The law says that a person is innocent until proven guilty. In my case I feel as though the world perceived me as a guilty man and that I had to try and prove that I was innocent.

This is the first time in my life to be in prison and it's been the worst experience and I hope any human being doesn't experience what I did because it was dreadful and awful. There's no word to describe it. I couldn't breathe, I couldn't think, I couldn't dream, I couldn't eat... as a person and as a human being I am shattered because all my thoughts and sympathy are with the American people. I repeat that all my thoughts and sympathy were with those innocent people and the families of those innocent people who died in that atrocity...I felt sympathy, especially as a pilot. There are no words to describe it.

As I believe British justice is the best in the world, and the expertise of Scotland Yard, and I believe the FBI, their expertise, I said that it's an atrocity and I'm a pilot and a pilot instructor, they have a right to do an investigation. I thought it would take two or three days. I thought they would come back and apologise and say bye bye Charlie. I was shocked [when they didn't]. I was fascinated with flying. Fascinated with Charles Lindbergh. I wanted to become a pilot. Not just a pilot, but a good pilot, a captain, a chief pilot. I wanted to go all the way in the aviation industry. I worked very hard. I woke up breathing aviation, I slept aviation. I dreamed aviation. That was my focus.

I don't have a job, I can't even support my family, and I'm very concerned for my future with the reputation I have. A number of my family because of this already lost their jobs and the humiliation we went through. I was Muslim, Algerian, Arabic and a pilot - it just gave them a licence to discriminate. I am a victim of my nationality. I am a victim of my religion. I am a victim of my ethnicity and I am a victim of the September 11 atrocity."

Religious Discrimination: The New Racism

LORRAINE SHERIDAN

Very little academic or other materials are available on the subject of religious discrimination (Malik, 2001), making it difficult to precisely quantify its incidence and nature and to identify potential contributory factors. What is clear, however, is that religious discrimination is a widespread problem throughout England and Wales, so widespread that it may now be more prevalent than racial abuse.

The evidence for this assertion derives from a number of sources, and will be reviewed here. The line between racism and religious discrimination is often blurred (e.g. Allen & Nielsen, 2002), with the result that measures of the former can serve to highlight the existence of the latter. The British Crime Survey 2000 (Clancy, Hough, Aust & Kershaw, 2001) estimated that during 1999, the number of racially motivated offences experienced by ethnic minorities in England and Wales was 280,000. Victimisation rates were highest among ethnic Bangladeshis and Pakistanis, who are primarily Muslim. Among British Hindu, Indian Muslim and Pakistani schoolchildren, Eslea and Mukhtar (2000) found that 57% of boys and 43% of girls aged 12-15 had been bullied within one school term. In each case the bullying was likely to have been related to religious or cultural differences. Inter-Asian bullying was seen as well as White-Asian bullying. For instance, Hindus most frequently bullied Indian Muslims and Pakistanis. This illustrates the early onset of discrimination on the grounds of religious and cultural differences.

What is 'Islamophobia'?

The first known printed usage of the word 'Islamophobia' appears to be in

February 1991, when it was published in a periodical in the United States (Insight, 1991). It has been included in the Oxford English Dictionary since 1997. Islamophobia is thought to constitute a two-stranded form of racism – rooted in both the 'different' physical appearance of Muslims and also an intolerance of their religious and cultural beliefs, and should be considered as a modern epidemic of an age-old prejudice towards and fear of Islam. Malik (2001) notes that such attitudes are still manifested in modern society which in itself is not considered 'religion friendly'. Islam is erroneously regarded as backward and chauvinistic compared to 'enlightened' modern Western values (Runnymede Trust, 1997). The word 'Islamophobia' is functionally similar to 'xenophobia' and offers a useful shorthand way of referring to a dread or hatred of Islam, and therefore a fear or dislike of Muslims (Runnymede Trust, 1997).

When exploring the processes that underlie religious discrimination, it is important to investigate where discriminators obtain information relating to the target group. Altareb (1998) examined attitudes towards Middle-Eastern Muslims held by non-Muslim undergraduates in the USA. It was found that although participants possessed little information about Muslims and Islam, they did hold definite attitudes towards Muslims. Further, much of this information was gleaned from film and media sources. Madani (2002), analysing newspaper headlines from between 1956 and 1997, found that the US media depicted Muslims and Arabs more negatively than Western Europeans and Israelis. Following the events of September 11, Allen and Nielsen (2002) reported that although the majority of European politicians publicly offered conciliation and solidarity with Muslim communities, some remained silent and a few made negatively charged statements. Both stereotypical and sensationalist depictions of Muslims were noted in the mass media. Negative images of Muslims promoted by the media and by political leaders may serve to build or provide 'evidence' for existing Islamophobic prejudices.

Evidence of Islamophobia
In the United States of America, a study by Omeish (1999) directly addressed religious discrimination, finding that Muslim students perceived prejudice and discrimination to be a common feature within their higher education establishments. Here in the United Kingdom, a recent survey indicated that a full 69% of Muslim interviewees said that they felt excluded from mainstream British society, and that 41% believed that their own communities should do more to aid integration (ICM, 2002). A Home Office study (Weller, Feldman & Purdam, 2001) examined religious

discrimination in England and Wales across more than 20 faith groups. Via questionnaire responses, meetings and interviews, Weller et al. ascertained that ignorance of and indifference towards religion were a widespread concern across all faith groups, but that Muslim organisations reported a consistently higher level of unfair treatment than did the majority of other religious groups, both proportionally and in terms of frequency. A majority of Muslim organisations reported that their members experienced unfair treatment in education, employment, housing, law and order and in respect of local government services. Further, Muslims were the most likely faith group to state that religious discrimination had worsened since 1996.

Islamophobia post-September 11 2001
It has been widely speculated that the events of September 11 have led to an increase in attacks on Islamic targets. Anticipating such an increase, the European Monitoring Centre on Racism and Xenophobia implemented a system to record anti-Islamic reactions across the 15 EU member states, producing a summary report in May 2002 (Allen & Nielsen, 2002). Although variations in methodologies employed between member states did not allow any reliable pan-European comparisons to be made, overall, Allen and Nielsen (2002) reported that Muslims, as well as members of other vulnerable groups, had experienced increased hostility post September 11 – a fuller account of their work appears elsewhere in this book. Although relatively low levels of violent abuse were reported, verbal abuse, harassment and aggression were far more prevalent.

Religious versus racial discrimination
One English study has provided comparators of both before and after September 11 levels of religious discrimination. Sheridan, Blaauw, Gillett and Winkel (2002) assessed whether members of religious and racial minority groups experienced an increase in racism and discrimination following the events of September 11. The highest proportion of the 451 participants were Muslim (50%). The next most frequently occurring religious grouping were Sikhs (17.3%), followed by Hindus (14.3%), Jews (11.8%) and Christians (6.5%). The majority of respondents (85.7%) resided in two English cities, Leicester and Stoke-on-Trent. According to the 1991 population census, 71.5% of Leicester people were white, and 22% of the population of the city were of Indian origin. The latter figure is believed to have risen markedly since 1991, and it is predicted that by 2011, Leicester will become the first UK city where 50% of the population will hail from a non-white background. Stoke-on-Trent, on the other hand, was

reported by the 1991 census to have a total ethnic minority population of just 3.1%.

Main results

Given that racist attitudes tend to be disguised by social sensitivities (e.g. Dovidio & Fazio, 1991), this research focussed on both (i) general religious/racial discrimination and (ii) 'implicit' religious and racial prejudice before and after September 11 2001. Implicit racism is where people deny having overt prejudices, but still react to members of racial, ethnic and religious minorities differently than to members of their own group. Of the five religious groups assessed, Muslims were found to have not only the greatest risk of being victims of both implicit racism and general discrimination before September 11, but also the highest increase in experiences of racism and discrimination since the events of that day, and, consequently, the greatest risk of being victims of both implicit racism and general discrimination after September 11. Sikhs and Hindus also reported increases in experiences of implicit racism post-September 11, but these increases were not as great as those reported by Muslims. By comparison, Christians and Jews reported a decrease in implicit racism experiences. In terms of ethnic origin, the most at risk groups of the seven examined appear to be Pakistanis and Bangladeshis, supporting findings from 2000 British Crime Survey. Overall, one of the most important findings was that religion was more important than ethnicity in indicating which groups were most likely to experiences religious and racial discrimination. When added to the evidence outlined above, this strongly suggests that religious discrimination may be more prevalent among certain minority groups than discrimination on racial grounds.

More on implicit racism

Participants reported high levels of negative daily life experiences on the 'implicit racism experiences' scale that they believed were directly related to cultural, racial and religious differences. The degrees to which respondents were subjected to such experiences were clearly associated with their race or religion. For instance, on the basis of religion Muslims reported experiencing more implicit racism both before and after September 11 than did other religious groups, whilst Pakistanis and Bangladeshis reported the highest levels on the basis of ethnicity. Importantly, the current work has clearly identified that 'implicit racism experiences' exist on religious, not just racial, grounds. This new finding indicates the existence of 'implicit religious discrimination'. Moreover, given the stronger relations found between religion and respondents' experiences of racism and discrimination, it appears that again, religion can be a stronger motivator for discriminatory sentiment and behaviour than race or ethnicity.

General discrimination

In terms of experiencing or witnessing general discriminatory practices after September 11, the biggest rise was recorded in ethnic Pakistanis. Prior to September 11, Bangladeshis had reported the highest levels of general discrimination, followed by Pakistanis. After September 11, these positions were reversed. Interestingly, 100% of respondents of Pakistani ethnic origin were Muslim, as were all except two of the Bangladeshi respondents. It is not clear why Pakistanis reported such a great increase in general discrimination. One possible reason is that following September 11 Pakistan saw a number of protests against military action in Afghanistan, perhaps leading some westerners to believe that all Pakistanis were supportive of the Taliban or the attacks on America. This explanation would, however, assume that those who behaved in a discriminatory manner were aware of the target's precise ethnic origin. UK whites also reported a rise in after September 11 discrimination – equivalent to that reported by ethnic Indians. Analysis of the religious orientation of the ethnic UK whites provides a probable reason for this reported increase in that almost half (15 of 37) were Muslims. These findings support the conclusion that Islamophobia is the primary factor in after September 11 discrimination in England.

Primary implications

Religion appeared to trigger both implicit racism and general discrimination to a greater extent than did race or ethnicity, both before and post September 11. Research on religious discrimination is severely limited, clearly indicating the need for an expansion of interest in this vastly neglected area. Further investigation into and delineation of the course and nature of religious discrimination in England and Wales requires immediate attention. Outlawing religious discrimination at an everyday level would highlight its status as an important social problem faced by a significant proportion of the English and Welsh population, and trigger much needed research. Some examples of the specific nature of these problems are provided by the following quotations (obtained during the research conducted by Sheridan et al., 2002):

"I had to go to Coventry. I missed the first bus and thus had to wait 40 minutes at the bus stop at Digbeth Coach Station, Birmingham. It was very disappointing for me that the bus driver, with the consent of English passengers, did not allow me to board the bus, only because that I was an Asian Muslim."

Pakistani Muslim male, 38 years, teacher

"I used to receive orders for ready made garments from many English stores, but since the 11 September incident, English stores have stopped giving me orders. The America incident has really affected the Pakistani businessman. Many of my friends also have the same problem and are worried."

Pakistani Muslim male, 35 years, businessman

"I am an English Muslim, and I wear a head scarf and long coat. Whenever I walk I get stared at. Whilst walking around supermarkets people turn their heads and look back at me as if I have just stolen something from them."

White Muslim female, 35 years, housewife

"When I was at college a girl said to me that all Muslims should be killed, that all Muslims are evil. The lecturer overheard but did nothing."

Pakistani Muslim male, 17 years, student

"I have been called a 'ninja' because of the headscarf that I wear, even though I do not wear a veil. I have also been called a 'Paki' and a 'lesbian' when gathering with other girls at prayer times."

Indian Muslim female, 12 years, school student

"I am afraid to mention on my CV that I was an active member of my University's Islamic Society, or to tell that I am a Muslim, for fear of being looked at as though I am a terrorist. I feel that this would increase if I was to wear a Hijab. I went for an interview recently, and was asked what other things I did at University, and I mentioned that I was a member of the Islamic Society, and felt that the tone of the lady interviewing me had changed."

Pakistani Muslim female, 24 years, PhD student

"I was travelling on the bus and about to open up my bag when a voice from behind me said 'Go on then, take out that bomb!' He repeatedly told me to '(expletive) off back to your country'. He said repeatedly that I don't belong here. He accused me and 'my people' to be behind the (September 11) attacks. He tried to racially incite the other passengers against me. He kept swearing at me and said things like 'why do you keep a beard?'. He got up a few times and came close to me as if he was going to become physical but at the end sat back down. One of the worst things was that nobody was saying anything to him. It was as if they cared more about their own safety. Some shook their heads disapprovingly but that didn't help me at all but in fact their silence helped him instead!"

Pakistani Muslim male, 27 years, student

"Whilst working in a kebab house, people came in calling us Usama Bin Laden and broke all our windows in the shop and caused a lot of damage."

Pakistani Muslim male, 20 years, Caterer

Others have attested to their belief that there is little recourse for the victims of religious discrimination:

"Every day I hear that another one of my friends or family has been insulted, has been laughed at, or has even been physically attacked. The worst part is that we can't do anything about it. Nobody seems to care about us, which of course the perpetrators are aware of."

Indian Muslim female, 20 years, student

"After September 11, a poor Sikh man was the first to feel the wrath of the racists, when he was killed in America. He was mistakenly thought to be a Muslim, because of his appearance, i.e. beard, turban. This event sparked a massive educating programme in America to distinguish Sikhs from Muslims. (Maybe America was saying shrewdly that if you're going to kill someone, at least kill the right people, i.e. Muslims)."

Indian Muslim female, 26 years, finance agent

Conclusion
Although much legal and academic attention has been afforded to racism,

religious discrimination has been largely ignored. The recent evidence reviewed here indicates not only that religious discrimination is commonplace in England and Wales, but also that it represents a significant social problem. Unless discriminatory activity on the grounds of religion is outlawed at an everyday level, members of the British public will continue to suffer without adequate recourse.

References

Allen, C. & Nielsen, J.S. (2002). Summary report on Islamophobia in the EU after 11 September 2001. European Monitoring Centre on Racism and Xenophobia. Vienna.

Altareb, B.Y. (1998). Attitudes towards Muslims: Initial scale development. Dissertation Abstracts International: Section B: The Sciences and Engineering, 58, 7-B, 3960.

Clancy, A., Hough, M., Aust, R. & Kershaw, C. (2001). Crime, policing and justice: The experience of ethnic minorities – findings from the British Crime Survey. Home Office Research Study 223. London: HMSO.

Dovidio, J.F. & Fazio, R.H. (1991). New technologies for the direct and indirect assessment of attitudes. In J.M. Tanur (Ed.). Questions about survey questions: meaning, memory, attitudes and social interaction. (pp. 204-237). New York: Russell Sage Foundation.

Eslea, M. & Mukhtar, K. (2000). Bullying and racism among Asian schoolchildren in Britain. Educational Research, 42, 207-217.

CM Research. (2002, June). Muslims poll. London: ICM Research.

Madani, A.O. (2000). Depiction of Arabs and Muslims in the United States' news media. Dissertation Abstracts International: Section B: The Sciences and Engineering, 60, 9-B, 4965.

Malik, N. (2001). Religious discrimination: historical and current developments in the English legal system. Encounters, 7, 57-78.

Omeish, M.S. (1999). Muslim students' perceptions of prejudice and discrimination in American academia: Challenges, issues and obstacles and the implications for educators, administrators and university officials. Dissertation Abstracts International: Section A: Humanities and Social Sciences, 60, 2-A, 0360.

Runnymede Trust (1997). Islamophobia: A challenge for us all. London: Runnymede Trust.

Sheridan, L., Blaauw, E., Gillett, R. & Winkel , F.W. (2002). Discrimination and implicit racism on the basis of religion and ethnicity: Effects of the events of September 11 on five religious and seven ethnic groups. Article submitted to Journal of Applied Psychology.

Weller, P., Feldman, A. & Purdam. K. (2001). Religious discrimination in England and Wales. Home Office Research Study 220. London: HMSO.

Hamidullah Gharwal
An Afghan taxi-driver - An Early Victim

On Monday 17 September 2001, Hamidullah Gharwal, 28, an Afghan taxi driver picked up three male passengers and one female passenger in Acton, West London before dropping them off in Twickenham, Middlesex. He was then dragged out of his vehicle in London and set upon outside the Prince Blucher pub. A Scotland Yard spokeswoman said, "During the incident we believe that some comments referring to the recent tragic events in America were made." He had been assaulted, racially abused, hit over the head with a bottle, kicked and punched by the three passengers, who shouted about the destruction of the World Trade Centre while he lay on the ground. Witnesses have told detectives there had been an argument over the fare. He was found by officers lying in the street outside his vehicle just after 3am. Police said that if passers-by had not intervened he would probably have been killed.

The victim was taken to the West Middlesex hospital, but after his condition deteriorated he was taken to Charing Cross hospital. At the time of the incident, Inspector Clarke Jarret said: "The victim is in a stable condition in a high dependency unit. He is paralysed from the neck down." The three men who carried out the assault were held by detectives in London who have treated the attack as a racially motivated one, charging them with grevious bodily harm.

His brother-in-law Naser Afzaly described his injuries: "Hamidullah is in a very, very bad condition and is too weak to speak very much... He has lost a lot of blood from his scalp and his back is badly damaged. The doctors think they will have to operate on his back." Afzaly added, "We are shocked at what has happened... Hamidullah was a student when he left Kabul seven years ago to escape the civil war... He was not involved in politics. He was just an ordinary student trying to get his qualifications. He was studying leisure and tourism."

Violence against ethnic minority taxi drivers – and indeed all taxi drivers – is nothing new. The very nature of the job – working nights, picking up strangers who are often drunk – means that taxi drivers are vulnerable to insult and attack. However the violence inflicted on Hamidullah was part of the pattern of harassment, verbal abuse and physical attacks reported across Britain since the September 11 atrocity. At the time, the Muslim Council of Britain observed: "This is what we feared could happen, that some extreme racist element would carry out this sort of attack using what happened at the World Trade Centre as an excuse...Partly it is the fault of how the media has reported it, which does not distinguish between the extreme elements which may have been involved in the bombing, and the rest of Islam which is nothing to do with them...there has been an increase in attacks. The community must take the necessary precautions and be more vigilant."

5

Providing Context

The Violation of International Law and the UN Charter

KHURSHID AHMAD

September 11, 2001 was a dark day at the dawn of the twenty-first century because of the terrorist acts on the World Trade Centre and the Pentagon. October 7, 2001 was even darker because of US and British aggression and bombardment of a poor and already ruined Afghanistan.

After the incidents of September 11, world sympathy was with the USA and the innocent victims of the tragedy. Muslims throughout the world, including the Taliban government of Afghanistan, shared the American grief and unequivocally condemned the terrorist acts. In the moments of grief and anguish, all peoples – whether in the east or west, rich or poor, developed or developing – who had suffered at the hands of the US leadership because of its military and financial manoeuvrings ignored their own afflictions and miseries.

The US leadership however, overwhelmed by arrogance, revenge, and the pursuit of its own 'special interests' adopted a strategy that came as second nature. President Bush's declaration of the 'first war of the twenty-first century' came on 13 September and on 14 September the US Senate gave full authority to President Bush to take any action against terrorism. Instead of identifying the perpetrators of the attacks on the World Trade Centre and the Pentagon through an unprejudiced, just and legal system and probing into the causes and reasons of terrorism, it launched its aggression against the Afghan people and embarked upon a grim and brutal plan to maintain its domination through the use of sheer force and strengthen its grip on the rich resources of Central Asia.

A 'world coalition' was stage-managed by enticements, cajoling, influencing and threats. Britain was at the US's side, vassal-like, standing shoulder to shoulder from the very first day. NATO's 18-member countries had to join in this operation, willingly or unwillingly. Article 5 of its Treaty, which states that war on a member would be considered as war on all member states, was invoked without any regard to the meaning of 'war' and 'attack' in the light of international law and the UN Charter. The events of September 11 were considered enough in themselves to serve as a 'declaration of war' from the alleged perpetrators, and the 'war against terrorism' was launched with unseemly haste. Political pressure and blackmail was employed to get the rest of the world on board. Weak countries were cajoled and bullied: side with America or be ranged against it; count as US allies or as supporters of terrorists. A world that had been divided into White and Red in the cold war was now partitioned into White and Black. Many countries, including Pakistan, became victims of, or surrendered to, this threatening posture.

US aggression against Afghanistan however was part of a well thought out plan and had hardly anything to do with the events of September 11. It was an abominable example of 'might is right'. It was an open violation of all political ethics, international law, and the UN Charter. It was the prelude to a new colonial era.

The need for a judicial commission

While the events of September 11 might have badly bruised the ego of the USA, the killing of 'over 6,000 people' (estimate at end of October 2001 but subsequently revised, the final figure being 2,819) originating from some 80 to 90 countries of the world were not only extraordinary but also a crime against humanity. It was as much a crime in Islamic law as it was in the American Constitution, international law and covenants. This is why all Muslim governments, Islamic movements and ulama condemned it without any reservation. The Taliban government condemned it. In spite of all this, and after just one hour of the events, former Israeli Prime Minister Barak was reading from a written speech during a BBC programme naming specific individuals and groups. Then, everyone started repeating the mantra that the Afghan government should hand them over to the USA immediately and unconditionally, without any research, scientific investigation, inquiry, judicial commission or hint of a trial.

Kennedy's assassination, the Oklahoma bombing, and the killings of school children in the USA were all probed into. Commissions were set up, court proceedings held, Senate and Congressional Committees carried out their own investigations and presented their results in these cases. In contrast, the facts, the causes and the implications of such a big, cataclysmic incident as September 11 that gravely impacted on global economy and politics are being covered up.

There were, and remain, numerous unanswered questions to warrant a thorough and transparent enquiry. For example, how could intelligence agencies with an annual budget of $50 billion not provide forewarnings? It is said that the events of September 11 took two years of planning, involving more than fifty people in addition to the hijackers – yet these people have yet to be traced. If the perpetrators are dead, how come their minders in the US have melted away so effectively? No significant information has come to light from the 2,000 that have been detained so far in the United States or elsewhere. How come a host of experts, all Americans, have asserted that amateur pilots trained on small civilian airplanes cannot fly 757 jetliners and keep them under control after killing or removing their own pilots? Nor can they hit, with precision, a specific building surrounded by so many other skyscrapers in a city like New York. Moreover the way in which official circles of Saudi Arabia have challenged the identity of the hijackers, and their lifestyle of wining and dining, raise further question marks.

The veteran Egyptian commentator and former minister Muhammad Heikal, in an interview with Stephen Moss published in *The Guardian*, alluded to the possibility of involvements beyond the oft-mentioned US-named individuals and groups: "When I hear Bush talking about al-Qaida as though it was Nazi Germany or the Communist party of the Soviet Union, I laugh because I know what is there. Bin Laden has been under surveillance for years, every telephone was monitored and al-Qaida has been penetrated by American intelligence, Pakistani intelligence, Saudi intelligence, and Egyptian intelligence. They could not have kept secret an operation that required such a degree of organization and sophistication…"

There was only one reasonable way out: a judicial commission should have been formed without delay that would have conducted an independent investigation and held open hearings. And, where solid evidence is uncovered, any accused could have either been extradited to the USA through the legal process according to internationally established laws of extradition or the case would have been referred to an international court or some neutral judicial commission with the help of the governments concerned. The Taliban repeatedly asked for evidence and went as far as to say that they were ready to present those responsible before a court or a judicial commission of non-partisan Muslim countries.

Senior British parliamentarians, such as 'father of the House of Commons' Tam Dalyell supported the case for respect for international conventions and the rule of law:

"British reaction to the terrorist attacks in New York on September 11 was exactly what bin Laden had wanted. The Anglo-American offensive against terrorism could lead to reprisals against British and American ex-partite access to the world. It is absolutely essential that the United Nations is brought in as soon as possible and not sidelined. Even now there ought to be an effort to offer to the Taliban for bin Laden to face a trial in a court under the auspices of the UN with both Islamic and non-Islamic judges." (*The News International*, London, 9 October, 2001, p. 9)

Bush's fixation with one individual and colonial designs did not let him take this reasonable course. His trite response was:

"When I said: no negotiations, I meant no negotiations. We know he is guilty. Turn him over. There is no need to discuss innocence or guilt." (*The Independent*, 15 October, 2001, p.1)

The USA has justified its stand by stating that all information cannot be made public, but this runs against the principles of justice, basic rights and judicial norms. One cannot be the accuser, the prosecutor, the presenter of evidence, the judge and the executioner. That is a travesty of justice. The recourse to bloodletting is perhaps to satisfy the ego and the sense of revenge, to cover up the failures of the intelligence and security systems, or to exploit the emotions of the people in the name of patriotism. But the United States in fact is also using the opportunity to achieve geo-strategic and economic objectives in Central Asia for which the ground was being prepared for years.

Consequences of war

While distinguished journalists and political veterans were expressing their apprehensions, President Bush was bent on imposing a deadly war on Afghanistan and subjecting its people to destruction. The attackers were exuberant on achieving 'air superiority' – against a country with no roads and railways, where even the facilities of electricity, water and food are not available, and with no air force. Towns and villages, and even mosques, schools, dispensaries, UN and Red Cross depots were levelled to the ground in the name of 'targeted bombing'. As a result, more than ten thousand people including over four thousand civilians, children, women, the sick and old have been killed and the entire country destroyed and thrown back into insecurity, political instability and perpetual warfare. The USA stands guilty of aggression against a sovereign state. Pakistan's 'General President' Musharraf had asserted that the campaign would be "short and targeted" - for which he claimed he was given guarantees – but it has instead turned Afghanistan into a land of continuing turmoil with no signs of stability in sight.

Afghanistan's Rightful Stand

Every sovereign country of the world has the right to refuse handing over its own citizens or those to whom it has given shelter or asylum to any other country, if this means breaking its laws or international covenants. If a person is required by some country, then there is only one way of doing this: his extradition is sought through the proper judicial process in line with ethics and the norms of international law. Even then, the court of the country whose citizen's extradition is sought has the power to decide on handing or not handing him over only after it has satisfied itself on the basis of evidence submitted to it.

Britain, of all nations, well understands these responsibilities. It has a laudable tradition of not extraditing accused persons willy-nilly. It refused to extradite Chile's former ruler Pinochet to the US, because he was wanted there for crimes for which capital punishment was applicable. Britain abides by the European conventions on human rights, under the terms of which an accused cannot be extradited to a country if a death sentence can be passed. As a European delegate declared on the Pinochet case, "We are fully and deeply on the American side on the fight... But we have a position of principle against the death penalty and there can be no exception on it" (*The Sunday Telegraph*, 7 October 2001). In siding with US aggression against Afghanistan, and shutting the door to the judicial route, Britain was unfaithful to values that it cherishes.

It appears that since the European countries are 'civilized', they have the right to hold their law supreme; Afghanistan, Pakistan and other 'eastern' countries are 'uncivilized' - their national law, religion, and tradition have no sanctity! The USA has the right to get the people it requires expelled from any country, be it Pakistan or the Philippines. It even kidnapped Panama's President after sending in some 25,000 troops, and then initiated legal proceedings in the USA. On the other hand, other countries cannot proceed against an American required in connection with some crime in their own territories. The USA has the audacity to claim that even verdicts of the International Court of Justice (ICJ), established under the UN Charter, are valid for other member countries but do not hold good for

America. It did so in 1996 when it refused to accept the court's decision regarding American military intervention in Nicaragua. It has now in 2002, un-signed its allegiance to the ICJ on the grounds that American armed personnel cannot be tried, even for crimes against humanity, at an international judicial forum. It is manifest global vandalism, not the mark of a civilized country.

Afghanistan fought for its sovereign right that the person it gave shelter to cannot be handed over to the USA on its demand without any clear evidence and judicial process. It lost that war, as it was destined to against the only super power, but it vindicated a principle. The USA's war against Afghanistan would be regarded in history as an act of aggression. Running amok with power, it is trampling upon the UN Charter, the Geneva Convention, and all international norms.

Violation of International Law

It is an established principle of law that a country or a person cannot be punished for someone else's crimes. Abetting a crime and giving shelter to someone are two different issues, especially when responsibility is not established and conclusive evidence not presented. The mere presence of a person in some country does not entitle another country to attack the asylum-giver simply because he is sought by it. The International Law Commission has distinct laws in this regard which have been accepted by all countries of the world including the USA and Britain. Article 11 of the Law states:

> The conduct of a person or group of persons not acting on behalf of the state shall not be considered an act of the state under international law.

Similarly, Article 14 says:

> The conduct of an organ of an insurrectional movement that is established in the territory of a state, or in any other territory under its administration, shall not be considered an act of that state under international law.

In the case of the Nicaragua government mentioned earlier, the USA was indicted by the ICJ in some matters but was absolved in others because of this principle. The judgment reads:

> The court finds that the USA, by producing a manual...and disseminating it to the Contra forces, has encouraged the commission by them of acts contrary to the general principles of

humanitarian law but does not find a basis for concluding that any such acts which might have been committed are imputable to the USA as acts of the USA.

In the light of these principles it is clear that even if a person in Afghanistan had committed, or was alleged to have committed, a crime against humanity, the responsibility could not be put at the door of the Afghan government. It should be clearly borne in mind that these laws are to prevent governments, especially those who wield great power, from arbitrary use of force against others under the excuse of some provocative acts. These laws are to block such military adventures. But the US deliberately ignored them all and acted as a rogue state.

Requirements of the UN Charter
The UN Charter's very purpose is to prevent the one-sided and arbitrary use of force by nations. Article 33 clearly says:

> The parties of any dispute, the continuance of which is likely to endanger the maintenance of international peace and security shall, first of all, seek a solution by negotiation, enquiry, mediation, conciliation, arbitration, judicial settlement, resort to regional agencies or arrangements, or other peaceful means of their own choice.

Subsequent articles call on member states to resolve issues through talks and peaceful means, and if these fail, it is incumbent on them to refer the matter to the Security Council. No country can take action against another country on its own, nor through a coalition that neglects the United Nations. The Security Council has the mandate to impose economic sanctions and also approve military action, under the UN Military Staff Committee.

Article 51 of the UN charter provides for an inherent right of self-defence in the face of military attack. Even in case of assumed threat, it is incumbent upon the country that is subject to attack to inform the Security Council. Moreover it must accept whatever the Council decides for restoring peace, without seeking to interfere or tamper with the UN's decision-making process. The US's invocation of Article 51 as justification for the military action against Afghanistan is a travesty. It was not under armed attack from Afghanistan, and it could not launch a strike merely on the basis of imaginary or assumed threat perceptions.

The Security Council resolution of 28 September, 2001 did not define terrorism in the first place, nor was it directed against a particular country. It asked all member countries to observe a 7-point demand that included preventing financial support to terrorist activities, freezing of assets of terrorist organizations, checking individuals and groups from providing financial support to terrorists, recruitment of new blood or providing arms to these organizations, a ban on co-operation to those who shelter terrorists and terror organizations, preventing terrorists' movement by effective border controls, and assistance in connection with criminal investigations.

The USA and Britain have violated each and every article of the comprehensive framework for international relations determined by the UN, in pursuance of their ulterior objectives. In the light of the UN Charter and international law, the American and British stand on Afghanistan was not based on justice. It was open aggression. It has set a bad precedent: a cruel and one-sided approach that is harmful for world peace.

Furthermore, keeping the Security Council uninformed even after military action and the Secretary General's own inactivity were violations of the Charter. This clearly means that whatever went on in the name of the 'international community' was neither a genuine international operation nor was it in accordance with the UN Charter. It was an act of state terrorism by a superpower, and by all who co-operated in this terrorism. This aggression was committed against an oppressed country, and the government of the country was changed by foreign intervention. The guilt is shared by all those who participated in or facilitated this oppression, in proportion to their contribution in perpetrating this military adventure.

The conscience of humanity is being aroused to recognise this naked aggression by super-powers, although the voices of protest are no more than subdued murmurs. The statement of over one hundred German intellectuals to the US President entitled 'A world of justice and peace would be different' is worth reflecting on:

"The mass murder by the terrorist attack on September 11 in your country, and the US war in Afghanistan as a reaction to that terror also affects Europe, the Islamic world, and the future of all of us. We think it especially important that an open and critical dialogue take place throughout the world among intellectuals of civil societies about the causes and consequences of these events, to assess them and judge their significance...there can be no moral justification for the horrible mass murder on September 11. We agree with you wholeheartedly about that. We also share the moral standards that you apply, namely that human dignity is inviolable, regardless of sex, colour of skin, or religion, and that striving for democracy is an important foundation for the protection of human dignity, of individual freedoms, of freedom of religion, and of the human rights specified in the UN Charter.

But it is precisely these moral values, which are universally valid in our eyes, that cause us to reject the war that your government and its allies (us included) in the "alliance against terror" are waging in Afghanistan - and which has cost the lives of more than 4,000 innocent to date, including many women and children - with the same rigorousness with which we condemn the mass murder of innocent bystanders by the terrorist attack. There are no universally valid values that allow one to justify one mass murder by another. The war of the 'alliance against terror' in Afghanistan is no 'just war'." (*Frankfurter Allgemein*, 2 May 2002)

Acting with impunity against Afghanistan has emboldened the USA to continue in this vein with others – military intervention in sovereign countries without legitimate authority, pre-emptive action on unproven apprehensions, and the right to 'change regimes' it regards as unacceptable. This is a recipe for international disaster and global destabilisation. Even Henry Kissinger is uncomfortable with this licence to murder and conquest. In his article on President Bush's impending attack on Iraq, he says that it cannot be justified as self-defence (*Los Angeles Times*, cited in Dawn 13 August 2002).

It is time the world community awakens to this menacing threat to world order.

Forging an
Alternative Civilization
CHANDRA MUZAFFAR

Once again, this issue of the clash of civilisations has been thrust upon us, in the wake of the September 11 tragedy. Is the tragedy and the Afghan war a witness to a clash of civilizations? I do not think so. The Muslim world together with the Western world has condemned the senseless slaughter of September 11. In other words, they have taken positions that transcend civilisational boundaries.

A lot of people in the West, together with Muslims, wanted the war on Afghanistan to stop. There were thousands and thousands of people in the West who, like the Muslim world, felt that this was an unjust war. By taking such positions, people of both sides of the divide once again crossed a civilisational boundary. No, it is not a clash of civilizations. It may be perceived as such if we are not careful.

If the dominant elites of the West continue to give the impression that terrorists are somehow Muslims and Muslims are somehow terrorists, if all the terrorist bases they are concerned with are located in Muslim countries, that sort of perception may develop - that it is a clash of civilizations. If Muslims are singled out in the capitals of the West as individuals who are somewhat problematic when it comes to such matters as visas and immigration, then such perceptions will get stronger. If certain countries regard Muslims within their boundaries as a challenge to the authorities and begin to target them because of the aftermath of September 11, if Moscow does this, if Beijing does this, if India does this, if Tel Aviv does this, then Muslims will begin to wonder whether they are being singled out once again.

If, let us say, after the bombardment of Afghanistan, the powers that be in Washington and London decide that other Muslim countries should also be attacked, because of harbouring terrorists, in other words if the war was to extend to Iraq, Iran, Sudan, Syria, Libya, then lots of Muslims are going to say this is a clash of civilisations. This is why the onus is on the power elites of the West.

The UN should perhaps think of various ways of fighting terrorism, non-violent ways – diplomatic, political, legal, financial and economic measures, that is a challenge that faces the UN. We cannot do it through violence.

World public opinion would be on the side of UN if it chose to embark upon this course of action. Will the US allow the UN to play this role? It was the UN that adopted a resolution in December 1987 on combating terrorism, a comprehensive resolution that addressed not only the issues that we have talked about, but also the root causes of terrorism. We cannot run away from addressing the root causes of terrorism.

When you begin to address the root causes of terrorism, you will realize that perhaps one of the most fundamental causes of the desperations, the frustration and the anger that has given rise to terrorism in certain parts of the world is linked with the global system. And all of us, wherever we are, have to address this challenge. The challenge of evolving a more just, equitable and democratic global system founded upon humane, universal, spiritual and moral values - that is the challenge that confronts us.

It is not the clash of civilization that we should be concerned about; it is the challenge of the dominant civilisation of forces that dominate the existing global system that is the real challenge. It is because there is such a global system that the tragedy of Palestine continues to stalk us after 53 years. It is because there is such an unjust global system that 5000 children die each month in Iraq. It is because there is such a global system that Chechens continue to fight for their freedom. It is because of such a global system that Tibetans continue to yearn for independence. It is this global system that we have to address.

It is a global system which concentrates political, military, cultural, economic and informational power in the hands of a few, a few who dominate many - that is the global system that confronts us, a global system which concentrates political power in such a manner that the vast majority of human kind have no role at all in shaping their destiny. They do not participate in matters that affect them or their children. It is a global system that marginalizes popular dissent at the level of the nation state. It is a global system which today seeks to militarize space, the last frontier, in the name of global security, in the name of global peace. It is a global system which has led to a situation where more than 1.3 billion people live on less than one US dollar a day, where the gap between the rich and the poor has been growing at a phenomenal rate. In 1960, the gap between the top 20% and the bottom 20% was 30 times, today it is more than 74 times. It is a global system which has marginalized other cultures, languages and religions other than the language and culture of the dominant force of the West. It is a global system which has rendered meaningless values and ideals that have sustained civilization for thousands of years. It is the global system which today threatens the family and threatens sacred relations between elders and the young in a community. It is that global system that confronts us, that challenges us.

Islam as a civilisation has resisted this global system. Let us not forget that before the Bolshevik revolution, before the so-called East-West confrontation, the civilization which challenged dominant imperialist western powers was Islam in the form of Islamic movements. That was the real challenge to Western imperialists.

Today, after the end of the so-called Cold War, we are witnessing again, a confrontation of sorts initiated by the dominant civilisation which does not do any justice to its own people.

My hope and my dream is that we will continue to resist this dominant civilisation not just because of it, but in the interest of us all, including the people of the West. Our dream is that we would continue to fight for justice, we would continue to seek to eliminate the injustices that are so deeply ingrained in this global system. This is the challenge we face now.

But we must do it, friends, with humanity. Knowledge will play a big role in our struggle against injustices. Ideas - the pen - will be a cardinal weapon in this struggle. We should not seek easy recourse to violence and thereby discredit ourselves. But in resisting oppression we should not hesitate to defend ourselves with whatever means available. The coming decades and centuries will be a struggle of ideas - ideas translated into action. This is the way by which we would be able to achieve justice for human kind and in the process, we may be able to go for an alternative civilization.

And what is the alternative civilization for the whole of humankind, a civilisation that embraces everyone, a civilisation that will oppose the present civilization - a civilization that submits to power, wealth and prestige. Ours will be a civilization that submits to God. It will be a civilization that understands the destiny of human beings and relations between people from the perspective of submission to the ultimate power, God. It will be a civilisation that understands justice, love, compassion and virtue through the prism of submission to God. It will be a civilization that will understand power, and wealth and knowledge through submission to

God. That will be the strength of our civilisation. That is the civilization humanity is waiting for. That was the civilization that lit the skies more than 1400 years ago. Over the centuries we have often failed that light. A time has come to restore that light. That is the challenge that confronts us. And this is the unique and distinctive contribution of Islam to humanity - submitting to God in such a manner that there is no parallel to God, submitting to God in such a manner that it provides us with strength and power that enables us to overcome every obstacle on our way - that is what we have to do again.

I am reminded of the beautiful words of the great European scholar, intellectual and statesman, Alijah Izetbegovic, who in his book, 'Islam between East and West', has this concluding line that says: Submission to God, Thy Name is Islam.

The Power of Dialogue

TARIQ MODOOD

For Western political leaders and commentators to keep politically repeating that the 'war on terrorism' is not a war on Muslims is of great importance. For the rhetoric associated with Samuel Huntington's 'clash of civilization' is thick in the air; just as it was politically being brought under control - at least as an official posture - the Italian Prime Minister, Silvio Berlusconi, reasserted the view that the underlying problem for the West is not terrorism or even Islamic fundamentalism but Islam, i.e. a rival and inferior civilization.

This pointing the finger at Muslims clearly will not go away and its denials are not believed by many Muslims throughout the world. Not just because all the countries, organisations and individuals that are being targeted are all Muslims (e.g., no one mentions the Tamil Tiger separatists in Sri Lanka, even though they pioneered the use of 'suicide bombers', not to mention the various groups that the CIA supports, as it used to support the Taliban). But also because Islam is so clearly evoked by many terrorist and jihadi organisations - bin Laden is perhaps the greatest advocate of the clash of civilisation thesis. Yet, we need to question whether the adjectives 'Islamic' or 'Arab' are appropriate in the common expressions 'Islamic/Arab terrorists'. When a fifth of contemporary humanity accepts the terms 'Islamic' and 'Muslim' as self-descriptions, to use the terms to characterise a limited number of lethal organisations is highly dangerous. Anything that frames the current crisis as war between rival portions of humanity is an act of gross escalation. We have to be careful not to cast our friends nor enemies in ethnic, religious or racial terms.

The 'clash of civilizations' idea poses a real danger of becoming a self-fulfilling prophecy in this moment when we are all trying to make sense of what is happening in the world, who is to blame and how can justice and peace be furthered. The one thing we are surely on sound intellectual, as well as practical, grounds to challenge is the idea of separateness. The idea of Islam as separate from a Judeo-Christian West is as false as it is influential. Islam, with its faith in the revelations of Abraham, Moses, Jesus and Muhammad, belongs to the same tradition as Christianity and Judaism. It is, in its monotheism, legalism and communitarianism, not to mention specific rules of life, such as dietary prohibitions, particularly close to Judaism. In the Crusades of Christendom and at other times, Jews were slaughtered by Christians and their secular descendants and protected by Muslims. The Jews remember Muslim Spain as a 'Golden Age'. Islam, indeed, then was a civilization, a 'superpower' and a genuine geopolitical rival to the West. Yet even in that period Islam and Christendom were not discrete nor mere competitors. They borrowed and learned from each other, whether it was in relation to scholarship, philosophy and scientific enquiry, or medicine, architecture and technology. Indeed, the classical learning from Athens and Rome, which was lost to Christendom, was preserved by the Arabs and came to western Europe - like the institution of the university - from Muslims. That Europe came to define its civilization as a renaissance of Greece and Rome and excised the Arab contribution to its foundations and well-being is an example of racist myth-making that has much relevance to today.

If in the Middle Ages, the civilizational current was mainly one way - from Muslims to Christians - in later periods the debt has been paid back. Yet this later epoch of West-Islam relations has been marked not by the geopolitics of civilizational superpowers but by a triumphant West. In terms of power, Muslim civilization collapsed under Western dominance and colonialism and it is a moot point whether it has since been revived or suitably adjusted itself to Western modernity. Anyway, the idea of a 'clash of civilizations' obscures the real power relations that exist between the West and Muslim societies. Whatever is happening in the latter today is in a context of domination and powerlessness - a context in which Muslim populations suffer depredations, occupation, ethnic cleansing and massacres with little action by the civilized world or the international community. Indeed, the latter, especially American power and military hardware, is often the source of the destruction and terror. As with Iraq, it is no small irony that the US and its allies are waging a war against a Taliban in Afghanistan whose weapons the US itself supplied only a decade before.

Meanwhile, the creation of Israel, as an atonement for the Holocaust and more generally for the historical persecution of the Jews by Europeans, along with ongoing Israeli military expansion, have resulted in a continuing and deepening injustice against Palestinians and others. It is a conflict that has many of the motifs of late twentieth and early twenty-first century barbarities: ethnic cleansing, state terrorism against civilian populations, guerrilla action against civilians, increasingly in the form of suicide bombing. All this, and yet no intervention by any international alliance for justice, because of, it is widely and rightly perceived by everyone but Americans themselves, the power of the pro-Israeli lobby. The latter cannot be challenged in the US for domestic electoral reasons regardless of the harm it does to American interests and a balanced policy in the Middle East. Now that the terror has come home, it must be time to review this disastrous policy and seek justice.

My point is not that the attack on Manhattan and the Pentagon is directly linked to Palestine (at the moment, nobody knows), let alone that the violence in one in any way justifies the other. The point is that our shock and outrage at the murder of the innocents in America on September 11 must not obscure a wider analysis and a wider sense of humanity. The murder and terror of civilians as policy does not begin with the acts of September 11. If we attend to the news carefully, we will be reminded that they occur regularly in a number of places in the world, sometimes by, or at least supported by, western states. The perception of these victim populations often is that they matter less than when westerners are victims. It is this deep sense that the West is perceived by many to exercise double standards and that this is a source of grievance, hate and terrorism which is perhaps the most important lesson of September 11, not the division of the world into rival civilizations, civilized and uncivilized, good and evil. This perception has to be addressed seriously if there is to be dialogue across countries, faiths and cultures, and foreign and security policies need to be reviewed in the light of the understanding that is achieved. Our security in the West, no less than that of any other part of the world, depends upon (adapting a phrase from the British Prime Minister, Tony Blair) being tough on terrorism and tough on the causes of terrorism.

Nor are the issues just to do with foreign policies. Just as there were attacks on Japanese-Americans after Pearl Harbour, so now, presaged by the attacks after the bombing of the Federal Murrah Building in Oklahoma City in 1996, when the US media, politicians and experts assumed that Muslims were responsible for that attack, there are reports of racist attacks, harassment and vandalism. Over the weekend of 15-16 September, a Muslim storekeeper in Dallas and a Sikh (no doubt presumed to be a Muslim on account of his brown skin, turban and beard) storekeeper in Arizona City were shot dead in what the police believe were racist murders. Since then, attacks and harassment against Muslims, including other murders, have been reported in all parts of the US and throughout Europe. This is a further reason why we must be careful with the 'clash of civilizations' thesis: it furthers racist stereotyping and all attendant evils within what are attempting to be multicultural societies. Through recent and not so recent migrations and population movements, many societies, especially in the West, are multiethnic or contain settled diasporas. Groups such as Muslims in the West – encompassing many racialised ethnicities – are clearly vulnerable to scapegoating and 'revenge' attacks. Muslims across the West (and elsewhere) have condemned the attacks of September 11 and have denounced them as unIslamic but most Muslims opposed the bombing of Afghanistan. They believed that it created unnecessary deaths and prevented food from being delivered to millions on the brink of starvation. Yet many moderate Muslims, especially in the US, are intimidated from protesting against the military action being carried out or supported by their governments. In effect, therefore, by harassment, by accusations of being a fifth column, by the use of 'Middle-Easterner' racial profiling by the aviation industry and security services and by having to silence their opposition to a war that created a humanitarian catastrophe in Afghanistan and a more general Islam-West vicious circle of global violence - for all these reasons, Muslims in the West are second class citizens. Their presence in the West, in the present atmosphere, may come to be seen, even by themselves, as alien. But actually it can be an asset.

For, if indeed it is true that what we need today is greater understanding of the dispossessed and the powerless, especially when they seem culturally alien and mobilize around their group identities, then their diasporas in the West can also be a critical source of dialogue, understanding and bridge-building. To mention only one example, just as Irish-Americans have recently sensitised American foreign policy-makers to the concerns of Irish Republicans in Northern Ireland, terrorists and otherwise, and shifted US policy, with dramatic and beneficial effects in the mother country, so groups such as Muslims in the West can be part of transcultural dialogues, domestic and global, that might make our societies live up to their promise of diversity and democracy. Such communities can thus facilitate communication and understanding in these fraught and potentially destabilizing times.

Such dialogue – at a personal, local, national, transnational and international level – seems a tall order. But there are grounds for hope. One is that while it is certainly true that the sense of being besieged and insecure that contemporary Islam and Muslim societies feel is not conducive to dialogue, this can change. The 'closed-mindedness' of Islam has had much to do with colonialism and Western dominance. When Muslims do not feel threatened and powerless, they have been outward-looking and expansive, generous and universal; it is powerlessness that has made them closed-minded and repressive (especially in relation to women), suspicious of new ideas and influences. Hence, dialogue is possible but it must be under conditions of mutual respect and in a world order which addresses inequalities of wealth and power and allows Muslims the political freedom to develop their own societies rather than imitate the West or suffer dictatorships that further Western interests (much of which hinge on the failure to develop alternatives to dependency on cheap oil).

As a Briton who was a social science student in the early 1970s, my intellectual and political formation took place at a time when many intellectuals and students were attracted to and energised by an ideology committed to the overthrow of capitalism. For the most part this was confined to hero-worship of far-away terrorists (those ubiquitous posters of Che Guevara, for example), dangerous utopianism and violent slogans - as it is amongst many Muslim students and intellectuals today - but also physical confrontations in the street, seizures of buildings (leading to a temporary breakdown of government in Paris in 1968) and domestic terrorism in parts of Europe by the Bader-Meinhof gang and the Red Brigade (paralleled by the Black Panthers and others in the US). Some of my generation still look back fondly at that era, but I think most of us are relieved that the militant Marxism passed away. This gives me some hope that the same can happen with militant Islamism.

Bridge-building, however, does not simply mean asking moderate Muslims to join and support the new project against terrorism. Muslims must be at the forefront of asking critical questions such as why there are so few non-repressive governments in Muslim societies, and help to create constructive responses. But we must also ask where are the moderate western governments when moderate Muslims call for international protection and justice in Palestine, Bosnia, Chechnya and Kashmir or for the easing of sanctions against Iraq after it became apparent that it was the weak and the poor who were bearing the brunt of their effects? US policy in relation to the Muslim world and many other parts of the world has been far from moderate. Now that a terrible tragedy has happened to the US, the US is asking moderate Muslims to get on side. The fundamental question, however, is whether there is recognition by the US and its allies of a need to radically review and change its attitude to Muslims.

Embracing the Challenge of a Connected World

JEREMY HENZELL-THOMAS

In recent weeks we have seen a growing tide of racism, intolerance and xenophobia in Europe. Let us be very clear that this is in the main an Islamophobic tide, even though there are worrying signs of a resurgence of anti-Semitism too in the desecration of Jewish cemeteries and synagogues. The difference is that Islamophobia is not confined to the far-right and lunatic margins but flourishes on all political wings and at all levels in European culture and society. It would be unthinkable today, and rightly so, for a European leader to pronounce publicly that Jewish civilization was inferior to Western civilization, but, as we know, the Italian Prime Minister declared soon after September 11 that Islam was inferior to the West, even if he was roundly castigated for so doing.

What is worrying is that the tide of Islamophobia is beginning to carry with it even some of those we might have trusted in the past to resist it with intelligence, fairness and humanity.

It was predictable that in certain sections of the British press the anti-Semitism of Jean-Marie Le Pen would thankfully be beyond the pale while a measure of indulgence was accorded to the anti-Muslim demagogy of Pim Fortuyn.

Melanie Phillips (*Spectator*, 13 May), for example, believes that Fortuyn was right in believing that Muslim immigration, which makes up "most of the mass immigration now convulsing Europe", threatens Western liberal values because Islam is "fundamentally intolerant and illiberal". Further on in the article, in a paragraph making obeisance to Samuel Huntington's poisonous doctrine of the Clash of Civilizations, we are told in one sentence that it is "militant Islam" which poses the threat against "the West" and in the next sentence that it is "Islam" as a single monolithic entity.

This interchangeability between Islam and militancy, as if they are necessarily equated, is a classic demonstration of the dishonest intellectual sleight of hand which marks out the language of Islamophobia.

We might have expected, too, that the Queen Mother's funeral and the impending Golden Jubilee would give the old guard of the Conservative party an opportunity to exploit patriotism and love of tradition as an apparently respectable means of replaying their fusty critique of multiculturalism, if not the more caustic and disreputable variant we associate with Norman Tebbit.

Thus, Norman Lamont (*Daily Telegraph*, 8 May), re-ploughing the old furrow left by previous champions of "England for the English", such as Sir Richard Body, gives us the platitude, masquerading as insight, that "all human beings need to belong" and that the "Queen's Golden Jubilee gives people a chance to celebrate their real identity".

Lamont is careful, of course, to renounce in his very first paragraph the "hateful" policies of Le Pen and Fortuyn. Nevertheless, according to him, the "real identity" to which everyone is required to subscribe, is the "national identity" of "Britishness", the "adherence to the values of one community", as opposed to a "community of communities" based on "facile ideas of diversity" like those promoted by the Runnymede Trust's report on the future of multi-ethnic Britain – the very same report, by the way, which identified Islamophobia as a "challenge to us all".

So much we might have expected. But when Ministers in a Labour government ostensibly committed to fairness and respect for diversity begin to speak the same language, albeit less stridently, we have to agree with Inayat Bunglawala (*Observer*, 19 May) that the Muslim community is being singled out and scapegoated.

When Home Secretary David Blunkett warns of asylum seekers and refugees (most of whom are Muslims) "swamping" our schools and when the Foreign Office minister Peter Hain observes that Muslim immigrants tend to be "very isolationist in their own behavior and their own customs", we have to ask what is really behind such utterances.

We can argue for ever about the detail of what they said, the words they used and what they really mean, and about the relative degree of truth or untruth in each statement, but there is a much bigger picture here and we need to develop the vision which will enable us to see it.

Consider again the statement of Norman Lamont that we all need to "belong" and celebrate our real "identity". Now, it is ironic that opponents of multiculturalism often refer to the empiricism of Sir Francis Bacon as one of the key features of "Englishness". Bacon was one of the fathers of the scientific revolution in England. He held the view that we must purge the mind of prejudice, conditioning, false notions and unanalyzed authority – what he called the "Idols of the human mind" which distort and discolor the true nature of things – and rely instead on direct experience, perception, observation, and "true induction" as methods of gaining sound knowledge. In support of his ideas, Bacon draws on the view of the Greek philosopher Heraclitus that the limitations of the human mind cause us to seek truth within the confines of our own "lesser worlds" rather than in the "greater or common world".

And as you might expect, the England-for-the-English camp take the "lesser world" as the "isolated" immigrant community which either cannot or will not be assimilated to the values of the "greater world". Whether this is the "common culture" of Englishness or Britishness is still unresolved among the antagonists of multiculturalism. But let's not quibble. We're trying to catch a bigger fish in a much larger pond.

It is the grossest form of reductionism to equate the "lesser worlds" with the assumed "parochialism" represented by the imported cultures of immigrant ethnic minorities, and to equate the "greater common world" with a fixed nationalistic identity, as if that is any less parochial. There is a greater common world than the "common culture" of Englishness, whatever that may be. It is greater too than the assumption of shared values in the rhetoric about preserving the "way of life" in the West, even if we would agree that there are certain core values in Western civilization which are worth defending. It is at least as big as the increasingly connected global community, and this already transcends those dwindling national boundaries which are becoming impossible to police.

For people who seek a still larger identity, the "greater common world" is greater even than the global community. It is a world which Bacon associates with what he calls the Ideals of the Divine, not the Idols of the human mind. It extends further out beyond this planet to the universe, and to that sense of awe and wonder which its vastness, beauty, and mystery evokes in people of imagination and questing spirit. And for people of faith, the "real identity" which Norman Lamont restricts to national pride is the fully inclusive world of our true nature as fully human beings in harmony with God and the Universe. It can have countless cultural expressions. Celebrating the Golden Jubilee can be part of that, but to equate such a celebration with my "real identity" is to present to me a miserably stunted picture of myself.

I believe that we are on the brink of an exciting leap in human development, a true paradigm shift. This is an adaptive challenge which will define who is capable of moving forward and connecting with the rest of humanity. Impending paradigm shifts, those radical changes in the way we view the world and ourselves, are threatening to those who are incapable of adaptation. They prefer to remain locked and imprisoned within safe and familiar boundaries.

As the new paradigm emerges, they retreat further, redoubling their defence of the old model of reality. Xenophobia, which in its most virulent contemporary expression singles out and scapegoats Islam and Muslims, is the last refuge of those who are incapable of that expansion of the heart which enables us to engage with and to embrace the "other", to welcome and love the stranger in our midst, and, beyond that, to connect with the rest of humanity, wherever they may be.

Everywhere, boundaries are crashing down or melting away. This is the age of connectivity, of permeability. It is ironic that Islam is often stereotyped as being implacably opposed to modernity. True modernity, for all of us, whether Muslims or non-Muslims, is to embrace the challenge of a connected world, to identify and dissolve the forms of parochialism which limit us.

To cling to our lesser world, in the words of a group of children I once taught, is to be sad and out of touch. It is also to be old – not physically old, for there are many sparkling old people whose eyes still shine with curiosity and the spirit of adventure - but to be old, cramped and blinkered within, hanging on to a fusty world of outmoded and barren habits of thought. To borrow another of Lamont's misplaced adjectives, it is this fearful retreat which is truly "facile", not the engagement with diversity. And its most facile expression, so easy and unconscious, is to blame others for your own lack of development, to project cravenly onto others the least developed parts of yourself.

The growing tide of racism, xenophobia and intolerance is nothing less than a fearful retreat from an impending paradigm change which radically extends our boundaries. And the scapegoating of Islam and Muslims is the most convenient expression of that failure to extend ourselves. It is a failure on every level – a failure of the heart, of the mind, of the imagination – and it is a dismal failure to be truly modern in our outlook.

The real clash is not the bogus Clash of Civilizations, with its regurgitated clichés about the opposition between Islam and modernity, but the clash between a new way of looking at the world and our own crippling prejudices.

There, but for the grace of God, go you or I

M FAKHRY DAVIDS

The events of September 11 were brought home to us all by wall-to-wall television coverage of airliners crashing into the twin towers like giant guided missiles, followed moments later by the towers collapsing into heaps of rubble. These were awful, shocking images of devastation on a scale that was quite simply unbearable. It is one thing to think "It's just like a scene from a Hollywood disaster movie!", but how can you take in the fact that there, in front of you, a jumbo jet full of people is ploughing straight into offices also full of ordinary people? And that the explosion, flames and smoke you see speak of people being burnt and suffocated to an unimaginable death at that very moment? And, in the sequence showing the collapse of the towers, you were watching perhaps thousands of people being crushed to death under tons of shattered glass, mangled steel and broken concrete? And the chilling realisation that those tiny specks hurtling down beside the towers, moments before their collapse, were real people jumping to certain death a hundred floors below – a death that must have felt preferable to an infinitely more terrible and horrifying fate inside. For all of us living in the West, here was a human catastrophe that we could not keep at an emotional distance – it was all too obvious that there but for the grace of God go you or I.

As psychoanalysts we know that psychically unbearable events call into play powerful defences whose aim is to protect us from perceived danger. To the normal mind, racist modes of thinking constitute the most readily available constellation of such defences, and these have been evident from the very outset. Early that afternoon a close friend rang, deeply distressed that "they say Muslims have done it", terrified that they were about to bomb Pakistan (where she has relatives), and desperately praying that, like the Oklahoma bombing, this would turn out to be another home-grown attack. The following day a patient addressed this same issue from the opposite end. He hoped that the victims under the rubble would turn out to represent every colour, race, creed and nationality of the human family, thus giving the lie to any simplistic notion that it was an attack by "them" on "us".

That latter hope was in vain, and as events since September 11 have unfolded the extent to which the situation has been reframed in stereotyped racist terms has been apparent everywhere – the problem has now been reduced to a conflict between the enlightened, civilised, tolerant, freedom-loving, clean-living democrat vs. the bearded, robed, kalashnikov-bearing, bigoted, intolerant, glint-in-the-eye fundamentalist fanatic. Or, viewed from the other side, the humble believer with God on his side vs. the infidel armed with all the worldly might of the devil. As these battle lines have been drawn the near world-wide consensus that genuinely did exist in the immediate aftermath of the bombings has given way to a world sharply divided. Now, it is very difficult to find neutral ground – "if you're not with us, you're against us". The unseen pressure to locate one on a side is almost irresistible, and attempts at genuine dialogue are soon bedevilled by the hidden question "but, which side are you on?" For example, a colleague shared with me his regret that, rather than face and address the underlying causes of the atrocities, we seemed to be rushing headlong into a futile bombing campaign that would only make matters worse. Somehow a way would have to be found to address the mess in the Middle East. We both nodded, then he added "And I don't just mean Israel". I was taken aback since I had never discussed my views on the Israeli question, or on the current crisis, with him. On reflection, I considered it likely that a fleeting suspicion that I might be one of "them" had crept into his mind at that moment.

It has long been known that racist frames of mind involve splitting and projective identification, but today we understand more clearly their extraordinary power in reducing complex anxiety-provoking situations into more straightforward black-and-white accounts that sharply differentiate good from bad. A paranoid solution to intense anxiety, this makes us feel that we know where we are, which helps, and can further justify actions designed to make us feel better, rather than to face the real problem (which requires a full appreciation of its complexity). The effects of such polarisation are powerful and pervasive since racist thought seeks to present itself as the true picture of reality, sweeping up all in its path as it imposes its agenda and seeks to buttress its views. In the process alternative views are portrayed as being in the camp of the enemy (e.g. "Hitler appeasers"), which places their proponents on the back foot as they are forced to engage in a discourse constructed around the racism. This leaves no room for freedom of thought.

As clinicians we know that when racist mechanisms are mobilised in an analysis the ordinary analytic business of understanding is easily immobilised. For instance, a black patient complains of being misunderstood by the white analyst's interpretation, allegedly because of (unconscious) prejudice on the analyst's part: rather than see the patient as he is, the analyst is felt to be imposing a view of the patient refracted through a white lens (to which his own ethnocentricity blinds him). The analyst sees the problem differently: the interpretation is reasonable, but brings anxiety, hence the patient's objections are a form of resistance. These two positions become entrenched, everything said by one party is felt simply to restate his own polarised stance, and it becomes more and more difficult to find common ground on which to base communication. The result is a highly charged situation that causes us more problems than most – e.g. when we are accused of being sexist in our views. Even the most experienced and nimble clinicians can become extraordinarily flat-footed in the face of such unyielding polarisation, and often the result is impasse or unanalytical political correctness. Under these circumstances, just ensuring that an analysis survives, let alone move things on, requires a great deal of hard work, skill and perseverance.

Racist thinking causes similar problems when deployed within the broader socio-political context, where it constitutes a particular obstacle to constructive thinking. From the moment the suicide hijackers were known to be Arabs from the Middle East their religious beliefs have been held to be responsible for their murderous crimes. As psychoanalysts we know, of course, that motivation is a complex matter for any individual, and that elements of group psychology would be bound to add further complication. However, in the aftermath of September 11 the atmosphere has become pervasively racialised as the term terrorist has elided all too easily into fundamentalist, into Muslim. Hardly a day goes by without some article or report appearing in the popular press seeking to explain "the Islamic mindset" to its Western audience. It is not difficult to see that this racist abuse is a sublimated expression of moral abhorrence and condemnation of the group held responsible, in phantasy, for the atrocities. However, when ideas are used in this way they lose their ability to describe or illuminate – they become quite simply rocks hurled in anger, or are perceived as such.

Among the adherents of Islam is a spread of believers as regular, rich and varied as any. Some are immersed in their religion in a dedicated and thoughtful way that clearly benefits themselves and their community: they bring people together and help to ease the strains of communal living. Others are less preoccupied with their religion, but it nevertheless provides them with a way to structure and give meaning to their daily lives: good fortune allows gratitude to be felt (towards God in the first instance), and misfortune can be borne (in the knowledge that God is all-knowing and just). Yet others understand their religion literally, which is felt to be the purest way, hence the only one acceptable to a God free of imperfection: they tend to be intolerant of Muslims who hold less restrictive interpretations of their religion. In the present climate it this latter version of Islam that is presented as its essence (for instance, with literal quotations from the Qur'an apparently supporting it), which Muslims at large are constantly called on to disavow. Because of the racial dynamic that underpins this call, however, every restatement of Islam's ordinariness as a religion (which incorporates many views) can only have a limited and transient effect. In addition, it is a hallmark of racist stereotyping that when deployed it provokes the object to retaliate, and this in turn makes it more and more difficult for sane thoughts to be thought and sane voices to be heard.

This is further complicated by the fact that Muslims are among the poorest and most deprived peoples on the planet. In the UK there are two Muslim communities: the urban professionals and entrepreneurs gradually making inroads into British social, economic and cultural life, and the deprived inner city dweller with little such hope. This latter group is much more helpless in the face of the vicious force of Islamophobia extant in this country (The Runnymede Trust, 1997). To the disinterested observer it is clear that the despair and hopelessness of straitened economic circumstances are responsible for their plight. In a climate where they themselves are targets of racism, the individuals concerned are most likely to experience their plight in racial terms: "it was ever thus – this country hates Muslims". This, in turn, increases the attractiveness of intolerant versions of Islam as the only ones that adequately articulate their experience of being hated outsiders. Tragically, this in turn feeds a vicious cycle in which their religion is portrayed as something monstrous.

Psychoanalysis clearly has many vital contributions to make to the debate surrounding the current crisis. In addition to clinical expertise in the area of trauma, we have specific perspectives on concretised, fundamentalist states of mind, on the perverse excitement generated by human destructiveness, on the impulse to triumph over destructiveness, on the place of revenge in mental life (which compels us to make enemies out of potential allies) and other issues. However, the effectiveness of these contributions is constrained by the current racialised context in which they are formulated and presented, and in my opinion this has to be taken into account, much in the way that we take into account the atmosphere in a session, for at least two reasons. First, it determines how our contributions are likely to be received. Second, in a divided world any contribution is likely to be perceived as partial and, given that we ourselves cannot easily rise above or opt out of that divided world, we must consider whether ours too might be. In the face of the pervasive and intense anxiety present in our world today, do we become more emphatic or dogmatic than our evidence base permits, perhaps unwittingly pushing a socio-cultural-ideological, rather than scientific, agenda? Let me explore this through a brief example.

Most of us find it hard to imagine that a murderous suicide attack can be carried out other than in a psychotic or perverse state of mind – psychically this is necessary to overrule the ordinary attachment to life that most of us have. And we are inclined to dismiss the view (from the other side) that desperation can drive people to such horrific acts, on the grounds that they ignore our detailed understanding of normal and pathological states of mind. However, our view does come uncomfortably close to the rhetoric of politicians who maintain, for instance, that "Bin Laden is paranoid and psychotic", which is instantly recognisable as partisan propaganda in the midst of war. In any event, our views will be received differently on either side of the divide. Citizens of the West, besieged by a terrorist threat, will feel supported in facing something quite mad, while Muslims will feel accused of having a mad set of beliefs. This latter will be seen as an expression of prejudice or even blind hatred, dressed up as expert opinion. These positions are quite polarised, but notice how remarkably well each side complements the other in reducing complexity to a single issue – madness.

Psychoanalysts, unlike politicians, rely on evidence to support their propositions, but here we run into some difficulties. Suicide bombers are, of course, not available for detailed psychological study after they become identifiable as such, and we are forced to extrapolate from other work. In response to the objection that extreme frustration, deprivation etc. can produce despair, disillusionment and hopelessness so great as to lead to suicide attacks, we would answer that our view does draw on a body of work with patients from severely deprived and disadvantaged backgrounds. Though true, this glosses over the fact that this body of work has been carried out almost exclusively in the West, where the relatively stable political order provides a background of safety absent in much of the Third World. This absence is often compounded by the presence of malicious forces that become part and parcel of people's daily lives. Our discourse excludes detailed evidence of the prolonged impact on the mind of these external factors, whether they are internalised and if so, how? This is a serious gap in our knowledge base that limits our ability to comment authoritatively.

From a theoretical point of view, these issues are not without interest. We know that in our world, once the depressive position has been negotiated the normal mind is able to maintain a balance between paranoid-schizoid and depressive functioning. Does this observation hold equally well in the Third World settings I have just described? Or does the maintenance of this equilibrium depend not only on inner psychic achievements, but also on the existence in the environment of structures consonant with it? Under what circumstances does that equilibrium break down, and with what psychic consequences? The lack of evidence regarding such issues does not mean, of course, that we must abandon our views because they are based on limited observations. Rather, we must be particularly vigilant about keeping an open mind. However, a pervasively racialised climate restricts the scope for this.

I have gone into some detail regarding one compelling psychoanalytic proposition (that suicide attacks involve perverse or psychotic states of mind) in order to point to the complexity of the issues involved, and to underscore the need for us to be aware of the limitations of our knowledge base. One could do the same for any other potential contribution. It is as well to remember that psychoanalysis is at its best when its initial observations, as well as the thinking that follows, cover as broad a range as possible, so that we might illuminate, say, both civilisation and its discontents.

Finally, I would like to suggest a strand of thinking stimulated by the current situation. In one of its explicit references to human diversity, the Qur'an states "O mankind! We have created you as male and female, and have made you into nations and tribes, that you may know one another" (49:13). Today we live in a global village, and the twin towers, conjoined on the ground but each reaching independently to the heavens, may have been a most potent symbol of humankind's progress in sharing a basic humanity in a way that supports each to grow and develop in their own way. But this is a description of life in the metropolitan West, where progress towards cultural pluralism, though not without its glitches, has, on the whole, gone remarkably smoothly. Our cities today are increasingly multi-cultural and tolerant, and sometimes proud of it. Have we, the privileged few in global terms, achieved this by projecting the uncertainties and anxieties connected with ordinary human frailty into excluded groups around the world, whose lives then become less precious than ours? And might this contribute to our finding the reminder that there, but for the grace of God, go you or I, so brutally shocking and unbearable?

[1] Prejudice can take many forms, each involving distinctive dynamics (Young-Bruehl, 1996). Here I am referring to a form of prejudice against Muslims that has taken hold since September 11, which I see as underpinned by the specific dynamics of racism in the mind. These involve the use of an existing difference for the purpose of massive projective identification, resulting in fixed phantasy relationships with members of that group (Davids, 1992). This state of mind functions like a pathological organisation (Steiner, 1987), but one with a consensual gloss of normality. It is unlikely that all forms of religious prejudice involve such a mindset.

[2] This ignores the fact that in every religion the interpretation of scripture is a complex scholarly discipline in its own right.

References

Davids, M.F. (1992). The cutting edge of racism: an object relations view. *Bulletin of the British Psychoanalytical Society*. 28 (11) pp. 19-29.

The Runnymede Trust (1997). *Islamophobia: A challenge for us all*. London: The Runnymede Trust.

Steiner, J. (1987) The interplay between pathological organisations and the paranoid-schizoid and depressive positions. *International Journal of Psychoanalysis*. 68. Pp. 69-80. Reprinted in E. Bott Spillius (Ed.) (1988) *Melanie Klein Today*. vol. 1, *Mainly Theory*. London: Routledge.

Young-Bruehl, E. (1996). *The Anatomy of Prejudices*. Cambridge, Mass.: Harvard University Press.

6

The Global Impact

September 11 as a Cover for Mayhem

DAUD ABDULLAH

There were, naturally, many calls for retribution after the September attacks. Amid the uproar, however, several promissory political visions were unveiled. At his party's annual convention in 2001 Britain's Prime Minister Blair pleaded for the creation of a 'reformed world order' and 'justice' for the Palestinian people. One year on, the world has somehow witnessed more dramatic reversals than advances toward these ideals.

Inevitably, certain countries capitalized on the resultant American-led 'war against terrorism' to realise ambitions or settle old scores. In Palestine, Israel's ruling elite took license to subdue Palestinian aspiration to self-determination. The results were not isolated acts of human rights violations but a catalogue of war crimes and genocidal activity that looked as part of the thrust towards 'a final solution'. These were manifested in the form of extra-judicial killings, torture, inhuman treatment, collective punishments, unlawful deportation or transfer and the unlawful confinement of "protected persons" (all deemed "grave breaches" under the Fourth Geneva Convention).

Similar policies were conducted by the Russian authorities in the republic of Chechnya after the events of September 11. Though not a Russian people, successive Czars had since the 17th century attempted to exercise absolute rule over the Chechen people in the southern Caucasus. Thus, when Dzhokhar Dudayev declared Chechen independence in October 1991 Moscow swiftly responded with the full force of its military might. Caucasian oil is as much the lifeline of the Russian federation as Middle Eastern oil is vital to the American economy.

After September 2001 international criticism and censure of Russia's human rights record in the Caucasus faded into silence. By playing the 'war on terrorism' card Russia managed to deflect attention, criticism and sanction of its policies in the region. As a consequence, the war in Chechnya has produced widespread lawlessness characterized by extra-judicial killings, detentions, torture, disappearances, and sexual abuse.

The lethal weapon of sexual abuse, it would be recalled, was used with devastating effect by the Serbs against the Muslims in the Balkans throughout the 1990s. In the post September era its use has proliferated elsewhere. Hindu extremists in India, notably Gujarat, have resorted to this weapon in their campaigns against Muslims.

In Eastern Turkestan, international human rights organizations have since September 11 reported a marked escalation of abuses perpetrated against the Uighur people. Now part of what is called Xinjiang Uygur Autonomous Region, the predominantly Muslim Uighurs have been the target of China's brand of the 'war on terror'. As in all the other theatres of this open-ended war thousands of Muslims have been detained without trial and mosques closed across the region.

Whether conducted by countries, large or small, extra-judicial killings, torture, and the ill-treatment of prisoners must be regarded as forms of state-terror. They are subject to penal sanction under the laws of war (humanitarian law). The reason why they receive official endorsement, particularly in America, was explained by former US Undersecretary of State, Charles W. Yost several years ago: "We all righteously condemn it – except when we ourselves or friends of ours are engaging in it. Then we ignore it or gloss it over or attach to it tags like "liberation" or "defence of the free world" or "national honor" to make it seem something other than what it is." [*Christian Science Monitor*, 14 September, 1972]

No other theatre of conflict corroborates this view more poignantly than the Middle East. Given the sacred doctrine that the Jewish state must have a strategic "edge" or "advantage" over its neighbors, Israel has enjoyed an unlimited license to develop and deploy nuclear weapons. While some regional states namely, Iraq and Iran, are ostracized within the community of nations for their purported nuclear programmes, Israel has been singularly exempted from the rigors of international inspection, monitor and control.

To add insult to injury, the US has since September 11 supplied Israel with 228 guided missile systems, 24 Black Hawk helicopters and 50 F-16 fighter-bombers.[1] The Israelis used one such F-16 to drop a one-ton bomb on a residential quarter of the Gaza Strip in July 2002. Their declared reason for carrying out this act was to eliminate a single "terrorist leader".

It is significant to recall here that in 1973 the US Congress enacted a series of laws prohibiting economic or military assistance to any country that violated the human rights of people within its borders for political reasons. Similarly, the Foreign Assistance Act of 1974 entrusted the president with powers to "substantially reduce or terminate security assistance to any government which engages in a consistent pattern of gross violations of internationally recognized human rights".

Ironically, when the Palestinians allegedly tried to import 50 tons of weapons from Iran, there was a flood of international condemnation led by the United States. No mention was made of UN Resolutions 2955 and 3034 of December 1972, which affirm the "inalienable" right of all peoples, and in particular the Palestinian people to freedom and self-determination and the legitimacy of their struggle from alien domination and foreign subjugation "by all available means".

Palestine is not the only country where a campaign is underway to de-legitimize fundamental rights. The "legitimacy" of national liberation movements and their peoples' struggle against colonial and racist regimes and other forms of alien domination are also under attack in Kashmir. In effect, international standards and laws have been suspended and put on hold.

On legal obligations

The basic law or constitution of the organized world community is the Charter of the UN. Its preamble affirms faith in the fundamental human rights and equal rights for all nations rich or poor, north or south. It pledges to establish conditions under which justice and respect for international law can be maintained.

These pledges are not optional. They are so binding that if a clash of interest occurs between the obligations of the members of the UN and their obligations under any other international agreement, "their obligations under the present Charter shall prevail". [Article 103] Yet, after the atrocities in the Palestinian refugee camp in Jenin in April 2002, the UN could not even get a fact-finding mission into the illegally occupied territories, let alone prosecute those held criminally responsible.

With respect to humanitarian law, its guiding principle is the recognition that the purpose of all wars is to destroy governments and states and not peoples.[2] International jurists concur that the Geneva Conventions of 1949 reaffirm most of the rules contained in earlier conventions such as the Hague Conventions (1899 and 1907), the Geneva Protocol for the Prohibition of the Use in War of Asphyxiating Poisonous and Other Gases and of Bacteriological Methods of Warfare (1925) and the Geneva Conventions for the Amelioration of the Condition of the Wounded and Sick in Armies and in the Field and of Prisoners of War (1929). The Geneva Conventions of 1949, which incorporated the norms of these earlier conventions were motivated by a determination to prevent a repetition of the kind of barbarity that occurred during the Second World War. They have since become the cornerstone of international humanitarian law.[3]

Since the commencement of the global 'war on terror' grave breaches of these conventions were recorded in Afghanistan especially with regard to the treatment of prisoners and the indiscriminate killing of civilians. The scale of the 2001 massacres of Muslim prisoners in Qala-e Jhangi, Konduz and other parts of the country is now gradually coming to light. Of related importance, the treatment of prisoners held at the Guantanamo naval base in Cuba remains a cause of grave concern; of embarrassment on the part of the US there is none.

There were still other notable assaults and erosion of Muslim human rights. Moderate countries like Pakistan, Egypt and Saudi Arabia have come under ever-increasing pressure to reform their educational systems and this is being read partly as downgrading Qur'anic teaching, especially to youngsters. In Europe and America Islamic relief and charitable institutions have been closed and assets seized. The official reason is that they support or have links to terrorists.

The absence of impartiality and balance has naturally caught the eye. As the war on terrorism intensifies and Muslim bank assets are seized or frozen across the world America's strategic ally, Israel, remains prominent among 15 countries "black listed" two years ago by the OECD for acting as a cash haven for international criminals. The report confirmed that billions of dollars accrued from drugs, prostitution, bribes and various forms of criminal activity are laundered in Israel each year. It, moreover, accused the Tel Aviv establishment of refusing to tighten rules or to cooperate in international efforts to investigate suspicious funds.[4] Has the coalition used force or threatened the use of force to ensure Israeli cooperation? Such measures though desirable are highly unlikely under Blair's "reformed world order" and Bush's Pax Americana.

Whatever changes that may occur in the aftermath of September 11, 2001, one reality would remain constant. It is the inextricable link between the rule of international law, justice, and security. That security only comes about when there is respect for the law and the rights of all are guaranteed and protected by it. When this principle is violated and replaced by racist notions of superiority and privilege, insecurity and mayhem becomes the order of the day. This remains the underlying reason for the unfulfilled promise of a reformed world order.

Notes
1. See www. johnpilger.com, 25 July 2002
2. L. Takkenberg, The Status of Palestinian Refugees in International Law (Oxford, 1998), p.198
3. The four Geneva Conventions are: (1) the Geneva Convention for the Amelioration of the Conditions of the Wounded and Sick in Armed Forces in the Field (2) the Geneva Convention for the Amelioration of the Conditions of Wounded, Sick and Shipwrecked Members of Armed Forces at Sea (3) the Geneva Convention relating to the Treatment of Prisoners of War and (4) the Geneva Convention relating to the Protection of Civil Persons in Time of War. The four Conventions were approved on 12 August 1949
4. J. Lichfield, "Russia and Israel are Criminals' Cash Havens", *Independent*, p.16, 23 June 2000

Islamophobia in the EU
post-September 11

CHRISTOPHER ALLEN

From the most northerly member state of Finland and its largely assimilated Muslim community, to the southern-most tips of Spain, where the presence of Islam can be reached across a narrow stretch of the Mediterranean; from the most westerly of nations, where Eire struggles in its infancy as an immigrant rather than an emigrant nation, to the most easterly extremes of those such as Austria, where the spectre of fascism has again begun to raise its ugly head, Muslims in the European Union (EU) have never had such an intense scrutiny placed upon them. Amid the hyperbole and sheer overstatement that has become such a necessary requirement of any analysis of September 11 – where commentators regularly swing between the theoretical poles of 'the end of history' and the beginning of the long anticipated 'clash of civilisations'[1] – the consequential effect on European Muslims has been one that has permeated all levels of understanding, from the most basic of discourses at street level, to the highest echelons of national and pan-European governance. And to suggest that this permeation was almost entirely Islamophobic, is not to understate the issue.

The European Monitoring Centre on Racism and Xenophobia (EUMC) was quick to realise this and, as a result, commissioned its network of national focal points to monitor this wave of anti-Muslim feeling and produce a series of reports. Whilst some of these were initially published on their website [2], the vast majority of the findings were left unpublished: this was until Jorgen Nielsen and myself were asked to compile a synthesis of the material's entirety[3]. The resultant report, entitled "Summary report on Islamophobia in the EU after September 11, 2001"[4] was published in May 2002 and sought to provide a snapshot of the manifestations of

136

Islamophobia that were identified across the EU, whilst considering some of the catalysts underlying it. In summary, the report unequivocally highlighted the regularity with which ordinary Muslims throughout Europe became indiscriminate targets for abusive and sometimes violent retaliatory attacks against them. A new ferocity and dynamism was clearly identified in the way in which Islamophobia became much more extreme, explicit and accepted across European society as a result of the attacks in the United States.

Irrespective of the variable levels of violence and aggression identified within each member nation, the recurrence of attacks at street level upon recognisable and visible traits of Islam and Muslims was the report's most significant finding. Incidents ranged from verbal abuse indiscriminately blaming all Muslims for the attacks, women having their hijab torn from their heads, male and female being spat upon, children being called "Usama" as a term for insult and derision[5], and being randomly assaulted in the street, with some of the most extreme leaving victims paralysed or indeed, hospitalised for many days[6]. The reasoning behind the majority of these attacks was the belief that victims became legitimate if they could be identified as Muslims, whether in fact they were or not, by their external appearance: something that we termed visual identifiers[7]. For women this was primarily the hijab and other traditional Islamic attire, whilst for men the turban was most prominent. Surprisingly, only in France and Germany were Muslim men identified by their beards, despite this probably being much more common a characteristic than the turban. The focus upon the turban though was attributed to the images that were widely disseminated through the media of the traditional attire of both Usama bin Laden and that of the Taliban[8]. Whilst it was quite clear that the visual identifiers were not in themselves the reason for retaliatory and other attacks, they did provide the necessary identifiable stimulant for directing anger or some other violent sentiment. In addition, the idea of visual identifiers was also seen to apply to physical constructs as well, where mosques, cultural centres, Muslim-owned businesses and properties were also targeted.

Following the events of September 11, the report noted that the media increasingly cast its spotlight on Muslims, where speculation, sensationalism and genuine interest could be identified in each of the fifteen member states. Muslims in the media have always been a contentious and debatable issue and in the post-September 11 period, there is little if any evidence to suggest that this issue became any less so[9]. Whilst some medias attempted to differentiate between those Muslims that were perceived to have perpetrated the attacks in the US from those Muslims ordinarily citizens of Europe, this was not the case everywhere. Inherent negativity, stereotypical images, fantastical representations and grossly exaggerated and dangerous caricatures were all identified in media output. Balance, fairness and accuracy, whilst being present and identifiable in differing levels, was in the minority[10].

Media attention again surged following the realisation that some of the alleged perpetrators had been residing in Europe, that some Muslims had been arrested on suspicion of links with Al-Qa'ida and the detention of two UK Muslims in Guantanamo Bay. One significant consequence of this was the emergence of an increased sense of Muslims being posited as the 'enemy within'. This of course has always been an inherent stereotype of Islamophobia[11], but in the aftermath of September 11, the media increasingly used these incidents as inconclusive yet accusatory evidence against a seemingly unidimensional and transcendent Muslim community. What with the hugely disproportionate and inappropriate coverage that was extended to small and largely unrepresentative fringe groups that vociferously supported the attacks in the US and Usama bin Laden[12], trying to explain the subsequent role and impact of the media remains difficult. As the report stated, "whilst no evidence exists to suggest that medias are influentially causal, they also cannot be dismissed either"[13]. Substantiating such evidence is one that is to some degree, almost impossible.

In addition to questions about the role and impact of the various medias across the EU, similar questions were also raised in the report concerning politicians and other opinion leaders. At the level of mainstream political activity, there appeared to be at least in some quarters an awareness of the possibility of a very real negative backlash against Muslims. In order to try and lessen this, whilst some political leaders made immediate verbal statements stressing the need to differentiate between 'Muslims' and 'terrorists', others such as the Irish Prime Minister Bertie Ahern opted for a much more visible message by visiting the Islamic Cultural Centre in Dublin[14]. In countries such as Portugal, political leaders chose to remain silent on the issue, and whilst Portuguese Muslims condemned such inaction, there was no evidence to suggest that this lack of comment actually shaped public views or reaction either positively or negatively.

This however was not the situation in those countries where political leaders were much more vocal with their emotionally charged, anti-Muslim rhetoric. This was seen particularly in those countries that were governed by those on the right-wing of the political spectrum. Whilst much of the inflammatory rhetoric was constrained by the national borders, the words of Silvio Berlusconi, the Italian Prime Minister, did resonate across Europe.

When European and global medias reported Berlusconi's pronouncement that Western culture was superior to its Islamic counterpart, the same message was also being said, albeit less prominently, in other parts of the EU as well[15]. Denmark, a country where Jan Hjarnø stated that "there is now a tendency among many politicians and media to make Islam the explanation for all problems"[16], was one such country, and was the first to have national elections after September 11. Unsurprisingly, the main political thrust of the election was one based on anti-Muslim/anti-immigration campaigns, where right-wing parties saw a significant shift of the vote towards them. More recently, a similar pattern emerged following the assassination of the anti-Muslim, pro-liberalism politician, Pim Fortuyn in the Netherlands.

Whilst the term 'mainstream' was used to represent those political parties that had an impact on national government and the dissemination of ideas through the hierarchies of society, the report also highlighted a resurgence of far-right and neo-Nazi groups participating in 'street politics' across the EU[17]. An upsurge in activity saw those such as the quasi-legitimate British National Party (BNP) in the UK find a voice for their Islamophobic views, whilst other much more fluidly determined groups such as 'skins' in Spain gained a similar momentum. However, there was no evidence to suggest that there was any collaborative or pan-European co-operation between these groups, even though a recurrent feature in their activity was the re-establishment of a European Christian identity because of the threat that Islam was presenting to it. Whilst it is questionable how far into the mainstream of European society these groups have been able to go, it is worthy of note that they were able to find a platform by being entirely Islamophobic, despite failing to do so with similar racist and antisemitic endeavours. There would also appear to be some evidence to suggest that the gap between the acceptability of both the political mainstream and street extremities has begun to close, where Islamophobic language and ideas now bridge this essential divide.

The report concluded that, "a greater receptivity towards anti-Muslim and other xenophobic ideas and sentiments has, and may well continue, to become more tolerated"[18], and the preliminary impetus of this may now be coming to fruition. These sentiments, and indeed the earlier posited ideas relating to the emergence of the Muslim enemy within, have all had their role in determining and strengthening EU-wide anti-terrorism legislation. Equally seeming to reflect this same enemy 'Other' has been the changes in attitude and legislation in some countries where tighter controls on immigration, including the Dutch 'no Muslim immigration' campaign[19], have been made. Whilst campaigns against asylum seekers pre-existed

September 11, the growing overlap of issues and the blurring of difference between asylum seekers and Muslims since, has been significant. It is fair to say that there is now a much greater interchangeability, where issues of citizenship, social integration and cultural absorbency, national and European identity, and allegiance and loyalty are now recurrent features of societal discourse, and where each are imbued with a sense of 'Muslim danger'.

Perceptions of Muslims in Europe entered a critical period following the events of September 11, and the EUMC report has provided no more than a snapshot of this rapidly moving and protean time-frame. As Jorgen Nielsen recently described it, the aftermath of September 11 initiated a period of 'urgent history'[20], where considered analysis and reflective assessment have been quite impossible despite a pressing need to achieve otherwise, which is where serious concerns have arisen. Whilst the events themselves were geographically remote to the vast majority of Europeans, the aftershock has seen the conceptual borders of Fortress Europe being strengthened and an awareness of the resultant, somewhat conceptual enemy within being much more prevalent. Unfortunately, the enemy that is perceived to exist both inside and out, are now one and the same: a newly created and resurgent, chimeric, dangerous and unprecedentedly threatening, hyperreal Muslim 'Other' that is at once remote, but also attributable to *all* Muslims. Hyperreality and hyperbolic overstatement are now as integral to understanding contemporary Islamophobia, and applicable to all Muslims without differentiation, as indeed they are in understanding the fallout from September 11.

Yet despite this fact, Islamophobia remains overlooked and dismissed by a variety of detractors from unlikely sectors of society. At all levels of societal and political structures, an ambivalence exists towards Islamophobia that would be unacceptable if the same sentiment was expressed to other equally untenable prejudices or hatreds. Irrespective of the neologism that is used to describe it - Islamophobia, anti-Muslimism or anti-Muslim racism[21] - the phenomenon remains the same. They all equate to the same processes of Muslim vilification that have become increasingly acceptable across the spectrum of European society. Whilst this also pre-existed September 11, the speed with which Islamophobic stereotypes and chimerical fantasies have since been able to permeate the discursive structures throughout Europe's various modes of dissemination is one that points wholeheartedly towards a process of Islamophobia's eventual 'normalisation'. What is most worrying though, is that if anti-Muslim prejudice and hatred become normal, what will be the consequences for those Muslims that exist within the confines of

Fortress Europe, and potentially even more worrying, Fortress USA?

Islamophobia therefore has to some extent been condensed into the visual identifiers that were so vital in pinpointing victims for retaliatory attacks and infringements. Where particular Europeans were identified, or indeed presumed Muslim, subsequent attacks were witnessed. Where however, Muslims did not possess those same external visual identifiers of Islam, attacks were drastically reduced and hostility was minimal. As both the EUMC's Luxemburgish and Portuguese national focal points stated, the low levels of aggression and violence experienced in their respective countries was due "to the invisibility of the Islamic community"[22]. What this recognition seems to imply is that if Muslims therefore become invisible within Europe, then the problems will disappear. The question remains though, whose problems will disappear: those perpetuating Islamophobia, those accepting Islamophobia, or those that are the victims of Islamophobia? And does 'invisibility' mean assimilation or even eradication?

Maybe the visual identifiers remind Europeans just how close a proximity - both physically and conceptually - the archetypal enemy now is, where the atavistic monsters that previously existed only outside the barriers of Europe, either real or imagined, are now contemporarily far too close for comfort. Islamophobia is not an explicit hatred held by the vast majority of Europeans: such arguments are far too simplistic to suggest. However, the 'them' and 'us' dualism remains strong in the collective memory of the European psyche, and continues to shape the attitudes of contemporary Europe. As Asaf Hussain succinctly summarised, Europe has historically seen Muslims as peoples who are "either to be feared...or to be controlled"[23]. As the visual identifiers of Muslims and Islam are now commonplace in everyday European life, differentiating between Europe's attempts to 'control' and its need to 'fear' might only be identifiable if a much greater deconstruction of Islamophobia is undertaken. Only then will we have more than a snapshot of Islamophobia in Europe, and only then will it be contemporary rather than 'urgent'.

Historically therefore, lurking under the surface of European normality has been the existence and fear of the eternalised 'Other', typically one with fantastical Islamic attributes. Under the auspices of 'urgent history' however, whilst the 'Other' remains explicitly Muslim, contemporarily its attributes, capabilities and perceived threats have been inflated beyond all recognition, possibly because of the closeness of the spatial proximity that now exists. Whether the hyperrealistic 'Other' of urgent history is controlled or feared, remains to be seen, but what is for sure, is that in the foreseeable future, Europe's 'Other' will remain undoubtedly Muslim.

Notes

1. This refers to the many references made primarily in the media and political environs of both Europe and the United States (US) to the 'end of history' theory of Francis Fukuyama and the 'clash of civilisations' theory of Samuel P. Huntington.
2. http://www.eumc.eu.int
3. The research was completed at the Centre for the Study of Islam and Christian-Muslim Relations, University of Birmingham.
4. ALLEN, C. & NIELSEN, J. (2002) Summary report on Islamophobia in the EU after 11 September 2001. Vienna: European Union Monitoring Centre on Racism and Xenophobia. From here on, this will be known as the EUMC Report.
5. As reported in one of the unpublished Belgian national focal point reports
6. This refers to the incident of a taxi driver in London being left paralysed following a particularly vicious assault. The story was reported extensively in the British press, although this source refers to one of the unpublished reports compiled by the Commission for Racial Equality as national focal point for the UK.
7. p.34, EUMC Report.
8. pp.34-37, ibid. Whilst turbans are more popularly associated with the attire of the Sikh religion, this focus for attack may go some way in indicating a lack of knowledge about religious diversity, and the differences between religions that in some parts of Europe are all seen to emanate from the Indian subcontinent. Incidentally, the report also acknowledged the number of times that Sikh men became victims of attacks because of this very fact.
9. pp.46-48 ibid.

10. p. 47, ibid.
11. RUNNYMEDE TRUST, The (1997) Islamophobia: a challenge for us all. London: Runnymede Trust.
12. In Britain this was seen primarily with groups such as Al Muhajiroun, and Muslim individuals such as Shaykhs Abu Hamza al-Masri and Abu Qatada.
13. p.48 EUMC report
14. p.43, ibid.
15. p.44, ibid.
16. p.300, HJARNØ, J. (1996) Muslims in Denmark, in NONNEMAN, G. et al (eds.) Muslim communities in the new Europe. Reading: Ithaca.
17. p.42, EUMC report.
18. p.43, ibid.
19. This was one of the campaign ideas that resulted in the general election success of the recently assassinated Pim Fortuyn's political party, Leefbaar Nederland. This translates as, 'liveable Netherlands'.
20. As part of an as yet published research paper entitled, "Racist backlash and Islamophobia after 11 September - the UK record".
21. This point refers to a debate where the term 'Islamophobia' whilst becoming increasingly popular in common usage to describe anti-Muslim and anti-Islamic prejudice, hatred and fear, it is not without a number of detractors. Those such as Fred Halliday prefers the term 'anti-Muslimism' as he suggests that Islamophobia deflects legitimate criticism from Muslims and their respective communities, whilst in other parts of Europe, most notably France, the term Islamophobia is almost completely unrecognised, where 'anti-Muslim racism' is much preferred. Whilst each of these have their benefits, it is an argument that

needs to considered elsewhere.
22.pp.36-7, ibid, italics added.
23 HUSSAIN, A. (1990) *Western conflict with Islam: survey of the anti-Islamic tradition*. Leicester: Volcano books.

Bibliography

ALLEN, C. & NIELSEN, J. (2002) Summary report on Islamophobia in the EU after 11 September 2001. Vienna: European Union Monitoring Centre on Racism and Xenophobia.

FUKUYAMA, F. (1993) The End of History and the Last Man. London: Penguin Books.

HJARNØ, J. (1996) Muslims in Denmark, in NONNEMAN, G. et al (eds.) Muslim communities in the new Europe. Reading: Ithaca.

HUNTINGTON, S. P. (1997) The clash of civilizations and the remaking of world order. London: Touchstone.

HUSSAIN, A. (1990) Western conflict with Islam: survey of the anti-Islamic tradition. Leicester: Volcano Books.

NONNEMAN, G. et al (1996) Muslim communities in the new Europe. Reading: Ithaca.

RUNNYMEDE TRUST (1997) Islamophobia: a challenge for us all. London: Runnymede Trust.

European Survey

ZAHRA WILLIAMS

This survey presents some of the experiences of Muslim communities in ten European Union (EU) countries post-September 11. Information has been drawn from press reports and formal studies, including the EUMC survey (see article by Christopher Allen). It describes how Muslims have been targeted, through increased monitoring and observation by state apparatus, and also in the rise of hate incidents. It also notes some of the positive developments.

Austria

In Austria, women with headscarves were "increasingly insulted".

The Federal President, Thomas Klestil invited representatives from the Abrahamic traditions to participate in an inter-religious hour of commemoration from where he stressed the need for a continuation of dialogue between faiths. Voices from the Muslim community reiterated that legal recognition had dampened any hostility towards them. Austrian Muslims could identify with Austria much more easily and could play a more active and participatory role in public life.

The Netherlands

The lower house of Parliament called for a survey of beliefs of activities of its 800,000 Muslims which has alarmed human rights groups. The survey seeks to discover the funding and management of mosques and the training of imams and decide how many Muslims can legitimately be classed as "fundamentalists". The inquiry has been strongly supported by Jan Peter Balkenende's rightwing coalition government, led by Christian Democrats

144

and including Fortuyn's party.

'Islam and Citizenship', a lobby representing Muslims in the Netherlands, welcomed the investigation as an opportunity to show that most Muslims are moderates, but suggested that Muslims were being discriminated against. "One has to wonder whether the government applies different standards to different sections of the population," its spokesman Yassin Hartog said. "There has been no such investigation into fundamentalist Christian groups for example."

A former head of the immigration service, and one of the ministers from Fortuyn's movement, Mr Hilbrand Nawijn, said one of the first things he wanted to do was to get tough with immigrants, especially those with criminal tendencies. "I'm thinking about illegal immigrants who cause trouble in the Netherlands," he told the Nova TV programme. "They come from countries like Turkey, Morocco and North Africa and it is generally the criminal illegal immigrants that cause trouble here. We need to be as tough as possible." The carrying of identity papers is set to become mandatory.

Anti-racism groups said they were deeply concerned by the policy, which includes a plan to penalise newcomers who fail to complete Dutch language and citizenship classes: a key plank in Fortuyn's manifesto. "I think it's a sign of the new hard-line attitude towards foreigners in general, especially those perceived to be causing problems," said Dick Houtzager, a lawyer at the National Bureau against Racial Discrimination in Rotterdam. "I'm worried that this signals a total lack of consideration for humanitarian circumstances on the part of the new government. The immigration policy of the last government was already harsh and caused a lot of problems but this is harsher....We don't have anything against an open debate on foreigners and criminality but now it seems that all the hidden biases and prejudices are starting to come out in a very unsubtle way, and that's something we deplore."

A poll in the left-of-centre De Volkskrant said that 62 percent of the Dutch thought the attacks in New York and Washington damaged Muslims' integration process into Dutch society. Herman Vuijsje, an Amsterdam University expert on racism and immigration, said he was not particularly concerned by the polls showing Dutch willingness to expel Muslims who supported the raids on the United States. He said, "They just indicate that we are ... beginning to divest ourselves of our naiveté."

Sweden

Ingmar Karlsson, a Swedish diplomat who has written extensively on the subject of Islam in Europe, says that the effect of September 11 in Sweden has been almost entirely positive. "Interest in Islam is at a peak not seen before," he says, "and acceptance of Muslims - and we have 350,000 in a country with a small population - is as normal among ordinary people as it is among the highly educated." A number of interfaith initiatives were developed, including the co-operation of the Swedish Christian Council and the Muslim Council. The Swedish Committee Against Islamophobia was also launched.

There have however been reports of increased hostility to asylum seekers. Violent incidents have been noted, with an increase in verbal abuse towards Muslims and those of Arab descent. Islamic web sites have been targeted with explicit Islamophobic messages.

Muslim women and schoolchildren as well as mosques became the most identifiable targets. The far-right also significantly increased their activities, although there appeared to be a balance between groups becoming increasingly more Islamophobic, such as the Sweden Democrat group, whilst other neo-Nazi organisations including the National Socialist Front voiced support for the attacks on the US.

A particular incident concerning the ruling Social Democratic Party occurred where three Swedish residents of Somali descent - one of whom is a member of the party and prominent parliamentary candidate for the forthcoming general election - were named on a US State Department list of possible al-Qa'ida supporters. All assets and funds were frozen and the three individuals have subsequently been declared bankrupt. The State Department continued to refuse access to relevant documentation. At the time of the last report, the situation was still ongoing.

Spain

In Spain there are around 500,000 Muslims legally resident in a population of 40m. At first no identifiable incidents of aggression, hostility or changes in attitudes occurred. However a number of mosques have been attacked and verbal assaults and attacks on property are now being reported.

Much of this expression of anti-Muslim sentiment has been directed towards those of Moroccan descent, which drew upon a deeply embedded and pre-existent ethnic xenophobia that was in evidence long before September 11. Issues relating to immigration and asylum seekers have become entwined with the entire debate. Neo-Nazi groups have became much more active in areas with a high percentage ethnic population.

The media is displaying increasingly stereotypical language and images where Muslims are concerned and the Muslim community itself is reported

146

as living in fear of reprisal attacks, stepping up security around mosques. OThere have however been some positive contribution from the press, particularly *El Pais*, which sought to include Muslim voices and differentiation, discussed the coexistence of the Abrahamic traditions and provided an introduction to Islam and the Qur'an. The Council of Organisations for Immigrations (CEI) also attempted to present a more balanced understanding of Islam through various media.

Initial response from political leaders was limited and quiet, and mixed reactions from opposing voices were acknowledged. Some Muslims felt that the government had refrained from offering them support and called for them to be more vociferous in order to give the situation more attention. Similarly, a number of Muslim organisations asked the government to make a positive gesture towards them to support their own endeavours.

Italy

The Italian Prime Minister, Silvio Berlusconi, expressed the view that the underlying problem for the West is not terrorism or even Islamic fundamentalism, but Islam as a rival and inferior civilisation.

His statement had a significant impact both within Italy and internationally. He did later state that his words were taken 'out of context' and met with representatives from a number of Muslim countries. He also attended the Christian-Islamic summit in Rome. Some political parties reinforced their anti-immigrant campaigns with explicit anti-Muslim elements, the most prominent being the Northern League. Calling for Muslims to be refused entry into Italy, members of the party including an MEP, have remained active in seeking political capital out of the events.

Germany

A number of German politicians have expressed their solidarity with the Islamic community by visiting mosques and setting signs for tolerance, showing the necessity to differentiate between the Islamic Community and terrorists. In order to counteract negative trends, initiatives such as the constitution of the Muslims of Nurenberg have been organised to represent mosques and Muslim organisations.

The 'Day of the Open Mosque' was organised and had a record attendance level. A number of politicians and religious leaders emphasised the inappropriateness of equalling Muslims with terrorists and made use of the day to reinforce this message. However, much political debate was given over to the legislation relating to national security which in some ways overshadowed other political initiatives.

A computer-based investigation which locates suspects by looking systematically at certain selected categories of people has been introduced. The search has focussed on students from Arab countries who are kept under observation by the police. This has been widely criticised as it places all Muslim students under suspicion and has led to searches of apartments and interrogations.

Following the terrorist attacks, a number of legislative measures are being discussed. For example, the Federal Minister of Interior has submitted a draft for a change of the law of association wherein the "privilege of religion" shall be abandoned, which means that extremist associations would no longer enjoy protection as "religious communities" or could be entirely forbidden. Additionally the minister intends to introduce identity characteristics of all visa applicants such as fingerprints and other biometric characteristics. All applicants for German citizenship are also to be security checked by the Office for the Protection of the Constitution which will involve checks on any indications of unconstitutional activities.

France

Ecumenical, interfaith and a range of public debates were organised and the establishment of a new Islam Council of France has been suggested. Political leaders called for calm and distinguished between Muslims and terrorists, and Prime Minister Jospin congratulated the French population for its maturity in this crisis.

On a local level, a widespread response adopted by mayors was to take advantage of the situation by increasing their relations with the Muslim and other communities. However, in the light of September 11, concerns were expressed about the need to develop training programmes for French Imams and the need to organise Islam nationally as well.

Portugal

Overall the Portugese Government has asserted unity between creeds and inscribed a frontal repudiation of prejudiced and intolerant voices. A statement made by the Internal Affairs Ministry has underlined the issue of immigration: "Naturally the equation integration-migration has a counterpart in the equation liberty-security." Many right wing politicians such as the Popular Party (PP) have quickly made established a link between security and migration. The leader of the PP suggests the "instruction of the intelligence services in order to surveillance the movements" of people that "came from countries where the social base or the State are under the strong influence of the Islamic fundamentalists".

Denmark

A number of opinion polls confirmed that the Danish majority believed that September 11 had made them become more negative towards Muslims, where the vast majority of the population felt that Muslims should be made to take lessons in Danish democratic values. Another opinion poll showed that almost half the population believed the war against terrorism had a religious connection. The far-right was also increasingly more vocal, with the Dansk Forum calling for a boycott of Muslim businesses. Copenhagen police intensified patrols following a series of meetings with representatives from ethnic minorities. In support of an open air concert against xenophobia in Copenhagen, various human rights organisation began actively protesting against Islamophobia and other prejudices.

Denmark was the only country that had national elections during the reporting period and the aftermath of September 11 was a vital part of campaigning for this. Initially various positive statements were made by leading politicians, including the Prime Minister Poul Nyrup Rasmussen, although at the same time Danish Muslims were called upon to affirm that the Danish constitution is above the Qur'an. Many Muslims interpreted this as a stance that indiscriminately subjected them to suspicion.

Throughout the election campaign, the issue of 'foreigners' was central. Most political parties seized on the event of September 11, the Danish People's Party explicitly portraying Muslims as 'our enemy', so much so that the party leadership was reported to the police for violation of laws against hate speech.

Belgium

A collaborative platform was organised in Belgium from which to combat racism along with thirteen other umbrella organisations. Initiatives such as the "Racism Sucks" and "La haine? Je dis non" campaigns in the Flemish and French communities respectively. A smaller scale campaign had fifty three organisations, including trade unions, NGOs, immigrant organisations, foundations and integration centres, supporting a statement promoting democracy, peace and an open society.

Whilst the Prime Minister, Guy Verhofstadt declared that the war was against terrorism and not Islam, the NFP launched a campaign asking political parties to support a common declaration of mutual respect. All of the democratic parties, excluding Vlaams Blok, have signed the declaration. Muslim leaders also called for calm so that hostility and violence was not reciprocated.

Africa Events

ALI MAZRUI

Both the Middle East and Africa have been paying a price for anti-American terrorism. The violent price which the Middle East is paying is obvious, especially in Palestine, Iraq and in neighbouring Afghanistan. What is the price which Africa is paying for terrorism against the United States?

Firstly, there is the issue of being caught in the crossfire. Africa has been the victim of violent action intended by the terrorists for the United States; Africa has also been a victim of violent action taken by the United States and intended for the terrorists.

In order to kill twelve Americans, Middle Eastern terrorists killed about two hundred Kenyans in the streets of Nairobi a few years ago. This was the attack on the US Embassy in Nairobi in August 1998. There were also Tanzanian casualties when the US Embassy in Dar es Salaam was targeted at the same time.

On the other hand, Sudan was caught in the crossfire soon after when President Bill Clinton ordered the bombing of an apparently harmless pharmacy near Khartoum. President Ronald Reagan before Clinton had ordered the bombing of Tripoli and Benghazi in Libya because Reagan thought the Libyans were responsible for a bomb in a German bar which had killed Americans.

An unknown number of Africans were killed at the World Trade Centre, in New York on September 11, 2001 – Senegalese hawkers, Nigerian investors, Ethiopian or Eritrean drivers or professionals, Ghanaian students, Egyptian and South African tourists and others. Who knows for certain?

September 11, 2001, has had other consequences for Africa. The security forces of Africa have opened their doors to the United States' FBI and CIA. Africa has fewer secrets from the Americans than ever, if Africa ever had any.

The FBI reportedly arrived in Tanzania after September 11 with 60 Muslim names for interrogation and potential action. The Kenyan authorities have been so eager to please the Americans that they are tempted to repatriate their own Kenyan citizens to the United States on the slightest encouragement.

The President of Kenya marched in sympathy with the victims of September 11. The Muslims of Kenya marched against the American bombing of Afghanistan. President Moi asked "Why didn't the Kenya Muslims march when Nairobi was bombed by terrorists in August of 1998?" The Kenyan Muslims turned the tables on their President "Why didn't President Moi lead a march when Nairobi was bombed in August 1998?"

The President of Tanzania declared a day of mourning for the victims of September 11 in the United States. His critics retorted that they did not remember a day of public mourning in Tanzania when 800,000 Rwandans were killed in the genocide of 1994. Africans grieve when Americans are massacred, but do we grieve as much when Africans are massacred?

There is some anxiety that September 11 and its aftermath may exacerbate tensions not only between pro-Western and anti-Western schools of thought in this continent, but also between Christians and Muslims in Africa. A demonstration by Nigerian Muslims in Kano against the American war in Afghanistan provoked stone throwing by Nigerian Christians in Kano, which flared up into communal riots. Churches and mosques were soon being burnt. President Olusegun Obasanjo had to rush to Kano to contain the tensions before they spilled over into secretarian riots all over Nigeria.

The United States' efforts to unite African governments against terrorism may be dividing African people among themselves - a coalition of elites resulting in a contestation at the grassroots.

The pressure on many African governments to enact new legislation against terrorism may pose newer threats to civil liberties in Africa just at the time when democratization was gathering momentum in some African states. Nor must we forget that if America's own democracy decays, it makes it easier for Africa's own dictators to justify their own tyranny.

Extract from a presentation to the Ethiopian International Institute for Peace and Development, December 2001.

Guilty of Faith

TAVIS ADIBUDEEN

Imagine waking up in the middle of the night to the sound of armed men entering your house. You rush to your children to ensure that they are safe and prepare yourself for the worst. Then, you are suddenly seized and subdued by people in dark clothing and whisked away in an unmarked vehicle while your wife and children are left at home crying and terrified for your safety.

If this sounds like something out of a 007 movie, think again. Over a thousand Muslims in America have been arrested in similar fashion by the FBI, INS, and other governmental organizations with no explanation and without due process.

According to the Council on American-Islamic Relations (CAIR), over 1,000 Muslims have been "detained" in American jails since September 11. Most of them are still in custody, and very few of them have been charged with any crimes or given any chance to seek legal defence.

Using terrorism laws and the new US Patriot Act, the Department of Justice and the Federal Bureau of Investigations (FBI) have launched a campaign against law-abiding Muslims living in the US with complete disregard for their civil liberties and basic human rights. While these injustices of the state have now reached alarming levels, the government has actually been involved in such activities for several years.

In 1997, Palestinian Professor Dr. Mazen al-Najjar was arrested and subsequently imprisoned in a Florida jail for three years by the INS under "Secret Evidence". The secret evidence laws, signed under the Clinton Administration, allow the government to imprison individuals who are suspected of being "threats to national security" on the basis of evidence that is not released to the public or even to lawyers involved in the cases. As a result, the accused have no way of defending themselves against the charges.

After three years, al-Najjar was finally released after battling in court and after receiving the support of numerous human rights and religious organisations. Despite this, the court declined to overturn a ruling that he should be deported to the UAE, and al-Najjar was again arrested pending his deportation. On May 14, 2002, the American Civil Liberties Union (ACLU) reported, "The government acknowledged at the time that Al Najjar had nothing to do with the events of September 11, but in a press release issued on the day of his arrest the Department of Justice said that his detention demonstrated its "commitment to address terrorism".

Countless others have been held in United States prisons on the basis of "secret evidence" which neither they nor their lawyers have ever been allowed to see. The tragic events of September 11 have only given government agencies more excuses to detain Muslims without trial.

Since September 11 only one detainee has been charged with any crime. Human Rights Watch (HRW), in a letter to Attorney General Ashcroft states, "The danger to the United States posed by terrorist activities should not be used as a justification to expand these powers in ways that undermine the rights to liberty and due process possessed by citizens and non-citizens alike."

HRW also mentioned that the International Covenant on Civil and Political Rights (ICCPR), in Article 9, clearly states that everyone "has the right to liberty and security of person. No one shall be subjected to arbitrary arrest or detention". The United States is a party to ICCPR and agreed to adhere to its legislation.

Despite international consensus opposed to it, the United States has taken measures to give the INS and FBI sweeping authority to detain, question, and deport individuals deemed to support "terrorist activities". Many of these mandates and laws that have been passed are conveniently vague almost to the extent that anyone can be detained without explanation. The INS, for example, is allowed to detain people indefinitely for "questioning" as of an emergency regulation established immediately after September 11 (see 66 Fed. Reg. 48,334, September 20, 2001).

Perhaps the most precarious of this "anti-terrorism" legislation is the US Patriot Act. It is described in its text as, "Uniting and strengthening America by providing appropriate tools required to intercept and obstruct terrorism". While its first section begins with denouncing discrimination against Arabs, South Asians and Muslims (Section 102(a)1), it later gives the President and government agencies powers to spy on, arrest, deport, and seize assets of those individuals and organizations suspected of "terrorism".

The act never gives a clear definition of terrorism or terrorists. It does, however, give the President the power to "confiscate any property, subject to the jurisdiction of the United States of any foreign person, foreign organization, or foreign country that he determines has planned, authorized, aided, or engaged in such hostilities or attacks against the United States..."

The result of this US Patriot Act has been the closing and seizure of assets of several prominent Muslim charitable organizations, namely Al-Barakaat, Holy Land Foundation, Benevolence International Foundation, and Global Relief Foundation. All of these organizations have denied the charges against them and have filed lawsuits against the government to have their assets unfrozen due to the lack of evidence to support its claims.

The Global Relief Foundation, accused of funding terrorism, has recently had their numerous appeals to courts turned down by judges who are again using "Secret Evidence" to keep the organisation's assets frozen. In addition to this, the FBI arrested their public relations chair, Rabih Haddad and has kept him in custody since 14 December without bail, without charges, and without any evidence.

The United Nations Development Programme (UNDP) is currently attempting to legitimize Al Barakaat for fear that closure of the organisation, Somalia's largest money transfer system, "may cause a new humanitarian crisis in the war-ravaged country." The US shut down the organisation after suspecting that it had ties with Usama Bin Laden. The US government has stated that it has proof of these accusations, but no evidence has thus far been released.

Among the newest detainees since September 11 is Abdullah al-Mujahir (formerly Jose Padilla) who has been labelled by the American media as "The Dirty Bomber". Al-Muhajir was accused of plotting with terrorists in Pakistan to return to the US and detonate a "dirty bomb". While no evidence was presented by US officials to give credit to their case, al-Muhajir was nonetheless designated as an "enemy combatant" and thrown into a military jail.

Human Rights Watch became concerned by the government's total disregard for al-Muhajir's rights as a citizen who should at least be given a fair trial to determine his innocence or guilt.

Kenneth Roth, Executive Director of Human Rights Watch, contends, "There should be a strong presumption that anyone arrested in the US, far from any battlefield, be granted the full legal protections of the criminal justice system- including the right to counsel and not to be held without charges. Simply accusing someone of working with al-Qaida does not justify throwing him into a navy brig."

"Being an accused terrorist," Roth said, "is not synonymous with being an enemy combatant. Otherwise, the President could detain and hold anyone without charges simply by labelling him a member of al-Qaida."

As of date, Human Rights Watch has been denied access to the holding cells in their attempt to determine the quality of treatment and living conditions of the approximately 1,000 detainees since September 11. It is still unclear as to how long they will continue to rot in jail cells without justice (either of innocence or guilt). And in the case of al-Muhajir, President Bush has indicated that the accused "Dirty Bomber" will remain in the military jail for the "duration of the war on terrorism," a war that has already been called a war with "no boundaries" and thus no limitations.

Perhaps the most blatant of all US disregard for human rights was made apparent when the international community, on the verge of finalizing an International Criminal Court that would be capable of charging individuals for war crimes, asked the United States to agree on the provisions. The United States had signed and agreed to be a party in the criminal court under the Clinton administration, but then attempted a "withdrawal" under the Bush administration.

Their main reason for desiring exemption from the criminal court was that "peacekeepers" from the US, in various locations such as Bosnia, could in fact be charged for war crimes. In a recent interview, Secretary of State Colin Powell told reporters that the United States did not want US soldiers and officials to be charged in such a court. It is not a direct confession of guilt, but sometimes what is not said is equally revealing. Time will tell, and the truth will eventually be told.

And say: "Truth has (now) arrived, and Falsehood perished: for Falsehood is (by its nature) bound to perish." (The Qur'an, 17:81)

Why are You Smiling?

TOKUNBO OJO

In my several years of travelling around the world, I have never been subjected to humiliation and animalistic treatment as I was on 24 May, 2002 at the US-Canada border. Apart from questioning the authenticity of my Canadian passport, American immigration officers - D.R. Moore, J. Wilson and C. A. Racine - held me for over two hours, seized my mobile phone, and prevented me from contacting Canadian embassy or Immigration Canada.

As long as I live, this horrible ordeal shall remain fresh in my memory. Having dropped off my soccer clips for the Montreal Gazette Sports Editor, Mark Tremblay, I joined the 8:30pm Greyhound bus heading to New York at Berri Quam, Montreal. Arrived at the Canada-US border at 10:04pm. Everybody on the bus reported to the American Immigration Centre. Immigration officer Moore signalled to me to come.

"Where are you going tonight?"

"New York," I said

"For business or what?"

"To see a friend."

"Where do you live?"

"Montreal."

"Where were you born?"

"Montreal."

In my usual self, as I was responding to his questions, I had my smiling face on.

156

"Why are you smiling?" he asked.

"That's me."

"Do you know this being videotaped?"

"Yes, I know."

"So this is not funny."

It was at this stage that he got on my case. He scanned my passport and asked:

"Have you always been living in Canada?

"Yes, pretty much?"

"Do you live anywhere else?"

"I lived in Nigeria for a while."

"For how long?''

"For about 15 years or so."

"That's a significant amount of time. Do you have any other IDs?"

I gave him my Quebec driver's license, my Canadian Association of Journalists' membership card, my Investigative Reporter and Editor's membership card, and Washington D.C Library of Congress membership card. As if a bee strung him on his butt, he jumped off and walked swiftly to another computer at the other end of the room.

He asked immigration officer C.A Racine to come over. As she got closer, he whispered to her in an inaudible voice. Looking at my passport and other IDs, she asked:

"Do you speak French?"

"No."

"If you were born in Montreal, how come you don't speak French?"

"Well, I lived outside the province of Quebec for a while."

"So did you school in Canada?"

"Yes, I did."

"Which school?"

"Concordia"

Having ransacked my wallet, she took my mobile phone and went to join D.R Moore.

"Why this?" I protested. "I passed through this same border two weeks ago when I went to present a paper at MIT."

"It does not matter number of times you have entered in the past," another officer answered.

They searched my bag and could not find anything incriminating. As if I was a convicted fellow, I was taken back to the bus. The seat where I sat was thoroughly searched. Once again, nothing was found. I presumed that was the end of it. But I was wrong.

The bus driver and the rest on the bus were told to continue their journey while I was kept at the immigration centre. An officer named J. Wilson took my fingerprints and headshots. And at the back, Moore and Racine were giving out my passport number and driving license to several units and sections on the phone.

Looking frustrated after over ninety minutes of searching and phone calls, Moore announced to Wilson, Racine and other two officers, "They don't have any information on him,"

"What are your parents' names and date of birth," he asked in an angry tone.

Knowing fully well my parents (like I and the rest of the family) are law-abiding citizens, I was more than happy to give him the information. But I never failed to remind him and his gang that they were only wasting their time in making me a victim of racial profiling. Back to the phone again, he gave out my father's name. The atmosphere became tense when the response was still "no information".

Sensing that they were "up to something else", I demanded to use their phone to call the Immigration Canada or Canadian embassy in New York since they had already seized my mobile phone.

They denied the request and told me to "go" - "sit down".

"No, I am not going to sit down. I need to call my embassy now."

At the speed of light, Moore, Wilson and two officers with guns in their pocket pounced on me. They struggled so hard to put me on the seat, but they could not overpower me. As my emotions were running high, the memory of innocent Ahmadou Diallo, who was shot 41 times by four New York police officers in 1999, was flashing at my head. Since I didn't say a final good bye to my family, I allowed them to have their ways. Though physically I sat down, inside I was standing up.

After almost three hours of the so-called "inspection or investigation", they said that they could not allow me to enter the US.

"Why?"

"You're not co-operating with us," Racine said.

"Not cooperating with you? I gave you all the information you requested..."

"Sorry sir, we can't allow you to enter."

"Well, if that's the case, can I have an official form to make a complaint about your acts of unprofessionalism?"

"Sorry sir, we don't have the forms here. Call them in New York."

7

Looking Back and Forward

Historical Roots of Islam in Britain
JAMIL SHERIF

◆ ◆ ◆

Muslim Identity in Britain Today
M ABDUL BARI

◆ ◆ ◆

Raising Children as Citizens of the World
WAHIDA C VALIANTE

◆ ◆ ◆

Opening Up to the Wider Society
SHIBAN AKBAR

◆ ◆ ◆

The Exeter Experience
KAUSAR AHMED

◆ ◆ ◆

Historical Roots of Islam in Britain

JAMIL SHERIF

British Muslims today have a rightful sense of familiarity with their surroundings. The encounter of Islam and the British Isles goes back a long way. Just as under the surface of Britain's handsome landscape there is a complex geological interplay, similarly our cultural topology has been fashioned by diverse forces and interminglings, including the Muslim encounter for over millennium. What better indication than the English language itself: the philologist Richard Derveux has uncovered 600 loan words from Arabic – some of them listed in this book – noting "That, I submit, is not an insignificant number from any point of view, especially when one considers that the Basic English vocabulary, for example, includes only 850 words". Far from being an alien deposition in the topsoil, Islam in Britain has deep historical roots.

The First Contacts

Eighth – Fifteenth Century
Muslim cartographers were well aware of British Isles. Muhammad bin Musa al-Khwarizmi in his 'Surat al-Ard', written around 817 mentions a number of places in Britain.

Offa of Mercia (died 796) was a powerful Anglo-Saxon King who had coins minted with the inscription of the declaration of Islamic faith (None is worthy of worship but God) in Arabic.

The Ballycottin cross, found on the Southern coast of Ireland and dated around the 9th century also bears an Arabic inscription. At the centre of the

163

cross set in a glass bead in Kufic Arabic script is the phrase 'Bismillah' (in the name of God).

It is generally believed that the first Englishman known for certain to have been a scholar of Arabic was Henry II's tutor, Adelard of Bath (c. 1125) who travelled in Syria and Muslim Spain and translated a number of Arabic texts into Latin. In 1145, Robert of Chester translated Al-Khwarazimi's 'Kitab al jabr w'al-muqabal' from Arabic into Latin.

In the twelfth century, King John was excommunicated by Pope Innocent III. Matthew Paris, a contemporary monk, has left details of an emissary sent by King John in 1213 to the North African Amir, Mohammed An-Nasir. King John offered to help Muslims in their campaigns in Spain against the Catholic king of Aragon.

Muslim scholarship was well known among the learned in Britain by 1386, when Chaucer was writing. In the Prologue to the Canterbury Tales, there is among the pilgrims wending their way to Canterbury, a 'Doctour of Phisyk' whose learning included Razi, Avicenna (Ibn Sina) and Averroes (Ibn Rushd). Ibn Sina's canon of medicine was a standard text for medical students well into the Seventeenth Century.

Following Adelard's footsteps, others too sailed from Britain in the twelfth and thirteenth centuries in quest of Arabic learning and returned to enlighten their fellow countrymen. This included Danel of Morley and Michael Scotus, whose translations of Aristotle from Arabic were of great value during the Renaissance.

The first book ever to have been printed in England by Caxton in 1477 is considered to be 'The Dictes and Sayings of the Philosophers', which was a translation of a popular Arabic compilation entitled 'Mukhtar al-Hikam Wa mahasin al-Kalim', by Abul Wafa Mubashir Ibn Fatik.

Sixteenth and Seventeenth Century

This was a time when Muslim naval power dominated the Mediterranean. This expanse included Istanbul, the centre of the Ottoman Empire; Aleppo, a crucial link in the Silk Route; Beirut, "the Marte-towne whereunto all the ships coming from Europe doe arrive"; Jerusalem, the city of pilgrimage; Cairo, a centre of trade, witnessing "the greatest concourse of Mankind in these times", and Fez, "a world for a city". When the threat of the Spanish

Armada loomed in the mid-1580s, Queen Elizabeth did not hesitate to ask the Ottoman Sultan Murad for naval assistance against the Spaniards. Of all the countries of Europe, Britain enjoyed the most extensive trade with Muslim lands.

The first English convert to Islam whose name survives in an English source, 'The Voyage made to Tripoli (1583)', was a "son of a yeoman of our Queen's Guard...His name was John Nelson". A Chair of Arabic at the University of Oxford was established in 1636, and it was known that Charles I collected Arabic and Persian manuscripts. The Bodleian Library in Oxford has the manuscript of a letter to Charles from Sutlan al-Walid of Morocco – part of this reads, "To our exalted presence has come your noble servant, John Harrison, well and in good health and with far-reaching, sincere hopes. He has taken up residence with us, encompassed by kindness and treated with all manner of genorisity...."

The turmoil of the Civil War may have encouraged some Englishmen to break with tradition and an account written in 1641 referred to "a sect of Mahomatens" being "discovered here in London". By 1646, King Charles was holed up in Oxford under siege by Cromwell's army and the worst of the fighting was soon to be over with defeat for the Royalists. In December 1648, the 'Council of Mechanics' of the new Commonwealth voted for a toleration of various religious groups, including the Muslims. The next year, in 1649, the first English translation of the Qur'an, by Ross, was printed. It had two imprints, attesting to a wide circulation.

Following the regicide in 1649, sole authority now rested with Cromwell, 'Lord Protector'. Reference to Islam and Muslims was part of the discourse of the times. The Royalists attacked the revolutionaries for their disrespect of parish priests and rejection of the 'High Anglican' official tenets. Ross, who had lost his royal patron, observed: "And indeed if Christians will but diligently read and observe the Laws and Histories of the Mahometans, they may blush to see how zealous they are in the works of devotion, piety and charity, how devout, cleanly and reverend in their Mosques, how obedient to their Priests, that even the Great Turk himself will attempt nothing without consulting his Mufti." The revolutionaries, according to their critics, followed their own self-declared religious authorities, while even the Sultan heeded the advice of the Mufti on religious matters. Other writers who were unsympathetic to the revolution compared the 'Professours of Religion' amongst the Turks with 'the Puritans' of Cromwell. In Cromwell's camp there were men like the remarkable Henry Stubbe, scholar in Latin, Greek and Hebrew and friend of Pococke, the first professor of Arabic in Oxford.

According to a contemporary (English) Muslim scholar in Cambridge, Dr. Tim Winters, Stubbe "had sided with Parliament during the civil war, holding, with Cromwell, that the righteous man may sometimes justly bear the burden of the sword. An admirer of Cromwell, he became an admirer of the Prophet". Stubbe's circle must have known his private views on Muslims and Islam, which could not be publicly disclosed at the time: "their articles of faith are few and plain, whereby they are preserved from schisms and heresies, for altho' they have great diversity of opinion in the explication of their Law, yet, agreeing in the fundamentals, their difference in opinion do not reach the breach of charity so common among the Christians, who thereby become a scandal to all other religions in the world". At least six manuscripts of Stubbe's book 'An account of the Rise and Progress of Mahometanism, and a Vindication of him and his Religion from the Calumnies of the Christians' circulated in a clandestine manner (not to be published until 1911). Stubbe died in 1676, after having been accused of heresy, and spending some time in prison.

Cromwell, or his Secretary, John Milton, showed familiarity with the Qur'an in a letter to the ruler of Algiers in June 1656. "Cromwell expected the addressee to abide by the commercial agreements between their two countries because of the nature of Muslim religion: 'We now at this time require the like of you who have declar'd your selves hitherto in all things to be men loving righteousness, hating wrong, & observing faithfulnesse in covenant.' The last words repeat the exact description of Islam as a religion that advocates righteousness and repudiates wrong-doing." From secretary to antiquarian to Lord Protector, the Qur'an was a text widely consulted and quoted: it had legitimacy for addressing not only Muslims overseas but Christians in England and the rest of the British Isles.

Stubbe's contemporary at Cambridge, Isaac Newton, who was much influenced by Muslim Arab scholarship placed the offer of the Lucasian Professorship made to him in 1674 at risk by refusing to take holy orders, a mandatory requirement at the time. Newton secretly rejected Trinitarianism (according to his biographer, Michael White, Newton was 'fanatically opposed' to the concept of Trinity). Fortunately for science, King Charles II granted him a special dispensation and all subsequent holders of the chair were exempted from holy orders.

Texts in Arabic in mathematics, astronomy, chemistry and medicine were central to higher education in England in the seventeenth century. In order to obtain access to the advanced knowledge of the day, not only were translations commenced at Oxford and Cambridge, but preparations were made to train a generation of Arabic scholars. A visitor to Westminster School observed in his diary, "I heard & saw such exercises at the election of scholars at Westminster Schoole, to be sent to the Universitie, both in Lat: Gr: Heb: Arabic &c in Theames & extemporary Verses, as wonderfully astonish'd me, in such young striplings." Linguistic ability was important, because, in the words of Isaac Barrow, Cambridge Professor of Mathematics, 'the mastery of Arabic was necessary for the advancement of learning'. Muslim intellectual giants came to be known by their anglicised names 'Alfarabi, Algazel, Abensina, Abenrusd, Abulfeda, Abdiphaker, Almanzor, Alhazen'. Walter Salmon included among the authorities of his Practical Physik (1692) 'Geber Arabs', or the chemist (and alchemist) Jabir ibn Hayyam. Robert Boyle, the chemist known to every schoolboy, studied Arabic sciences in order to be able to challenge the 'groundless traditional conceptions' in contemporary learning. Boyle in turn acted as a guide for Isaac Newton, a seeker of the truth who naturally became drawn to the esoteric sciences (perhaps better called the mystical arts). Newton, in the words of Maynard Keynes, 'regarded the universe as a cryptogram set by the Almighty'. Newton left behind more than a million words on the subject of alchemy – itself an Arabic word.

An illustration from 1676 shows two Englishmen being served coffee, in the company of a turbaned Turk with twirled moustaches. The Turk is big and at ease, while his table companions are sitting in a demure fashion. It is an apt imagery that applies not just to the social interaction in the first coffeehouses that appeared in Britain around this period, but to the wider inter-relationships between Britain and Muslims in the seventeenth century.

Eighteenth Century
Simon Ockley was a noted Arabist of his time, in 1708 translated Ibn Tufail's philophical novel 'Hayy bin Yaqzan' to English. This was republished in 1711 and appeared in an abridged form in 1731. Hayy's adventures after being marooned on an island launched a new genre of adventure writing, of which Defoe's 'Robinson Crusoe' (published 1719) is the best known. Ockley also translated 'An Account of South West Barbary' to English –

Barbary was to feature prominently in subsequent English literature. Another learned figure in the latter half of the Eighteenth Century was Sir William Jones, a great Arabic and Persian scholar whose translations from Persian and Arabic were to influence Tennyson in several of his poems.

The Colonial Period

In 1897 a map of the British Empire would include Nigeria, Egypt, India and Malaya, all large territories with significant Muslim populations. Muslim lands provided the manpower and material resources that contributed to the prosperity of Victorian and Edwardian England.

The colonial encounter first brought Muslims to Britain as seamen, soldiers or students. The seamen, known as 'lascars', established the first communities in the main ports of England and Scotland. By the turn of the century there were also several hundred Muslim peddlers, who even ventured to the remoter parts of Scotland with their wares and medicines.

For a long period during her reign Queen Victoria employed two male Indian secretaries - Mohammed Buksh and Abdul Karim. They both entered the Queen's service three days after her Golden Jubilee in 1887, but while Buxsh remained at the rank of bearer, Abdul Karim became her secretary and an influential figure in the Royal Household.

The 'Muslim time-line' below describes how a Muslim community emerged in more recent times, with some facts on its most important personalities.

1860: Existence of a mosque at 2 Glyn Rhondda Street, Cardiff, recorded in the Register of Religious Sites (now maintained by the Office of National Statistics)

1886: Founding of the Anjuman-I-Islam in London, later renamed the Pan-Islamic Society.

1887: William Henry Quilliam (Shaikh Abdullah Quilliam) embraced Islam and led a small community in Liverpool. In 1891 the community rented a house in Brougham Terrace to serve as a prayer hall. He would personally call the adhan – the call to prayer – from one of its upper windows. Following a visit to Turkey he was given the title 'Sheikh-ul-Islam of the British Isles' by the Sultan. He founded a weekly journal, The Crescent, that was published from 1893 to1908.

1889: Establishment of the Shah Jehan Mosque, Woking, with an adjoining student hostel, under the patronage of the Indian Muslim princess, the Begum of Bhopal. It was the base for the journal 'Muslim India and The Islamic Review', re-named as 'the Islamic Review' in 1921. An early editor was the charismatic Khwaja Kamal-ud-Din, a barrister originally from Lahore.

1910: Syed Ameer Ali convened a public meeting at the Ritz Hotel for the establishment of the London Mosque Fund for "a mosque in London worthy of the tradition of Islam and worthy of the capital of the British Empire". He was the first Indian to be appointed Privy Councillor and to be given membership of the Judicial Committee, the then Supreme Court of the Raj. On retirement in 1904 he settled in Britain with his English wife. His sons Waris and Tariq would subsequently serve as trustees on a number of the first mosque projects in London.

1914: Friday prayers held under the auspices of the London Mosque Fund, first in Lindsay Hall, Notting Hill Gate, and later at 39 Upper Bedford Place. The venue then shifted to 111 Campden Hill Road, where prayers were conducted till October 1928.

1916: British Muslim Lord Headley (Al-Haj El-Farooq) writes to Secretary of State Austen Chamberlain for allocation of state funds for the purchase and construction of a mosque in London "in memory of Muslim soldiers who died fighting for the Empire".

1917: Marmaduke Pickthall, the son of an Anglican clergyman and distinguished poet and novelist, declared his Islam in dramatic fashion after delivering a talk on 'Islam and Progress' on 29 November 1917 to the Muslim Literary Society in Notting Hill, West London. Throughout the Great War (1914-1918), and even prior to declaring his faith as a Muslim, he wrote extensively in support of the Ottomans. When a vicious propaganda campaign was launched in 1915 over the massacres of Armenians, Pickthall rose to the challenge and argued that all the blame could not be placed on the Turkish government. At a time when many Indian Muslims in London had been co-opted by the Foreign Office to provide propaganda services in support of Britain's war against Turkey, Pickthall's stand was a most courageous one and of great integrity. When British Muslims were asked to decide whether they were loyal to the Allies (Britain and France) or the Central Powers (Germany and Turkey), Pickthall said he was ready to be a combatant for his country so long as he did not have to fight the Turks. He was conscripted in the last months of the war and became corporal in charge of an influenza isolation hospital. The Foreign Office would have dearly liked to have used his talents as a linguist, but instead decided to regard him as a security risk. His translation of the Qur'an is still in wide currency.

1928: Formation of the London Nizamiah Mosque Trust Fund by Lord Headley; these funds were subsequently transferred to the London Central Mosque Fund (present day Islamic Cultural Centre in Regents Park).

1930: A branch of the Western Islamic Association was formed in South Shields by Khalid Sheldrake. In 1936 there was also a sufi zawiya in South Shields at 45 Cuthbert Street. By 1938 the Muslim community was 700 strong.

1933: Muslim Society of Great Britain, under the presidency of Ismail de Yorke, organises Islamic events at the Portman Rooms, Baker Street.

1934: Formation of the Jamiat Muslimeen, East London, under the presidency of Dr. Qazi, with branches in Birmingham, Manchester, Glasgow and Newcastle. Following the death of Lord Headley, Sir Hassan Suhrawardy took over as chairman of the Nizamiah Mosque Trust.

1937: Abdullah Yusuf Ali, best known in the English-speaking Muslim world for his monumental translation and commentary of the Holy Qur'an, finally settles in Britain after years as an itinerant educationalist. British Muslims initiate their first political campaign by expressing opposition to the Peel Commission's proposals for the partitioning of Palestine. Yusuf Ali, drawing on his first-hand knowledge of the mandates prepared by the League of Nations, lectured widely on the injustice in Palestine, at venues in Brighton, Cambridge and London. Yusuf Ali was the only non-ambassadorial trustee of the London Central Mosque Fund, thus representing the British Muslim community.

1940: Churchill, at a war cabinet meeting on 24th October, authorises allocation of funds for the acquisition of a site for the London mosque.

1941: East London Mosque and Islamic Cultural Centre opened by the Egyptian Ambassador, Dr Hassan Nahjat Pasha. The Mosque was subsequently managed by the Jamiat Muslimeen.

1943: Formation of the Jamiat Ittihad Muslimeen, Glasgow. The Jamiat's first mosque was at 27/29 Oxford Street, Glasgow.

1944: King George VI visits the Islamic Cultural Centre - Regents Lodge in Regents Park - for its official opening.

1950 – 1978
If the main emphasis of Muslims in the earlier period was the establishment of proper prayer facilities, the emphasis would shift towards the establishment of social, educational and welfare institutions. While the 70s is not 'history' – it may well appear in the distant past to the majority of British Muslims today – half of whom are under thirty years old!

1962: Groups of students from six cities meet in Birmingham to form the Federation of the Students Islamic Societies in the UK & Eire (FOSIS). The UK Islamic Mission was also formed this year.

1969: The Muslim Educational Trust came into being, addressing the needs of Muslim schoolchildren, and publishing the landmark 'First Primer of Islam' in April 1969.

1970: Martin Lings (Abu Bakr Sirajuddin) appointed Keeper of Oriental Manuscripts at the British Museum. The Union of Muslim Organisations (UMO) was formed with Dr Syed Aziz Pasha as General Secretary. Bashir Maan elected the first Muslim councillor in Glasgow.

1971: Jamiat-ul-Muslimeen, Manchester, commence work on a purpose built mosque in Victoria Park; 'Impact International', the authoritative Muslim news magazine, launched in London in May; the association 'Jamiat Ulama Britain' formed.

1973: Establishment of the Islamic Council of Europe, with headquarters in London and diplomat Salem Azzam appointed Secretary General. The Islamic Foundation, Leicester (subsequently relocated in 1990 to Markfield) was also formed this year with Professor Khurshid Ahmed as its first Director General.

1974: Opening of the Dar-al-Uloom, Holmcombe Hall, Bury; publication of the 'Draft Prospectus of the Muslim Institute for Research and Planning', by Dr Kalim Siddiqui

1976: World of Islam festival in London

1977: Belfast Islamic Centre established.

1978: Completion of the new markaz of the Tableegh Jamaat in Dewsbury.

In his best-selling book 'The English', Jeremy Paxman offers a relatively well-known historical fact but then in his inimitable style concludes with a startling insight, "the first thing you discover about the English, is that they are not English – in the sense of coming from England – at all. They had arrived from Jutland, Anglen and Lower Saxony. The 'English race', if such a thing exists, is German. These first English people certainly demonstrated characteristics, which have reasserted themselves periodically through the English story.... they showed early symptoms of that urge to smash things which seizes the country from time to time, whether in the destruction of the monasteries or the levelling of town centres in the 1960s". But there can be other less destructive patterns in social and cultural history – the multicultural conviviality of the Elizabethan coffee houses are due for a comeback.

References

The Islamic Quarterly, London, Volume I, April-July 1957, 'The British Isles According To Medieval Arabic Authors' by D. M. Dunlop

The Islamic Quarterly, London. Volumes XVII, Nos. 1 and 2, January-June 1973, 'A letter to Charles I of England from the Sultan Al-Walid of Morocco' by D. S. Richards.

The Islamic Quarterly, London. Volumes XX-XXII, No. 4, December 1978, 'Some Oriental Elements in Islamic Scholarship in the West' by R. Hawari

The Islamic Quarterly, London. Volumes XXVIII, No. 3, Third Quarter 1984, 'The Arabic contribution to English' by Robert Devereux

Islam in Britain 1558 – 1685 (Cambridge University Press, 1998) by Professor Nabil Matar. The section above 'Sixteenth & Seventeenth Century' quotes extensively from this source.

British and Muslim? by Abdal-Hakim Murad
http://www.islamfortoday.com/murad05.htm

Some Arabic loan words in English

Admiral
Albatross
Alchemy
Alcohol (from al-kuhl, powdered antimony)
Alcove
Algebra (from al-jabr, the bone-setting or literally, the reduction
Algorithm
Alkali
Almanac (from al-manakh, calendar)
Amalgam
Ammonia
Antimony
Arsenal
Artichoke

Assassin
Aubergine, brinjal (from al-badhinjan)
Azimuth (from al-samut, the direction)
Baccalaureate
Ballyhoo
Benzoin
Camphor
Carafe
Coffee
Cork
Cotton
Crimson
Dhow
Fanfare
Garble
Gazelle
Genie
Ghoul

Giraffe
Guard (from al-garad)
Guitar
Hazard (from az-zahr)
Jar
Jargon
Lacquer
Laskar (from al-askar, the army)
Lemon
Lemon
Lute
Magazine
Massage
Mattress
Mohair
Mummification
Muslin
Nadir
Orange

Popinjay
Racket
Saffron
Sash
Sequin
Sesame
Sherbet
Shrub
So long
Sofa (from suffah or long bench)
Syrup
Talc
Talcum
Tambourine
Tariff
Zero, cipher (from sifr or empty)
Zircon
Zirconium

Muslim Identity in Britain Today

M ABDUL BARI

The race riots in some northern England cities in the summer of 2001 and the events following the September 11 atrocities have given rise to a debate on 'identity' within different communities. Muslim youth in particular are now at the sharp end of this debate. It is not the first time this issue has come to the surface in Britain. Over recent decades, comments of influential politicians like Enoch Powell and Norman Tebbit made headlines and set the agenda for the discussion on race and racism in Britain. What makes the present debate on identity so crucial is its global nature. Muslims or other civil rights campaigners may consider this debate patronising, but it is not going to go away in the foreseeable future.

From time to time, fingers are pointed at the Muslim community questioning whether they are or can be genuinely loyal citizens of the states, particularly in the western world, where they live. For Muslims, as for many others, the issue of identity is a critical and soul-searching one. If, however, it is addressed holistically and in its proper context, the outcome will definitely benefit not only Muslims but also all in the western hemisphere. Muslim communities should thus engage in contributing positively and effectively to this debate, although it might have started from the negative premise of putting Muslims in the dock.

Identity is essential for human beings. It gives them anchor, root and a sense of belonging. Identity is linked to one's background or history. It helps people in their present and leads them to the future. As such, the debate has a universal relevance and appeal.

What then is 'identity' and how does it affect an individual, a community or a nation?

From a sociological point of view identity is a sense of personhood that involves sameness as well as difference. It tells what kind of person one is compared to another. If I am a Muslim, I am like other Muslims and different from non-Muslims. At the macro level the issue could be linked to someone's geographical origin such as the continent or country from which he or his parents come. A person may thus be considered an Asian or a European, a Malaysian or a Nigerian. Identity could also involve a person's linguistic origin whereby he may regard himself primarily, for example, as Bengali or French. Identity often involves a person's racial or ethnic origin such as being Semitic or Anglo-Saxon. At a micro level there are other identities one could maintain. One could identify oneself with a locality and call oneself a Londoner or a Liverpudlian while maintaining a broader British identity. Then there are gender, social class, family, job and other factors that dictate one's identity on a regular basis. All of them have an important bearing on a person's life in different contexts. They do not have to clash with each other or be mutually exclusive.

Some aspects of identity such as race and colour are immutable. Others such as religion and faith are maintained through choice or action. Identities are linked with cultures and sub-cultures. People can change some aspects of their identity over the course of their lifetime.

The overriding identity, according to Islam, is one's religion or way of life where belief and conviction play a vital role. Religion is taken here in a very broad sense, encompassing all aspects of human life - from personal hygiene to international dealings. Religious identity is a matter of choice, free from one's ethnic, racial or geographic origin. In this sense, a Muslim or any other religious identity is dictated by one's conscious acceptance of a way of life.

While nationality, ethnicity and race have been a dominant feature of identity in post-enlightenment Europe, religious markers of identity have remained significant for many in their day-to-day life. At the beginning of the 21st century, we now see not only a multi-racial, but also a multi-faith and multi-cultural Britain, thanks to the presence now of many faith and ethnic communities. This may be a departure from the traditional mono-religious nature of British society, but it reflects the rainbow pattern of global humanity. This is something that we need to be proud of.

Religious or faith identity and racial or ethnic identity do not have to clash. In a plural society, with a positive social environment, they are complementary. It is only when religion turns to fanaticism and race turns to racism that society and the world turns ugly. The racist attitude, which says 'my nation, right or wrong', or the fanatic 'holier than thou' mentality

175

are the root causes of hatred, vengeance and acts of inhumanity between communities and nations. True, religion or faith could be claimed by extremists for political gains or spreading hatred among people. In the same way, race or ethnicity could also be used by bigots to create mayhem in society.

Muslim identity revolves around Islam's view of human beings and the concept of ummah or community. According to Islam, human beings have the status of vicegerency (The Qur'an, 2: 30) which gives them stewardship over the earth. God has created human beings from a single entity and caused them to inhabit the spacious earth (4: 1). God has honoured the children of Adam over other creatures (17: 70) and made subservient to them all that is in the heavens and all that is on earth, and has bestowed upon them His blessings (31: 20). He has created human beings as one community, an ummah (2: 213).

All these are manifestations of God's love for human beings. The variations of languages and colours (30:22), the differences in gender, and the variety of ethnicities and tribes are all for people to realise the richness of diversity and to get to know one other (49:13). Awareness of this unity in diversity elevates human beings to a state where they become grateful servants of God. The superiority of one person over one another has nothing to do with one's race, colour, language or wealth. True superiority, and it is not for any human being to detemine this, is based on piety, righteousness, or consciousness of God (30:22).

In the pre-Qur'anic period of Ignorance in Arabia, attachments to race, tribe or wealth were venerated to such an extent that people lived and died for aspects of their identity. The Arabs used to fight one another for their inflated sense of tribal dignity. Various tribes of Makkah were engaged in internecine feuds for generations. The same was the case with the people of Yathrib (which later came to be called Madinah). Asabiyah or tribal loyalty was at the root of their communal life and strife. Because they held on to the notion 'my nation, right or wrong', they could not even contemplate going against their own tribe even if they were wrong. This made them a doomed people for centuries.

When Islam arose with its universal message of brotherhood, Prophet Muhammad (peace be on him) dealt with tribalism in a delicate and enlightened manner. He did not seek to wipe out clannish or tribal bonds but sought to channel the vitality that was inherent in such a primary loyalty for the good of their own communities and for the benefit of the wider community especially when this was threatened from outside. The benefits of family, clan and tribal organisation and loyalties were recognised by the noble Prophet and used to create social cohesion.

However, with Islam as their primary identity the Arabs then became a nation within a generation. The asabiyah that caused havoc in the past proved decisive in the early period of Islam in encouraging different tribes to compete in good works and contribute in smaller and therefore more organised communities to the well-being and defence of the larger community. Such was Islam's power of inclusion and its concern for stable growth.

Muslim identity does not clash with any other identities so long as one's commitment to Islam remains authentic. One can be a confident Muslim and at the same time be British or Egyptian, Anglo-Saxon or Malay. Geographic nationality, race or language are not necessarily factors that make for divisiveness among Muslim peoples. However, in the last few centuries Arabs, Turks and Muslims of other 'nations' fought against one another on the basis of competing nationalisms based on geography, race and language and brought ignominy on themselves. With several 'independent' Muslim states, Muslims are now even weaker, because their Muslim identity has been superseded by nationalistic or other divisive identities. Border, sect and other barriers have become insurmountable for many Muslims.

Muslim identity should bring confidence, courage and humility among Muslims, especially the youth. It leads them to dynamic and pro-active engagement with others in humanity.

Of course, like other youth in a society, Muslim youth have their own problems. The reason a section of them resorts to delinquency is because of their gradual loss of links with Islamic roots, values and culture. Those who have a strong anchor in the family and community with strong faith in their hearts have enough self-esteem and confidence to stay away from the problems, such as underachievement in education, gangsterism and other social diseases that lead to violence. Disaffection and social exclusion linked with unemployment, poor housing, racism and other factors are alienating young people from Muslim and other minority communities as well.

The government is trying to address the issue of identity and citizenship in schools with the inclusion of Citizenship as a core subject from September 2002. At the same time, Local Governments are also acknowledging the contributions made by the minority faith and ethnic communities. In a book "Faith and Community: A Good Practice Guide for Local Authorities" the Local Government Association (LGA) has praised faith communities for contributing to 'good health, providers of pastoral care, promoters of citizenship, voices of social justice and as the locus of gathering of people'. This is an encouraging acknowledgement in the wake of an increased necessity of building cohesion among communities.

The Muslim contribution to modern Britain is enormous. As a significant minority community Muslims have brought many features that have enriched British society over many decades. Muslims are a diverse group of people with tremendous resource and potential. Their contribution can only be enhanced when they, as role models of Islam, are able to actively participate in the affairs of the wider society.

Islam encourages Muslims to interact with other people in humanity. This engagement with others, the positive and full participation in the affairs of the wider society, has been practised by Muslims in their heyday. By its very nature the religion of Islam is outgoing and, as such, it wants Muslims to create links with the Creator and His creation. This produces in them a sense of responsibility toward other human beings and the environment. With religious identity as the primary source of confidence and pride, Muslims are encouraged to make a meaningful contribution in the society they live in and work for justice and common values. Confident Muslims are not worried about their Islam or their survival as a community. Their job is not confined to protecting themselves alone, but promoting morality and justice for the benefit of all.

Raising Children as Citizens of the World

WAHIDA C VALIANTE

Only a short time ago the world was aghast at the atrocities, ethnic cleansing and genocide in Europe, when Bosniaks (Muslims of Bosnia-Herzegovina) and Kosovars (Muslim Albanians of Kosova) were the victims. But the maiming and killing of Palestinians, Chechnyans, Iraqis, Kashmiris and Afghanis still continue. The world may be inured to it because it has become routine, or because the victims are of a different faith and colour or race.

But parents wonder how to explain this collective human propensity for brutality and inhumanity, mass killing and extermination to their children. We may offer them intellectual justification or hide behind the historical reality of ancient hatred, but we can never convince them of the necessity of such brutality and inhumanity.

The children must wonder whether the leaders of the nations are capable of telling them the truth, or their parents have the ability to teach them how to create a world where peace, liberty, justice and equity, rule of law, economic fairness, human equality, and international human rights would prevail.

The racism, greed, and religious hatred that have fanned the fires of war are still alive on the pages of newspapers, magazines, films, and novels, and they continue to pose a threat to the cultural and religious identity and well being of billions of people worldwide. How to ensure that the children become upright world citizens and spared the vicious cycle of ethnic and religious hatred, human greed and lust for power?

Will the children, be able to transcend ethnic and religious hatreds, and the lust for power and wealth, to foster a global civil society based on the principles of fundamental freedom and human rights for all?

It will depend on what and how we teach and nurture our children, the future generation-in-the-making, to be good and worthwhile citizens of the world. There is indeed a way out of the vicious cycle.

Across the ages and throughout the world, parents, teachers, philosophers, religious and civic leaders have wrestled with the question of how to raise morally and ethically responsible citizens in every society and civilization. Today, the task before parents is greater: they have not only to raise good citizens of the state, but also to train them to be good citizens of the world, to be part of humanity and the community of nations.

These days, to meet their own needs, parents increasingly rely on day care centers, baby sitters, tutors, educators, health care providers, early childhood classes and organized social activities. As partners in our children's education, however, we simply cannot abdicate our nurturing responsibility and leave outside educators and other professionals to instill ethical and moral values in our children without reinforcement and role models at home.

Children need role models, and parents are their primary examples. To be good role models themselves, parents must also have models or mentors of their own whose example they can emulate. For Muslim parents, the ideal role model is the noble Prophet Muhammad. 'Indeed, in God's Messenger, you (men and women) have a good example for all whose hope is in God and in the Final Day and who remember God frequently.' (The Qur'an, 33:21) The Prophet's actions and deeds were local, but had global implications in terms of promoting social justice, economic equality, and harmony between different cultures, races, genders, and religions. We need to translate those Islamic global values into day-to-day reality for our children if they are to be worthy future representatives of God in the world community.

The most difficult and demanding challenge for parents today is not determining which civic or religious ideals to pass on to their children, but how effectively to translate them into daily routine. How can parents achieve this when both are juggling multiple jobs? Burdened by social and economic pressure, crime, violence, stressful family relationships, and a confusing political environment, they feel their confidence continually eroded as they try to be good nurturers and role models for their children. Therefore, parents also need guidance to help them translate Islamic ideals into daily life and the lives of their children. All this begins at home.

We must nurture and protect the family as the primary unit of social system and the natural environment for maximizing children's physical, psychological, and moral growth. Children need a safe, peaceful, tolerant, understanding, loving, free, and just environment in which to grow. As we move into the post-modern world of parenting, we must find fundamental universal principles to serve as signposts. A wealth of such principles, or signs (ayah), can be found in the Qur'an. While, these vital signposts already exist in our daily rhetoric, parents need actively to apply them in their own homes. They need to understand the concepts and underlying meanings of these Qur'anic principles, and translate them into everyday reality.

Children should be raised to understand fully their own rights, obligations and responsibilities as Muslims as well as of their parents, community, society and ultimately the world itself. The Qur'an directs the children persuasively, appealing to their emotions.

It asks children 'to show kindness to parents; and if one of them or both of them attain old age then not even a word of disapprobation or disgust be uttered, let alone repulsing them'. They should be addressed politely and graciously, lowering unto them the wing of humility and kindness. The Qur'an links worship of God with kindness to parents.

> "Your Sustainer has decreed that you worship none save Him, and that you show kindness to parents..."(17:23-24)

> "And We have enjoined on the human being to be kind to his parents..." (31:14)

Children must understand what it means to be a Muslim. It means, first and foremost, to believe in God, who is the Creator and Sustainer of all peoples and the universe. The Qur'an tells us that God's creation is 'for just ends' and not in 'idle sport'; humanity, fashioned 'in the best of moulds', is created to serve God.

According to Qur'anic teaching, service of God cannot be separated from service to humankind, or – in Islamic terms – believers in God must honour both their obligations to God and to His creatures. Fulfilment of one's duties to God and mankind constitutes 'righteousness' (2: 177).

These basic concepts are first put into practice in the home; among our extended families, our friends, schools, places of work and worship, our communities, our country, and, finally, in the world. It involves parents in setting limits, formulating rules and teaching children to take moral responsibility for their own behavior as 'vicegerents' of God as they prepare to inherit the global culture now being promoted so assiduously.

There are certainly no guarantees, but with these principles in mind, parents can expose the youth to basic global Islamic values and concepts, thus preparing them to be good citizens of the world. To achieve this goal, children need to know how to apply and integrate these basic Qur'anic principles to daily life:

1. Children must be able to think critically and rationally if they are to understand the Qur'anic principles governing human behavior in order to maintain a proper balance between knowledge ('ilm) and behaviour ('amal).

2. Children should know their rights and responsibilities, which according to the Qur'an, begin at home and continue in concentric circles, encompassing the local and global arena.

3. Children should understand the importance of volunteering: at home, regularly helping their parents; and in the community by helping neighbours, sharing their time with the elderly, visiting the sick, and sharing resources with others.

4. Children should learn to fit in with others. It means resolving conflicts with fair words, not clenched fists; it also means listening to one another, expressing oneself, developing self esteem, being a good team player, having good manners, and demonstrating civility to all.

5. Children should learn to participate actively in the political process, so as to improve economic and social conditions, both locally and internationally. They need to understand that global action has local impact.

6. Children should make the natural environment part of their entire life's concern. As stewards (or caring preservers) and inheritors of this planet, it is their task to take responsibility for the world's finite resources and seemingly infinite consumption habits. This means getting them committed to recycling, reusing materials, preparing and eating healthy and locally produced food, taking care of plant ecology and managing wisely the goods we have.

7. Children should be engaged in projects involving people in other countries to learn how to accept and celebrate human differences and gain self-confidence. They need to know that there are many others' with whom we share this planet earth and its resources.

182

8. Children should understand that history indeed matters. The Qur'an draws attention repeatedly to the misdeeds of previous peoples, and to their destruction as the consequences of those misdeeds. The warning is that if the past produced all those disastrous results, or if, conversely virtuous deeds in the past bore fruits in the form of good results, there is a relationship between the past, present, and the future - and it is significant in fashioning human life.

9. Children need to understand where they come from and feel sufficiently confident in their own religious and cultural identity to appreciate others' customs and practices.

10. Children should experience the continuing, stable love of family and friends. This means being able freely to express emotions - love, humor, and respect - within the family.

Throughout history, parents have been there to provide civil society well adjusted, hardworking and honest future citizens. Effective civic education based on Islamic concepts indeed begin and continue at home where the laying of foundations is a daily process for the development of ethical and moral values reinforced through interaction with school and the larger community. Regardless of what messages children receive from schools, day care, or pre-school, they learn many of their profound lessons at an early age from their own family members.

Therefore, the family must be protected as the fundamental unit in society, and as the natural environment for children's emotional, physical, moral, religious and social well being and growth. Since children learn their first lessons in citizenship at home, parents must take the initiative, and be fully engaged in this process as the driving engine of society.

Opening Up to the Wider Society

SHIBAN AKBAR

I was at a bus stop in Oxford town centre when a tourist came up to me to ask about the bus timings for the service that I was waiting for. From her accent I could tell that she was American and I took the opportunity to talk to her. Apart from the fact that we were both naturally chatty, we discovered that our academic background was in literature. However, we found that whereas she was pursuing a career in her field of study in her native country, I have had to change direction and re-invent myself professionally several times to remain in the job market in my adoptive country.

We continued our conversation on the bus. I asked her if she had visited ground zero and how she had been coping since. The account she gave of the events surrounding the Twin Towers mirrored my own sentiments and moved me. At the time I had thought of all my American friends, including two of my best friends with whom I had shared three wonderful years at Oxford. She in turn was touched by my account, saying: "When you come across genuine goodwill from complete strangers like yourself, one can start being optimistic about the future." She went on to say that people outside America had "of course suffered much more" but because this was concentrated largely in one particular area, the images left by the tragedy were enormously overwhelming. She was right. The American tragedy is enormously overwhelming in its own right.

Our brief time together was about to run out. As I got up from my seat I wished that God would grant us all the strength to come to terms with what had happened. She put her hand on my shoulder as she said, "You take care." I returned the gesture and wished I could do more. Encounters such as this one are what I would call momentary bursts of connection and they are certainly worth having. After all, what is life if not made up of moments.

Human relationships can be forged on various levels. It is the task of the society, its institutions, organisations and communities to attempt to come together and accept each other. There is no single prescription for achieving this.

In Islam the sacred is supposed to be intertwined with the ordinary. The Qur'an (4:36) lists different categories of people that Muslims are required to show kindness to, such as parents, near kindred, orphans, the needy, the neighbour who is of kin to us, the neighbour who is not of kin, the fellow-traveller, the wayfarer and so on. The easiest way to desecrate the land is to shed innocent blood and cause misery and pain to others. The Qur'an (53: 42) says, "To your Lord is the final goal." So with our Goal set and the Scene designated, all it remains for us is to work towards establishing understanding, justice and harmony between communities and people. If only we could 'listen without prejudice'; if only we could communicate with each other by endorsing and practising a process of transparency, the world would be a different place.

I am passionate about my Prophet. For practising Muslims our most important role-model should be the Prophet Muhammad (peace and blessings be on him). In his various roles as a private man, a public figure and above all as the Prophet and Messenger of God, perhaps the attribute that is his unique hallmark is that everything he did, he did in moderation and never swayed from the middle-path. And what better way to emulate this family man, this trusted companion, this humble shepherd, this successful businessman, this teacher, leader, statesman, general, social reformer and servant of God than to follow the middle-path in obedience to God.

If Muslims are to open up to the wider society as fully as possible, they should be allowed and encouraged to enjoy full membership in the community. This will enable them to consolidate their citizen status. Quite often highly educated and competent Muslims are having to settle for unsuitable jobs because they are rarely considered for positions in the mainstream environment. Many Muslims will tell you that they are seen to be fit only for jobs that cater to the needs of Muslims or minority ethnic members. They are rendered doubly disabled for both their ethnicity and their faith.

That Muslims are an integral part of this society can be demonstrated by simple gestures such as the announcement of major Muslim festivals like Ramadan and Eid. It would help schools, employers and other institutions to be sensitive to the needs of Muslims during their festive season.

The Government, the Civil Service, the Local Authorities and other appropriate agencies need to adopt a more inclusive agenda towards

Muslims and consult with them on policy issues. If a policy is to be introduced it should be the result of a serious consultation and partnership between Muslim professionals in the field; the different organisations with grassroot contact; representatives from the community and the authority. We need to feel that we are part of a larger scheme of things. I would like to see a hijabed woman as a television presenter or newsreader.

However the problems for Muslims remain numerous. With every change in the wider political climate the government and the Muslim community will be faced with new challenges. British Muslims will have to brace themselves for what lies ahead. The MCB will have to remain as poised as ever. Since September 11 we have been absolutely swamped with all kinds of demands. We have had to travel to numerous places nation-wide to give talks on Islam and participate in seminars, conferences and multi-faith events. I have made new acquaintances and have acquired friends, Muslim and non-Muslim.

Within a speech that I delivered at Cumberland Lodge, Windsor, I asked the question "How do Muslims fit in as members of the national collectivity?" and put forth the observation that "Citizenship means full membership in the community encompassing the civil, political and social dimensions. Muslims' second-order citizen status is legitimised by constructing our identity to our disadvantage and at times to our peril. Many Muslims feel that as long as their collectivity as a whole is subordinated and hegemonic socio-cultural structures imposed on them and implemented for them they will not enjoy full membership in the community.

"Muslims now occupy a subject position in major discourses. It would have been heartening when Muslims in cosmopolitan Britain did not have to struggle for their cultural space. The true test of being British will lie in our ability to forge alliances through reciprocal exchanges; and by focussing on difference and diversity as one of our principal organising themes; and in our willingness to seek out and recognize allies in different cultural communities, and to contrive to build a firm foundation of cooperation and partnership."

After every talk I have given I have been approached by people saying that if I had not quoted chapter and verse they would not have believed that Islam condemns and forbids wanton destruction and the killing of innocent lives. Many were incredulous when I said that an entire chapter of The Qur'an has been set aside for the account of Mary, mother of Jesus or that the Scripture for Muslims proclaims her the chosen, the pure and the preferred woman of all the women in creation. I have had people asking me to recommend books and I have been invited back.

If we are to look to the future, first and foremost we must acknowledge that the global community is plunged into a state of spiritual bankruptcy and moral impoverishment which has taken shape over a prolonged period of time. It is now the task of each and every one of us to get our respective houses in order.

The Exeter Experience

KAUSER AHMED

The Muslim community in Exeter is as diverse as could be found anywhere in Britain. The total number of attendees at the only mosque number just under six hundred but the number of people who would describe themselves as Muslim is nearer the nine hundred mark. A large percentage are students at Exeter University and there is a significant contingent who come from overseas, particularly from the Middle East.

The diverse ethnic backgrounds of the Muslim community do not give any one group greater influence over any other. With a Sudanese Imam and trustees who are of Bengali, Pakistani and Arab background, the Mosque has a very cosmopolitan feel and maintains an open and welcoming ethos. The Mosque itself comprises three large mid-twentieth century huts, utilitarian in both design and appearance. These are modestly huddled well away from the traffic on a side road, almost invisible to passers-by. This is the way the worshippers prefer it. Despite the present fund-raising for a purpose-built mosque, the quiet anonymity of the present Mosque affords a great deal of protection. The experiences of the community during the Gulf war of 1991 have left unpleasant memories. Graffiti had been daubed on walls and many Iraqi students and asylum seekers had either been deported or detained, with the corresponding human tragedies.

It was inevitable that there would be a backlash against Muslims after the perpetrators of the attacks in the United States on September 11 were declared as being Muslims.

Collectively, most Muslims felt resentment and horror at hearing Muslims associated with this awful crime; individually, many felt afraid and apologetic. The vitriolic pronouncements of commentators against Islam, particularly those from America gave a focus for the shock and anger of many people.

The reports of Muslim women being jeered at and abused in the street, of the beatings suffered by many Muslims in both the UK and the US, leading to the death of a Sikh mistaken for a Muslim because of his beard, fostered a climate of fear and trepidation.

In Exeter, the beat officer for the Mosque area was Muslim. His advice (and that of his superiors) to the congregation was to keep a low profile and avoid any insensitive remarks. It seemed as if we were all to be judged guilty by association. The Police had installed CCTV cameras at the Mosque on the 12 September and throughout were extremely supportive and showed much sensitivity to the needs of the Muslim community.

It was not totally unexpected then that an anonymous call was received at midnight by the Chair of Trustees of the Mosque at his home. The caller let out a stream of invectives and abuse, ending with the threat that supporters of Usama bin Laden would pay. Almost immediately there was a call from the police asking the trustee to go to the Mosque as there had been an incident.

Briefly, the incident in question was that a group of men had gone to the Mosque to desecrate it by throwing around a number of pigs' heads, red paint to look like blood and to pin an offensive banner to the perimeter fence which ended with the words "Nuck (sic) em George". By the time the Trustee arrived at the scene the Police had cleared up the mess. Eventually a man was apprehended and convicted for this crime.

In itself, this small incident would be taken in their stride by the Muslims of Exeter - after all, attacks on religious buildings are, sadly, common. Its significance lay in the effect it had on the Muslim and non-Muslim community. As soon as knowledge about the attack became public, the Mosque was inundated with letters and calls of support.

Church groups, the Hebrew congregation of Exeter, the Quakers and numerous individuals wrote, phoned and personally delivered letters of support and solidarity with the Muslims. Almost all of them offered to undertake a round- the-clock vigil to prevent further attacks to the Mosque. Many of these letters expressed dismay over the rise in Islamophobia and pledged themselves to work with the Mosque in confronting its growth.

Solidarity by other faith groups on a national level was very much in evidence in the aftermath of September 11, but our local support arose from more personal links.

Throughout the thirty-year existence of the Islamic Centre in Exeter, there has been constant dialogue between the Mosque and the Churches. Building on common spiritual outlook and shared heritage, it has been possible to go beyond dialogue and forge mutual bonds of friendship. It was therefore natural and easy for the community to acknowledge with gratitude the support and solidarity shown by Church groups at a time of great tension and uncertainty.

The link with the Synagogue came from the personal contacts with individual members of the Jewish community and coming to those friendships with mutually open hearts and minds. The demonising of a whole group has never enabled understanding to be established and meaningful dialogue to take place.

There are many within the Muslim community who see such fraternisation as akin to treason. The only dialogue they will have is of a one-sided variety, under the title of 'dawah'. The tendency to proselytise wins no converts and only alienates and fosters suspicion. Conducting a relationship based on openness and genuine concern for others is essential. Looking beyond stereotypes is even more important for Muslims as we are victims of it so often.

The support of the local non-Muslim community has been very important to us. Where the locality is hostile, acts of vandalism and hate will go unchallenged. Where the community is supportive, then it will be vigilant to such behaviour. The Mosque has very strong links with the Head of Religious Education in Devon. The Imam is on SACRE (Standing Advisory Committee for Religious Education). Through this, local schools make frequent visits to the Mosque to tie in with their studies.

After the attack on the Mosque there was an acknowledgement that schools needed to confront the racist and Islamophobic attitudes held by many pupils. The next three months saw members stretched to the full, in both responding to school visits to the mosque and also invitations to go to schools. An interactive multi-school linked workshop via the Internet was held under the auspices of the Education Authority, involving several schools discussing Islam and combating Islamophobia. This was a novel approach in itself in reaching the remotest schools in Devon.

Each school visit required the Mosque member be briefed in tackling topics with sensitivity and tact. There is nothing more intimidating than a class of thirty fifteen-year olds who are convinced of the soundness of their views and who often see events in monochrome.

The work with young people required a variety of approaches, discussions and workshops delivered in a spirit of collaboration. This meant that those taking part did not feel that they were being brow-beaten into hearing the "Islamic version" but that they had contributed to a discussion and a debate in which all sides had equal opportunity to participate.

Contacts with the local Arts Council allowed a project with Muslim young people to be funded looking at cultural identities. This project recognized the fact that Muslim youth would be feeling confused about their British and Islamic identities and this gave them the opportunity to explore their feelings through Art. Similarly, there was collaboration with a local gallery for the Mosque to jointly host an Exhibition of Afghan art. This brought many people to the Mosque who would not otherwise have ever dreamt of coming in.

What was happening was the breaking down of barriers between the community and the Mosque with the Muslims being part of the greater life of the wider community.

The challenge now is to retain the momentum and build on the good work that came out of our little incident. At the end of Ramadan, a reception for all our friends was held at the Mosque. Speeches were kept to a minimum; instead children sang nasheeds or religious songs, and others recited poems. Food is always a treat and having food from five different continents was an added attraction.

For the longer term, the channels of communication must remain open and partnerships with other organisations must be strengthened. Maintaining an open and welcoming attitude at the Mosque is vital.

In a strange shift of positions, a few months ago, an American came to the mosque bearing a placard stating "An American prepared to listen". She set up in a hall after the Friday Prayer and soon attracted a sizeable audience. She also received a severe barracking from a few of them. Some accused her of being an American spy amongst other things. The fact that she felt confident enough to come to the Mosque is a testament not only to her courage but also the courage of the Muslim community, who despite feeling emotionally battered by international and national events, could make their hearts big enough to allow her the opportunity to come and take part in a discourse so painful to all. Islam teaches the peaceful approach.

Winning hearts and minds requires a fearlessness to confront bigotry and hate, from wherever it may spring.

8

Islamic Values

The Words of an Asylum Seeker
◆ ◆ ◆

Pluralism Enshrined – On the Constitution of Madinah
ZAKARIA BASHIER
◆ ◆ ◆

The Prophet of Mercy
◆ ◆ ◆

War and Peace
MUHAMMAD ABDEL HALEEM
◆ ◆ ◆

Tolerance
MUHAMMAD ABDEL HALEEM
◆ ◆ ◆

Human Rights – Islamic and Secular Perspectives
AZZAM TAMIMI
◆ ◆ ◆

Hope for a Troubled World – A Reflection on the Qur'an
ABDULWAHID HAMID
◆ ◆ ◆

The Prophet's Farewell Sermon
◆ ◆ ◆

Endpiece – Beyond Blindness
KAAMILEH HAMID
◆ ◆ ◆

Some Recommended Books – Notes on Contributors
◆ ◆ ◆

The Words of an Asylum Seeker

In the year 616 CE, a group of asylum seekers fled their homes in Makkah and sailed across the Red Sea to Abysinnia. This was a Christian land ruled by a Negus or King. The group made their way to the court of the Negus. Before an assembly of bishops and courtiers, the spokesman of the group, Ja'far ibn Abi Talib, addressed the Negus:

> "O King," he said, "We were a people steeped in ignorance, worshipping idols, eating the flesh of dead animals, committing abominations, neglecting our relations and ill-treating our neighbours, and the strong among us would oppress the weak.

> We were in this state when God sent to us a messenger from among us, whose descent and sincerity, truthfulness, trustworthiness and integrity were known to us.

> He summoned us to worship the One True God and to renounce the stones and idols that we and our fathers used to worship apart from God.

> He commanded us to speak the truth, to fulfil all that is entrusted to us, to care for our relatives, to be kind to our neighbours, and to refrain from what is forbidden and from bloodshed.

> He has forbidden us from engaging in shameful acts, from speaking falsehoods, from devouring the property of orphans,

and from vilifying virtuous women.

He has commanded us to worship God alone and never associate anything with Him, to pray, to pay the purifying dues and to fast.

We deemed him truthful and we believed in him and have followed the message he brought to us from God.

Thus we worshipped God alone and we did not associate anything with Him. And we held as forbidden what God has forbidden, and lawful what He has made lawful.

Then our people turned against us and tormented us and persecuted us, to compel us to forsake our religion and go back to the worship of idols instead of the worship of God, the Exalted, and to compel us to indulge in the evil deeds we used to indulge in.

So when they oppressed us and treated us unjustly and made life difficult for us and denied us our religion, we came to your land and have chosen you above all others. And we are hopeful for your protection, and request that we do not suffer injustice with you."

The Negus evidently was a humane and cultured person and a man of principles. He was impressed by what Ja'far had to say. He granted the small band of Muslims asylum in his country and refused to extradite them to Makkah. The noble Prophet, through emissaries, kept in touch with the Negus and with the community of believers who stayed on in Abyssinia. The Negus eventually became part of this community and when news of his death reached the Prophet in Madinah, the Prophet was saddened. He performed the Funeral Prayer for him.

From Ja'far's speech on the mission and method of the Prophet, we see that the first thing he stressed was pure monotheism, the belief in the absolute Oneness of God. To be on the straight and natural way, the human being's first duty is to gain or regain a correct knowledge of and belief in God. From this knowledge he will come to accept the wisdom and authority of God. From this will spring correct action.

From Ja'far's speech, we learn that the Prophet encouraged all the natural inbuilt moral virtues such as truthfulness, kindness, generosity, and justice. And he condemned all the naturally repugnant vices such as falsehood, shamelessness, ignorance, and oppression.

There is also the testimony of Ja'far on the truthfulness and trustworthiness of the Prophet. Both before and after he became a Prophet, Muhammad had the unchallenged reputation of a person who was always truthful and trustworthy. These qualities adorned the character of all Prophets of God and should be the distinguishing marks of all God-conscious persons.

Whereas the Qur'an is the final expression of God's message and guidance to humanity, the life and example of Muhammad as the last Prophet of God represents the way or the method in which God's message has been and can be implemented. The importance of the Prophet's example has been stressed in the Qur'an:

> 'Indeed in the messenger of God, you will find an excellent example for whoever hopes for God and the Last Day.'

And the Prophet himself said shortly before he died:

> 'I am leaving behind me two things which if you hold fast to them, you will never go astray – the Book of God (the Qur'an) and my example (Sunnah).'

The Qur'an and the Sunnah are thus the two primary sources for an understanding of Islam and the Muslim way of life. The Sunnah or Example of the Prophet includes what he said, did or agreed to.

Pluralism Enshrined –
On the Constitution of Madinah

ZAKARIA BASHIER

After thirteen years of struggle and persecution in his home town of Makkah, the Prophet Muhammad made the Hijrah (Relocation – literally, migration) to the northern city of Yathrib where a group of its inhabitants had become Muslims and had pledged to support him.

One of the first things he did there was to build a place of prayer – a mosque. Then he set about the task of getting all groups and communities in the city-state to commit themselves to a new legal and political framework that would guarantee mutual rights and obligations and protect the interests and well-being of all groups. The main groups were the Arab tribes of the Aws and the Khazraj, several Jewish tribes chief of which were the Nadir, the Qaynuqa and Qurayzah, and lastly the Muhajirun or the largely destitute Muslim immigrants from Makkah.

The Prophet consulted the various groups and drew up a document called the Sahifah that was to guarantee each group autonomy and rights and create a single, unified ummah or community with the Prophet as its leader and arbiter. All parties readily declared their acceptance of the Sahifah and their commitment to it. This document has been called the first written constitution in the world and is remarkable for its precision, its comprehensiveness and the vigour of its language.

This was the foundation of the Madinan State which came into existence in the wake of conflict and revolution. The constitution gave legal form to a pluralist, multi-racial and multi-cultural society, comprising two distinct religious communities, Muslim and Jewish.

The three main groups or communities, Ansar (Muslims native to Madinah), Muhajirun (immigrants from Makkah) and Jews (native to Madinah) were accorded local and communal autonomy with regard to

198

certain matters. They had:

1. the freedom to practise their religious rites as they saw fit.

2. the obligation to enforce law and order, prevent crime and punish criminals and wrong-doers.

3. the freedom to carry out commercial and economic activities and earn a living as they chose.

4. provision for the management of communal affairs and solidarity and mutual support for all members. Prisoners were to be ransomed and compensation collected and paid out when due. No member of the community was to be left in destitution.

5. the right of the various parties, at least by implication, to make legal decisions. A dispute was to be referred to the Prophet only if it proved too difficult and prolonged, otherwise it could be resolved locally, at the level of the community. However, two matters must be dealt with at the central level by the Prophet himself: these were (i) matters pertaining to war and peace in general, and (ii) matters pertaining to the relationship of Madinans with the Quraysh.

Relations with the Quraysh were also put under the jurisdiction of the central authority of the Prophet. In particular, it was not permitted that any party to the Sahifah should extend friendship, protection or assistance to the wealth or persons of the Quraysh. It was failure to honour this restriction that brought so much doom and destruction to the Jewish party to this Sahifah.

The Sahifah is remarkable, also, for the very high place it gives to the issue of law and order, and the firmness which it shows vis-a-vis crime and disorder. Rebellious actions against the authority of the Prophet would not be tolerated, according to the tone of the document, even if the rebels were sons of the covenanted parties. It was not lawful to give protection of any sort to rebels or criminals, nor was it lawful to shelter them or render any other assistance to them.

A vital provision of the Sahifah was that all covenanted parties had to join in the defence of the city of Madinah if it were exposed to external aggression, as well as contribute to the cost of any such defensive action. The Jews were not excluded from this vital provision of the Sahifah. The city of Madinah was declared a sanctuary whose sanctity must not be violated.

The covenanted Jews were given full citizenship in the state. There was no sign of any distinction between first or second-class citizens.

The peace of Madinah was declared one and indivisible, every individual of the city must make peace and war in harmony with the state. However, should an individual Muslim extend his jiwaar (protection) to anyone, not guilty of any crime or an injustice, all Muslims must honour this jiwaar.

The Sahifah declared that the basis for legal responsibility is the individual. Each person is responsible for his own deeds. No-one shall be punished for the deeds of his allies or even his next of kin. The emphasis on personal responsibility is an important break from the tribal conception of collective responsibility, which was widespread in pre-Qur'anic Arabia. Then, if a member of a tribe killed a man from another tribe, the killer's tribe as a whole were held responsible. Anyone of the killer's tribe could be taken and killed in retaliation. The shift away from the tribal bonding of collective responsibility was an important objective of the Sahifah as a whole. Perhaps for the first time in history, we have the example of a state founded on the basis of ideology, and contractual agreement as to the rights and obligations of its citizens.

To the bonding on the basis of faith and law afforded by the conclusion of the covenant of the Sahifah, we must add a third unifying factor in the foundation pillars of the new Muslim state. This third factor was the territorial base of the new Muslim Ummah emerging as a multi-racial and multi-cultural society which now had secure, defensible territory. This was one of the considerations which persuaded the Jews to endorse the Sahifah of Madinah.

The state of Madinah extended to areas on its immediate outskirts where clients and confederates of the Aws, the Khazraj and the Jews lived. The Prophet also made treaties with some tribes living near Madinah, and these too could be included within the jurisdiction of the city.

The Sahifah is also noteworthy for the protection it accords to strangers travelling in Muslim lands. Hitherto, such strangers had been considered fair game for highway robbers and the violent, aggressive bedouins of the desert. Only within Makkah, did the Quraysh and the Hashimites in particular, manage to secure some rights of security for strangers. They had however to conclude a special alliance before they could extend such rights to strangers. The Sahifah must be praised for this important provision, and for the related but significant provision that any Muslim had the right to grant his jiwaar (protection) to any such stranger, provided that the protected strangers were innocent of crimes and wrong-doing. Moreover, all Muslims were called upon to honour this jiwaar, irrespective of the social status of the Muslim granting it. The protection of Allah and His Messenger is one and indivisible, and so is the protection of all Muslims.

The Lasting Significance of the Sahiifah

The Sahifah was perhaps the first-ever document governing the political conduct of a state, with a clear declaration of its main constituting principles and objectives. In modern terminology, it represents the first written constitution known in history.

But the Sahifah is also very significant for the lofty principles, the humane and just relations it ordains with regard to the different religious and ethnic groups living in the city of Madinah. As a matter of fact, it is the first known attempt to create a multi-cultural and multi-racial society with different religious denominations living alongside one another. Basic human rights were granted in a fashion unprecedented in history. Every individual, Muslim or Jewish, was granted freedom of worship and freedom to live and work in peace and dignity. His livelihood and property were protected, and his rights to be treated with equity and justice firmly established. To reinforce the concept of equal citizenship to all persons living in Madinah, irrespective of their religious affiliations, the Jews of Madinah were formally committed by the provisions of the Sahifah to participate in the defence of the city, should it be exposed to outside aggression. They were obligated both to take part in the actual fighting, should it break out, and to contribute towards the cost of such fighting.

The Sahifah has a strong commitment against crime and lawlessness. All citizens were bound to fight criminals and law-breakers, even if those were the sons of anyone of the covenanted parties.

Thus the Sahifah affords the unique possibility of a pluralist state, founded on a sound legal document. The degree of liberty and tolerance implied by the various provisions of the Sahifah is truly amazing. It promotes the Islamic ideals of peaceful and fruitful co-existence among different ethnic and religious groups.

(Adapted from Zakaria Bashier, *Sunshine at Madinah*, Islamic Foundation, Leicester.)

The Prophet of Mercy

For thirteen years in his birthplace of Makkah, the Prophet Muhammad called people to the worship of the One True God, to do good and renounce all that was false. But the powers with interests to protect remained implacably hostile and made life intolerable for those who had submitted to the truth.

In constant search for fertile soil to plant the message of truth, the noble Prophet eventually migrated - not fled - northwards to Yathrib. The green oasis became known as the Madinah or the City of the Prophet and was to become the territorial base from which he won the hearts of multitudes and consolidated Islam's place in the landscape of the peninsula.

The leaders of Makkah and a large part of its citizenry remained stubbornly hostile and sought - through wars, siege and alliances - to destabilise the fledgling community. The Prophet, who desired security and peace for people, negotiated a truce with the pagan Makkans on terms that many of his followers were deeply unhappy about. This was in the fifth year after the hijrah or migration to Madinah.

The truce turned out to be beneficial to the whole peninsula but the Makkans eventually broke it by mounting a bloody aggression against an ally of the state of Medina. The Prophet could not overlook this breach and in the eighth year after the hijrah, he mobilised an impressive force and moved on Makkah. Ten thousand converged on the city, reaching there in the month of Ramadan, the month of fasting. The Quraysh realised that there was no hope of resisting, let alone of defeating, the Muslim forces. What was to be their fate – they who had harried and persecuted the believers, tortured and boycotted them, driven them out of their hearths and homes, stirred up others against them, made war on them, and killed many?

They were now completely at the mercy of the Prophet.

Revenge was easy. He could have laid waste the city and wiped out its inhabitants. But revenge was not his object. He did not lead his confident army into Makkah like any tyrant, full of arrogance, forgetting the Almighty, the Cause of all causes, and intoxicated with self-conceit.

Far from it. In the words of an early biographer, he entered with great humility and gratitude, prostrating himself repeatedly on the back of the camel he was riding, before the One God, thankful to Him for all He had provided, declaring an all-embracing amnesty and peace, in place of any thought of avenging past material or mental afflictions, and in fact demonstrating what God wills of Godly men: "… enter the gate prostrating and say 'Amnesty'." (The Qur'an, 2: 58; 7:160).

He ordered Bilal, the Ethiopian, to go on the rooftop of the Ka'bah to call the adhan. The noble Prophet led the congregational prayer and then addressed the assembled citizens in the compound around the Ka'bah. He reminded them of what they had done to him and the Muslims, and said, "The arrogance and racial pride of the heathen days has been wiped out by God today. All human beings are descended from Adam, and Adam was made of clay."

He recited the following verse of the Qur'an:

> "O human beings! We have indeed created you of a male and a female and made you into nations and tribes so that you may know one another. Surely the most honorable of you with God is the one among you who is most deeply conscious of Him. Surely, God is Knowing, Aware. (The Qur'an, 49:13)

He then asked them in a voice full of compassion and tenderness:

> 'O people of Quraysh! What do you think I will do with you?'

One of them, Suhayl ibn Amr, who had fought against the Prophet, replied on behalf of the Makkans:

> 'We think (you will treat us) well, noble brother, son of a noble brother.'

A radiant smile flashed across the face of the beloved Prophet of God and, in a spirit of magnanimity and tolerance, he said:

203

"I shall speak to you as Yusuf [Joseph] spoke unto his brothers: 'There is no reproach against you today; God will forgive. He is the most Merciful and the most Compassionate.'" (Qur'an,12:92)

And he added:

'No more responsibility burdens you today.
'Idhhabuu... wa antum at-tulaqaa - Go, for you are free.'

Instantaneously Makkah was transformed, and overnight practically the entire population was won over to Islam. Nothing else could have won them over so profoundly and sincerely. They were not the inhabitants of a defeated and occupied country, but equals with the victors in rights as well as obligations. When a Messenger of God is the liberator of a town, nothing less exalted could be expected.

Without leaving a single companion of his to garrison the city, the Prophet soon returned to Madinah, leaving Makkah to be governed by a Makkan just converted. He never had to regret this later. This is how human hearts are won. In the entire episode, thirteen lives were lost.

'I am the Prophet of Battle; I am the Prophet of Mercy,' he is reported to have said. But it was destined for Muhammad to demonstrate that even in battle, he was the "Prophet of Mercy".

The above account has been partly compiled from the book, *Battlefields of the Prophet*, by the renowned scholar Muhammad Hamidullah. This book lists the number of people killed in battle on both sides in all the engagements led by the Prophet. This number is given as less than 500 (see box). It is clear neither revenge nor hatred, greed nor domination was ever the driving passion in the wars that the

Casualties in the main military expeditions led by the Prophet				
Engagement	Enemy force	Enemy killed	Muslim force	Muslims killed
Badr	950	70	313	14
Uhud	3,000	22	700	70
Khandaq	12,000	8	3,000	6
Khaibar	20,000	93	1,500	15
Mu'ta	100,000		3,000	13
Hunain		70	12,000	70
Taif			12,000	12

noble Prophet engaged or were forced into. His purpose was primarily to win over people to the truth. He did not see his enemies as irredeemable infidels, but as potential forces for the good, for their own selves and for others. And he gave them the opportunity and the space to transform themselves.

Casualties in Twentieth Century Conflicts

'I have lived throughout most of the twentieth century without, I must add, suffering personal hardship. I remember it only as the most terrible century in western history.'
  –Isaiah Berlin

	Military & civilian deaths
Belgian repression in the Congo Free State 1886-1908	6,500,000
First World War 1914-1918	8,500,000
Russian Civil War 1917-1922	2,825,000
Stalin's regime 1924-53	20,000,000
Italian campaign in Abyssinia 1935-1936	160,000
Second World War 1939-1945	71,000,000
Post-War Expulsion of Germans from East Europe 1945-47	2,384,000
Chinese Civil War 1945-1949	3,000,000
Mao Zedong's regime 1949-1975	40,000,000
Korean War 1950–1953	1,200,000
Tito's Regime 1944-80	250,000
French repression in Algeria 1954-1962	1,000,000
Vietnam War 1965-1973	1,033,000
Cambodia, Khmer Rouge 1975-1978	1,500,000
Soviet Union war against Afghanistan 1979-1989	2,000,000
Iran-Iraq War 1980-88	1,000,000
Gulf War 1990-1991	150,000
Bosnia 1992-1995	280,000

Sources: Britannica & other Internet resources including
http://users.erols.com/mwhite28/warstatx.htm

War and Peace

Muhammad Abdel Haleem

The Sources of Islamic law

The Qur'an is the supreme authority in Islam and the primary source of Islamic Law, including the laws regulating war and peace. The second source is the hadith, the traditions of the Prophet Muhammad's acts and deeds, which can be used to confirm, explain or elaborate Qur'anic teachings, but may not contradict the Qur'an, since they derive their authority from the Qur'an itself. Together these form the basis for all other sources of Islamic law, such as *ijma'* (consensus of Muslim scholars on an opinion regarding any given subject) and *qiyas* (reasoning by analogy). These and others are merely methods to reach decisions based on the texts or the spirit of the Qur'an and hadith. The Qur'an and hadith are thus the only binding sources of Islamic law. Again, nothing is acceptable if it contradicts the text or the spirit of these two sources. Any opinions arrived at by individual scholars or schools of Islamic law, including the recognised four Sunni schools, are no more than opinions. The founders of these schools never laid exclusive claim to the truth, or invited people to follow them rather than any other scholars. Western writers often take the views of this or that classical or modern Muslim writer as 'the Islamic view', presumably on the basis of assumptions drawn from the Christian tradition, where the views of people like St Augustine or St Thomas Aquinas are often cited as authorities. In Islam, however, for any view of any scholar to gain credibility, it must demonstrate its textual basis in the Qur'an and authentic hadith, and its derivation from a sound linguistic understanding of these texts.

Ijtihad – exerting one's reason to reach judgements on the basis of these two sources – is the mechanism by which Muslims find solutions for the ever-changing and evolving life around them. The 'closing' of the door of ijtihad is a myth propagated by many Western scholars, some of whom imagine that 'the door' still remains closed and that Muslims have nothing to fall back on except the decisions of the Schools of Law and scholars of the classical period. In fact, scholars in present-day Muslim countries reach their own decisions on laws governing all sorts of new situations, using the same methodology based on the Qur'an and hadith and the principles derived from them, without feeling necessarily bound by the conclusions of any former school of law.

In the Qur'an and hadith, the fundamental sources of Islamic teachings on war and peace are to be found.

Normal Relations

The Islamic relationship between individuals and nations is one of peace. War is a contingency that becomes necessary at certain times and under certain conditions. Muslims learn from the Qur'an that God's objective in creating the human race in different communities was that they should relate to each other peacefully (49:13).[1]

The objective of forming the family unit is to foster affection and mercy, and that of creating a baby in its mother's womb is to form bonds of blood and marriage between people:

> It is He who created the human being from fluid, making relationships of blood and marriage. (25:54)

Sowing enmity and hatred amongst people is the work of Satan:

> Satan wishes to sow enmity and hatred between you with intoxicants and gambling. (5:91)

Division into warring factions is viewed as a punishment that God brings on people who revert to polytheism after He has delivered them from distress:

> ... He is able to divide you into discordant factions and make you taste the might of each other ... (6:65)

War is hateful (2:216), and the changing of fear into a sense of safety is one of the rewards for those who believe and do good deeds (24:55). That God has given them the sanctuary of Makkah is a blessing for which its people should be thankful (29:67). Paradise is the Land of Peace – Dar al-Salam (5:127).

Justifications and Conditions for War

War may become necessary only to stop evil from triumphing in a way that would corrupt the earth (2:251). For Muslims to participate in war there must be valid justifications, and strict conditions must be fulfilled. A thorough survey of the relevant verses of the Qur'an shows that it is consistent throughout with regard to these rulings on the justification of war, and its conduct, termination and consequences.

War in Islam as regulated by the Qur'an and hadith has been subject to many distortions by Western scholars and even by some Muslim writers. These are due either to misconceptions about terminology or – above all – using quotations taken out of context.[2] Nowhere in the Qur'an is changing people's religion given as a cause for waging war. The Qur'an gives a clear instruction that there is no compulsion in religion (2:256). It states that people will remain different (11:118), they will always have different religions and ways and this is an unalterable fact (5:48). God tells the Prophet that most people will not believe 'even if you are eager that they should' (12:103).[3]

All the battles that took place during the Prophet's lifetime, under the guidance of the Qur'an and the Prophet, have been surveyed and shown to have been waged only in self-defence or to pre-empt an imminent attack.[4] For more than ten years in Mecca, Muslims were persecuted, but before permission was given to fight they were instructed to restrain themselves (4:77) and endure with patience and fortitude:

> Pardon and forgive until God gives his command.
> (2:109; see also 29:59; 16:42)

After the Muslims were forced out of their homes and their town, and those who remained behind were subjected to even more abuse. God gave His permission to fight:

> Permission is given to those who fight because they have been wronged, and God is indeed able to give them victory; those who have been driven from their homes unjustly only because they said, 'Our Lord is God' – for had it not been for God's repelling some men by means of others, monasteries, churches, synagogues and mosques, in which the name of God is much mentioned, would certainly have been destroyed. Verily God helps those that help Him – lo! God is Strong, Almighty – those

208

who, if they are given power in the land, establish worship and pay the poor-due and enjoin what is good and forbid iniquity. (22:39-41)

Here, war is seen as justifiable and necessary to defend people's right to their own beliefs, and once the believers have been given victory they should not become triumphant or arrogant or have a sense of being a superpower, because the promise of help given above and the rewards are for those who do not seek to exalt themselves on earth or spread corruption (28:83).

Righteous intention

Righteous intention is an essential condition. When fighting takes place, it should be *fi sabil illah* – in the way of God – as is often repeated in the Qur'an. His way is prescribed in the Qur'an as the way of truth and justice, including all the teaching it gives on the justifications and the conditions for the conduct of war and peace. The Prophet was asked about those who fight for the booty, and those who fight out of self-aggrandisement or to be seen as a hero. He said that none of these was in the way of God. The one who fights in the way of God is he who fights so that the word of God is uppermost (hadith: Bukhari).

This expression of the word of God being 'uppermost' was misunderstood by some to mean that Islam should gain political power over other religions. However, if we use the principle that 'different parts of the Qur'an interpret each other', we find (9:40) that by simply concealing the Prophet in the cave from his trackers, after he had narrowly escaped an attempt to murder him, God made His word 'uppermost', and the word of the wrong-doers 'lowered'. This could not be described as gaining military victory or political power.

Another term which is misunderstood and misrepresented is *jihad*. This does not mean 'Holy War'. 'Holy War' does not exist as a term in Arabic, and its translation into Arabic sounds quite alien. The term which is specifically used in the Qur'an for fighting is *qital*. Jihad can be by argumentation (25:52), financial help or actual fighting. Jihad is always described in the Qur'an as *fi sabil illah*. On returning from a military campaign, the Prophet said to his followers: 'We have returned from the minor jihad to the major jihad - the struggle of the individual with his own self.'

Jihad as an obligation

When there is a just cause for jihad, which must have a righteous intention, it then becomes an obligation. It becomes an obligation for defending religious freedom (22:39-41), for self-defence (2:190) and defending those who are oppressed: men, women and children who cry for help (4:75). It is the duty of the Muslims to help the oppressed, except against a people with whom the Muslims have a treaty (8:72). These are the only valid justifications for war we find in the Qur'an. Even when war becomes necessary, we find that there is no 'conscription' in the Qur'an. The Prophet is instructed only to 'urge on the believers' (4:64). The Qur'an - and the hadith at greater length – urge on the Muslim fighters (those who are defending themselves or the oppressed) in the strongest way: by showing the justice of their cause, the bad conduct of the enemy, and promising great rewards in the afterlife for those who are prepared to sacrifice their lives and property in such a good cause."[5]

Who is to be fought – discrimination and proportionality

In this regard we must discuss two verses in the Qur'an which are normally quoted by those most eager to criticise Qur'anic teachings on war: 2:191 ('slay them wherever you find them') and verse 9:5, labelled the 'Sword Verse'. Both verses have been subjected to decontextualisation, misinterpretation and misrepresentation. The first verse comes in a passage that defines clearly who is to be fought:

> Fight in the way of God those who fight against you, but do not transgress. God does not love the transgressor. (2:190)

'Those who fight against you' means actual fighters – civilians are protected. The Prophet and his successors, when they sent out an army, gave clear instructions not to attack civilians – women, old people, religious people engaged in their worship - nor destroy crops or animals.

Discrimination and proportionality should be strictly observed. Only the combatants are to be fought, and no more harm should be caused to them than they have caused (2:194). Thus wars and weapons of destruction that destroy civilians and their towns are ruled out by the Qur'an and the word and deed of the Prophet, these being the only binding authority in Islamic law. The prohibition is regularly reinforced by, 'Do not transgress. God does not love the transgressor'. Transgression has been interpreted by Qur'anic exegetes as meaning, 'initiation of fighting, fighting those with whom a treaty has been concluded, surprising the enemy without first inviting them to make peace, destroying crops or killing those who should be protected' (Baydawi's commentary on 2:190).

210

The orders are always couched in restraining language, with much repetition of warnings, such as 'do not transgress' and 'God does not love the transgressors' and 'He loves those who are conscious of Him'. These are instructions given to people who, from the beginning, should have the intention of acting 'in the way of God'.

Linguistically we notice that the verses in this passage always restrict actions in a legalistic way, which appeals strongly to Muslims' conscience. In six verses (2:190-5) we find four prohibitions (do not), six restrictions: two 'until', two 'if', two 'who attack you', as well as such cautions as 'in the way of God', 'be conscious of God', 'God does not like aggressors', 'God is with those who are conscious of Him', 'with those who do good deeds' and 'God is Forgiving, Merciful.' It should be noted that the Qur'an, in treating the theme of war, as with many other themes, regularly gives the reasons and justifications for any action it demands.

Verse 2:191 begins:
> Slay them where you find them and expel them from where they expelled you; persecution [*fitna*] is worse than killing.

'Slay them wherever you find them,' has been made the title of an article on war in Islam.[6] In this article 'them' is removed from its context, where it refers back to 'those who attack you' in the preceding verse. 'Wherever you find them' is similarly misunderstood: the Muslims were anxious that if their enemies attacked them in Makkah (which is a sanctuary) and they retaliated, they would be breaking the law. Thus the Qur'an simply gave the Muslims permission to fight those enemies, whether outside or inside Makkah, and assured them that the persecution that had been committed by the unbelievers against them for believing in God was more sinful than the Muslims killing those who attacked them, wherever they were. Finally, it must be pointed out that the whole passage (2:190-5) comes in the context of fighting those who bar Muslims from reaching the Sacred Mosque at Makkah to perform the pilgrimage. This is clear from 'verse 89' before and verse 196 after the passage. In the same way, the verse giving the first permission to fight occurs in the Qur'an, also in the context of barring Muslims from reaching the Mosque to perform the pilgrimage (22:25-41).

The 'sword' verse
We must also comment on another verse much referred to but notoriously misinterpreted and taken out of context – that which became labelled as the 'Sword Verse':

Then, when the sacred months have passed, slay the idolaters wherever you find them, take them and besiege them and prepare for them every ambush. (9:5)

The hostility and 'bitter enmity' of the polytheists and their *fitna* (persecution) (2:193; 8:39) of the Muslims grew so great that the unbelievers were determined to convert the Muslims back to paganism or finish them off.

They would persist in fighting you until they turn you back from your religion, if they could. (2:217)

It was these hardened polytheists in Arabia, who would accept nothing other than the expulsion of the Muslims or their reversion to paganism, and who repeatedly broke their treaties, that the Muslims were ordered to treat in the same way – to fight them or expel them.

Even with such an enemy Muslims were not simply ordered to pounce on them and reciprocate by breaking the treaty themselves; instead, an ultimatum was issued, giving the enemy notice, that after the four sacred months mentioned in 9:5 above, the Muslims would wage war on them. The main clause of the sentence 'kill the polytheists' is singled out by some Western scholars to represent the Islamic attitude to war; even some Muslims take this view and allege that this verse abrogated other verses on war. This is pure fantasy, isolating and decontextualising a small part of a sentence. The full picture is given in 9:1-15, which gives many reasons for the order to fight such polytheists. They continuously broke their agreements and aided others against the Muslims, they started hostilities against the Muslims, barred others from becoming Muslims, expelled Muslims from the Holy Mosque and even from their own homes. At least eight times the passage mentions their misdeeds against the Muslims. Consistent with restrictions on war elsewhere in the Qur'an, the immediate context of this 'Sword Verse' exempts such polytheists as do not break their agreements and who keep the peace with the Muslims (9:7). It orders that those enemies seeking safe conduct should be protected and delivered to the place of safety they seek (9:6). The whole of this context to verse 5 with all its restrictions, is ignored by those who simply isolate one part of a sentence to build their theory of war in Islam on what is termed 'The Sword Verse' even when the word 'sword' does not occur anywhere in the Qur'an.

Cessation of hostilities

Once the hostility of the enemy ceases, the Muslims must stop fighting (2:193; 8:39):

> And if they incline to peace, do so and put your trust in God. Even if they intend to deceive you, remember that God is sufficient for you. (8:61-2)

When the war is over, the Qur'an and hadith give instructions as to the treatment of prisoners of war and the new relationship with the non-Muslims. War is certainly not seen as a means in Islam of converting other people from their religions. The often-quoted division of the world into *dar al-harb* and *dar al-Islam* is seen nowhere in the Qur'an or hadith, the only authoritative sources of Islam. The scholars who used these expressions were talking about the warring enemies in countries surrounding the Muslim lands. Even for such scholars there was not a dichotomy but a trichotomy, with a third division, *dar al-sulh*, the lands with which the Muslims had treaty obligations.

The Qur'an and hadith talk about the different situations that exist between a Muslim state and a neighbouring warring enemy. They mention a state of defensive war, within the prescriptions specified above, the state of peace treaty for a limited or unlimited period, the state of truce and the state where a member of a hostile camp can come into a Muslim land for special purposes under safe conduct.[7]

Treaties

The Prophet and his companions did make treaties, such as that of Hudaybiyya in the sixth year of the hijra and the one made by 'Umar with the people of Jerusalem.[8] Faithfulness to a treaty is a most serious obligation which the Qur'an and hadith incessantly emphasise:

Believers, fulfil your bonds. (5:1)

Keep the agreements of God when you have made them and do not break your oaths after you have made them with God as your bond ...(16:91)
Covenants should not be broken because one community feels stronger than another. (16:92)

Breaking treaties puts the culprit into a state lower than animals (8:55). As stated above, even defending a Muslim minority is not allowed when there is a treaty with the camp they are in.

213

Prisoners of war

There is nothing in the Qur'an or hadith to prevent Muslims from following the present international humanitarian conventions on war or prisoners of war. There is nothing in the Qur'an to say that prisoners of war must be held captive, but as this was the practice of the time and there was no international body to oversee exchanges of prisoners, the Qur'an deals with the subject. There are only two cases where it mentions their treatment:

> O Prophet! Tell the captives you have, 'If God knows goodness in your heart He will give you better rewards than have been taken from you and forgive you. He is forgiving, merciful. 'And if they intend to be treacherous to you, they have been treacherous to God in the past and He has put them into your hands. (8:70-1)

> When you have fully overcome the enemy in the battle, then tighten their bonds, but thereafter set them free either by an act of grace or against ransom. (47:4)

Grace is suggested first, before ransom. Even when some were not set free, for one reason or another, they were, according to the Qur'an and hadith, to be treated in a most humane way (76:8-9; 9:60; 2:177). In the Bible, where it mentions fighting, we find a different picture in the treatment administered to conquered peoples, for example:

> When you march up to attack a city, make its people an offer of peace. If they accept and open their gates, all the people in it shall be subject to forced labour and shall work for you. If they refuse to make peace with you in battle, lay siege to that city. When the Lord your God delivers it into your hand, put to the sword all the men in it. As for the women, the children, the livestock and everything else in the city, you may take these as plunder for yourselves. And you may use the plunder the Lord your God gives you from your enemies. This is how you are to treat all the cities that are at a distance from you and do not belong to the nations nearby.

> However, in the cities of the nations the Lord your God is giving you as an inheritance, do not leave alive anything that breathes. Completely destroy them – the Hittites, Amorites, Canaanites,

Perizzites, Hivites, and Jebusites - as the Lord your God has commanded you. Otherwise they will teach you to follow all the detestable things they do in worshipping their gods, and you will sin against the Lord your God. (Deuteronomy, 20:10-189)

Resumption of peaceful relations

We have already seen in the Qur'an 22:41 that God promises to help those who, when He has established them in a land after war,' ... establish worship and pay the poor-due and enjoin what is good and forbid iniquity'.

In this spirit, when the Muslim army was victorious over the enemy, any of the defeated people who wished to remain in the land could do so under a guarantee of protection for their life, religion and freedom, and if they wished to leave they could do so with safe conduct. If they chose to stay among the Muslims, they could become members of the Muslim community. If they wished to continue in their faith they had the right to do so and were offered security. The only obligation on them then was to pay jizya, a tax exempting the person from military service and from paying zakat, which the Muslims have to pay – a tax considerably heavier than the jizya. Neither had the option of refusing to pay, but in return the non-Muslims were given the protection of the state. Jizya was not a poll-tax, and it was not charged on the old, or poor people, women or children.[10]

Humanitarian intervention

Humanitarian intervention is allowed, even advocated in the Qur'an, under the category of defending the oppressed. However it must be done within the restrictions specified in the Qur'an, as we have shown above. In intervening, it is quite permissible to co-operate with non-Muslims, under the proviso:

> Co-operate in what is good and pious and do not co-operate in what is sinful and aggression. (5:2)

International co-operation

In the sphere of war and peace, there is nothing in the Qur'an or hadith which should cause Muslims to feel unable to sign and act according to the modern international conventions, and there is much in the Qur'an and hadith from which modern international law can benefit. The Prophet Muhammad remembered an alliance he witnessed that was contracted between some chiefs of Mecca before his call to prophethood to protect the poor and weak against oppression and said:

I have witnessed in the house of Ibn Jud'an an alliance which I would not exchange for a herd of red camels, and if it were to be called for now that Islam is here, I would respond readily."[11]

There is nothing in Islam that prevents Muslims from having peaceful, amicable and good relations with other nations when they read and hear regularly the Qur'anic injunction, referring to members of other faiths:

> God does not forbid you from being kind and equitable to those who have neither made war on you on account of your religion nor driven you from your homes. God loves those who are equitable. (60:8)

This includes participation in international peace-making and peace-keeping efforts. The rule of arbitration in violent disputes between groups of Muslims is given in the Qur'an:

> If two parties of the believers take up arms against one another, make peace between them. If either of them commits aggression against the other, fight against the aggressors until they submit to God's judgement. When they submit, make peace between them in equity and justice. God loves those who act injustice. (49:9)

This could, in agreement with rules of Islamic jurisprudence, be applied more generally to disputes within the international community. For this reason, Muslims should, and do, participate in the arbitration of disputes by international bodies such as the United Nations.

Modern international organisations and easy travel should make it easier for different people, in accordance with the teachings of the Qur'an, to 'get to know one another', 'co-operate in what is good' and live in peace. The Qur'an affirms:

> There is no virtue in much of their counsels: only in his who enjoins charity, kindness and peace among people ... (4:114)

Notes

1. See article on Tolerance below.
2. 'Slay them wherever you find them: Humanitarian Law in Islam,' by James J. Busuttil, Linacre College, Oxford, in *Revue de Droit Penal Militaire et de Droit de la Guerre*, 1991, pp.113-40.
3. See article on 'Tolerance' below.
4. See A. M. al-'Aqqad, op.cit. (Cairo, 1957) pp. 187-91, quoting a survey by Ahmad Zaki Pasha.
5. See for example 3:169-172; 9:120-1 and many *hadiths* in the chapters on *jihad* in the various collections of *hadiths*.
6. Busuttil, op. cit. p. 127. The rendering he uses runs: 'Idolatry is worse than carnage'. This corrupts the meaning. It is clear from the preceding words, 'those who have turned you out' that *fitna* means persecution. This meaning is borne out by the identical verb (turning out/expelling) preceding the only other verse (2:217) where the expression, '*fitna* is worse than killing' appears. Here the statement is clearly explained: 'Fighting in [the prohibited month] is a grave (offence) but graver is it in the sight of God to prevent access to the path of God, to deny Him, to prevent access to the Sacred Mosque and drive out its people.'
7. 'Aqqad, op.cit., pp. 204-9.
8. See article on 'Tolerance'.
9. In the New Testament Jesus gives the high ideal that if someone hits you on one cheek, you should turn the other cheek. Pardon and forgiveness on the individual level is also highly recommended in the Qur'an. 'Good and evil deeds are not alike. Requite evil with good, and he who is your enemy will become your dearest friend, but none will attain this attribute save those who patiently endure; none will attain it save those who are truly fortunate' (41:34-5). And see 45:14. But when it comes to the places of worship being subjected to destruction and when helpless, old men, women and children are persecuted and when unbelievers try to force believers to renounce their religion, the Qur'an considers it total dereliction of the duty for the Muslim state not to oppose such oppression and defend what is right.
10. See article on 'Tolerance'.
11. Red camels were proverbial in Arabia as the best one can have.

Tolerance

MUHAMMAD ABDEL HALEEM

Islam is generally regarded in the West as being anything but tolerant - a religion of the sword and belligerency. This is the result of misinterpretation. A Muslim may wonder why this subject has assumed so much importance, but reference to European history shows that the history of the Christian West with regard to tolerance, by the admission of Western authors themselves, is shocking. In fact, it is this background that makes people now insist on tolerance and campaign for it to an extent for which Muslims, with their different background, do not see such a need.

Under the heading 'Tolerance' or 'Toleration', Western history books and encyclopaedias actually recount a long history of intolerance, and hesitant movements – only in recent times — of attempts to alleviate it. The Toleration Act of 1689 passed in England granted to religious dissenters freedom of worship, under certain conditions. Roman Catholics and those who did not believe in the Trinity were not covered by the Act. Political disqualifications were not removed by the Act and dissenters were not allowed to hold public office until the Occasional Conformity Act of 1711. The Catholic Emancipation Act of 1829 came to repeal earlier penal laws, which subjected the Irish Catholics to persecution. Such was the state of intolerance even within Christianity itself, let alone towards non-Christians.

What is Tolerance?

The lexical meaning of 'tolerance' is 'to bear, to endure, to put up with'. In the Encyclopedia Americana we read:

> Toleration, however, has a peculiarly limited signification. It connotes a refraining from prohibition and persecution.

Nevertheless it suggests a latent disapproval and it usually refers to a condition in which the freedom which it permits is both limited and conditional. Toleration is not equivalent to religious liberty, and it falls far short of religious equality. It assumes the existence of an authority which might have been coercive, but which, for reasons of its own, is not pushed to extremes ... However lamentable the fact may be, it should not surprise us that greater intolerance has been found amongst the Christian nations than among any other people.[1]

Traditionally, campaigns for tolerance were confined to the sphere of religion in a limited sense. In recent years, however, the meaning and the scope of the concept have become much wider, as we shall see later.

When we come to consider the issue of tolerance in Islam we find a different situation altogether. First of all there was no ready equivalent term in the Arabic language to mean what is traditionally understood in English by 'tolerance'. When Muslims began to talk about this subject as a reaction to its use in English, the word they used in Arabic was *tasamuh*, which has become the current term for 'tolerance'. The root form of this word has two connotations: 'generosity' (*jud wa karam*) and 'ease' (*tasahul*).[2] Thus the Muslims in Arabic talk about *tasamuh al-Islam* and *al-tasamuh al-dini*, in a quite different way from the English usage. Where 'tolerance' indicates a powerful authority grudgingly 'bearing' or 'putting up with' others who are different, the Arabic term denotes generosity and ease from both sides on a reciprocal basis. The term is always used in the reciprocal form.

In fact, tolerance is born out of the very nature of Islam – which seems to be the only religion that is not named after a race of people, like Judaism and Hinduism, or after any single person like Buddhism or Christianity. 'Islam', the name given to the religion in the Qur'an by God Himself, means 'devotion to God', 'dedication to God alone', conventionally translated as 'submission to God'. God, in Islam, is not the Lord of the Arabs or the Muslims but the Lord of all human beings and all the worlds, *Rabb al-'alamin*, who states in the Qur'an, 'We have honoured the Children of Adam' (17:70) – all the Children of Adam are 'chosen' by God to be honoured.

Islam, moreover, is not an exclusive or novel religion; it is part of the whole history of religion. Its book, the Qur'an, 'continues' and 'confirms' the previous scriptures (12:111), and its Prophet is only one in the long line of prophets Muslims have to believe in. For example, eighteen prophets are mentioned in one place in the Qur'an, and Muhammad is told:

These are the people God has guided. Follow the guidance that has been given to them (2:136; 6:83-96)

The Qur'an declares: 'Muhammad is but a messenger, before whom other messengers were sent' (3:144) and he never said, 'No man cometh to the Lord except by me.' Christians and the Jews who lived among an overwhelming Muslim majority are referred to in the Qur'an by the honorific term *ahl al-kitab* (the 'People of the Book') not as 'minorities', in the way that other religious groups in the Christian West, are described. The Qur'an does not brand the 'People of the Book' as a whole as unacceptable. It says:

> They are not all alike. Of the People of the Book there is a staunch community who recite the revelations of God in the night season, falling prostrate [before Him]. They believe in God and the last day, and enjoin right conduct and forbid indecency, and vie one with another in good works. These are of the righteous. And whatever good they do, they will not be denied the reward thereof. (3:113-5)

It does not brand them all as dishonest. It says:

> Among the People of the Book there is he who, if you trust him with a weight of treasure, will return it to you. And among them there is he who, if thou trust him with a piece of gold, will not return it to you unless you keep standing over him. (3:75)

Similarly, the Qur'an allows Muslims to eat the food of the 'People of the Book' and to marry their women who remain Christians and Jews (5:5). It does not allow Muslims to be carried away by fanciful hopes, but says:

> It will not be in accordance with your desires, nor the desires of the People of the Book. He who doeth wrong will have the recompense thereof, and will not find against God any protecting friend or helper. And whoso doeth good works, whether of male or female, and is a believer, such will enter paradise and they will not be wronged [by so much as] the groove in a date stone. (4:123-4)

It instructs Muslims not to argue with the 'People of the Book' except in the fairest manner and to say to them:

> We believe in what has been revealed to us and in what has been revealed to you. Our Lord and your Lord is one and the same, and to Him we submit ourselves. (29:46)

Muslims are instructed to appeal to the 'People of the Book' through what is common between them and Islam.

> Say, 'O People of the Book! Come to common terms as between us and you: That we worship none but God; that we associate no partners with him; that we erect not, from among ourselves. Lords and patrons other than God.' If then they turn back, say: 'Bear witness that we submit to God's Will'. (3:64)

In the Qur'an, God addresses Muslims and the followers of other religions, saying:

> We have ordained a law and assigned a path to each of you. Had God pleased. He could have made you one nation, but it is His wish to prove you by that which He has bestowed upon you. Vie, then, with each other in good works, for to God you shall all be returned, and He shall declare to you what you have disagreed about. (5:48)

This command, to leave differences to be settled on the Day of Judgement, is repeated many times in the Qur'an. Even in their relations with polytheists, who stand as the extreme opposite of the fundamental Islamic belief of monotheism, Muslims are instructed in the Qur'an:

> God does not forbid you, to be kind and equitable to those who do not fight you for [your] faith, nor drive you out of your homes: for God loves those who are just. (60:8)

Addressing all people, God says:

> O mankind! We created you from a single pair of a male and a female, and made you into nations and tribes, that you may know each other. Verily the most honoured of you in the sight

of God is the most righteous of you, and God has full knowledge and is well acquainted [with all things]. (49:13)

The variety of their colours, tongues, and races are regarded as a sign of God's power and mercy (30:22; 49:13), and as such should lead to closeness, rather than to discrimination or intolerance.

These instructions are not isolated or casual instances in the Qur'an, but are repeated many times and are part of the whole fabric of the message of Islam. On this basis, tolerance has been, from the beginning, a natural, inseparable part of Islam. It did not tolerate non-Muslims grudgingly, but welcomed them to live freely in Muslim society. At the height of Islam's success, the Qur'an set the principle, *la ikraha fi'l-din*, 'there is no compulsion in religion' (2:256). Here it employs the strongest and most permanent negative form in Arabic, the *la* of absolute negation, used in the Qur'an for such fundamental negations as: 'There is no god except God', and 'There is no changing the words of God' (47:19; 10:64). We also find the repeated pattern:

'To me is my religion; to you is yours,' (109:6); 'To me is my work, to you is yours' (10:41).

The Qur'an affirms that God has created people to be different, and they will always remain different, not only in their appearance but also in their beliefs (11:118-19) and it is up to each person whether to become a believer or not.

Had your Lord wished, all people on earth would have become believers. Will you [Muhammad] then compel all people to become believers? (10:99)

The two key expressions: *wa law sha'a rabbuka* (had your Lord wished) and *fa man sha'a* (whoever wishes to) occur more than twenty times in the Qur'an.[3]

The Qur'an not only 'tolerates' Christians and Jews who live in a Muslim society, but instructs the Prophet:

Say: 'O People of the Book! You have naught of guidance, till you observe the Torah and the Gospel and that which was revealed to you from your Lord'. (5:68)

God speaks, saying:

222

We have revealed the Torah. There is in it guidance and light. By it, the Prophets who have surrendered themselves to God judge the Jews and so do the Rabbis and divines. Those who do not judge in accordance with God's revelation are unbelievers. (5:44)

Let the followers of the Gospel judge in accordance with what God has revealed therein. Evil doers are those that do not judge in accordance with God's revelation. (5-47)

In accordance with the instructions of the Qur'an, in AD 638 when the Muslims, under the Caliph 'Umar, entered Jerusalem, then called Aeilia, 'Umar made the following covenant with the inhabitants:

In the name of God, the Merciful, the Compassionate! This is the security which Umar, the servant of God, the commander of the faithful, grants to the people of Aeilia. He grants to all, whether sick or sound, security for their lives, their possessions, their churches and their crosses, and for all that concerns their religion. Their churches shall not be changed into dwelling places, nor destroyed, neither shall they nor their appurtenances be in any way diminished, nor the crosses of the inhabitants, nor aught of their possessions, nor shall any constraint be put upon them in the matter of their faith, nor shall any one of them be harmed.[4]

This was not a freak piece of history: it is modelled on what the Prophet said and did, in obedience to the Qur'an, the authority for all Muslims at all times.

Another example of Islamic treatment of non-Muslims is the generosity shown by Saladin in 1188, when he repossessed Jerusalem from the Crusaders. In the first campaign (1096), the Crusaders had ransacked the city and slaughtered a great number of Muslims and Jews. One of the Frankish chronicles records that:

They also ordered that all the corpses of the Saracens should be thrown outside the city because of the fearful stench; for almost the whole city was full of their dead bodies. The Saracens who were still alive dragged the dead ones out in front of the gates, and made piles of them, as big as houses. Such a slaughter of pagans no one has ever seen or heard of; the pyres they made were like pyramids.[5]

When Saladin came, he found the Crusaders defiling the mosque by keeping pigs in it. Even European historians concede that he did not retaliate, but forgave the Crusaders, with the exception of a very few individuals who had been more vicious. He accepted ransom money from some of these and let others who could not pay go free.

Again, in 1492, when the last Muslim king of Granada surrendered the city to the Christian King Ferdinand, with a treaty that stipulated that all Muslims in the city should not be harmed, the Christians ignored the treaty and started the infamous Inquisition. Muslims in their own lands did not take revenge on any Christians living there. Moreover, Jews who were forced to flee from Spain came to the Muslims in North Africa and Turkey to continue enjoying the protection they had always received under Muslim rule in Spain.

Islamic tolerance allows non-Muslims to live according to their customs, even if these are forbidden in Islam. Thus Christians are allowed to breed pigs, eat pork, make and drink alcohol in Muslim countries even though such things are forbidden in Islam and it would not be asking Christians too much to refrain from such practices out of respect for Islam. In Egypt, for example, courts administer to non-Muslims laws of their own religious denominations, which are all incorporated into Egyptian law.

Some people in the West quote, as an example of Muslim intolerance, the fact that in the past they called Jews and Christians *dhimmis* (ignoring the real sense of this term which means 'those who enjoy protection') and the fact that Muslims collected *jizya* tribute from them. The jizya was one dinar a year for every able-bodied male who could fight in the army - monks were exempted. As non-Muslims they were not obliged to fight for the Muslim armies. This is a liberal attitude, which recognised that it would be unfair to enlist people who do not believe in Islam to fight for the Muslim state, something which their own religion and conscience might not allow them to do. The jizya was their contribution to the defence of the Islamic state they lived in. Muslims, on the other hand were obliged to serve in the army, and all Muslims had to pay the much higher zakat tax, part of which is spent on defence. When non-Muslims chose to serve in the Muslim army they were exempted from the jizya, and when the Muslim state could not defend certain subjects from whom they had collected jizya, it returned the jizya tax to them giving this as a reason. In return for the jizya non-Muslims also enjoyed state social security.[6]

The Muslims charged Christians one dinar a year and allowed them to live in Muslim society and practise their religion freely; the Christians, in Jerusalem, Spain and other places, did not charge Muslims one dinar a year

– instead they wiped them out.

It is a fact that there have always been Christians and Jews living among the Muslims, some even serving as members of the government at the height of the Islamic state; but no Muslims were left, for example, in Spain, Sicily, and other places from which Christians expelled them, and genocide was still practised in Europe in the twentieth century.[7]

Within the Muslim world itself, people are aware of the magnanimous nature of Islam as expressed by the Prophet, who called it *hanifiyya samha* 'lenient and magnanimous'. There have always been different *madhhabs*, or schools of law, which accept each other, enlightened by the statement attributed to the Prophet: 'Differences of opinion in my community are a mercy'. There is nothing in Islamic history similar to what happened between the Protestants and the Catholics, or the conformists and non-conformists in the West.

Leniency marks Islamic teachings, even in strictly legal matters. In the Qur'an, the door is always open for repentance and making amends for major penal offences like premeditated murder, highway robbery, theft and adultery, as well as in all offences that require punishment in this world and the next. Apostasy has no punishment in this world specified in the Qur'an; the penalty is left to the Day of Judgement:

> But whoever of you recants and dies as an unbeliever his works shall come to nothing in this world and the world to come. Such people shall be the tenants of Hell. 2:217

> If any of you renounce their faith God will replace them with others who love Him and are loved by Him. (5:54)

> Those who return to unbelief after God's guidance has been revealed to them, are seduced by Satan and inspired by him. (47:25)

In the Bible the situation is different:

> If you hear it said about one of the towns the Lord your God is giving you to live in, that wicked men have arisen among you and have led the people of their town astray, saying 'Let us go and worship other gods' (gods you have not known) then you must enquire, probe and investigate it thoroughly. And if it is true and it has been proved that this detestable thing has been done among

you, you must certainly put to the sword all who live in that town. Destroy it completely, both its people and its livestock. Gather all the plunder of the town into the middle of the public square and completely burn the town and all its plunder as a whole burnt offering to the Lord your God. It is to remain a ruin for ever, never to be rebuilt. (Deuteronomy: 13:12-16)

A man or woman who is proved to be worshipping other gods is to be stoned to death to 'purge the evil from among you'.[8]

The death penalty mentioned in the hadith of the Prophet Muhammad was not just for apostasy but for those who commit high treason against the Muslims by joining the enemy at war with them, or who commit other crimes against Muslims. The Qur'an itself tells us that a group of 'People of the Book' schemed to enter Islam at the beginning of the day and renounce it at the end of the day so that the Muslims themselves might abandon Islam (3:72).

The current meaning of tolerance

'Tolerance' now refers to tolerating the views, beliefs and practices of others that differ from one's own. This is dictated by the demands of the spirit of globalisation, pluralism, democracy, campaigns for human rights, non-discrimination laws, freedom of expression, secularisation, and the dwindling influence of religion in the life of the West. In the light of this there has been more emancipation for women, campaigns against discrimination on grounds of ethnicity, class and more recently sexual orientation, as well as for the protection of minorities. This new sense of tolerance is broadening so fast that there are people now, even in the West, who are worried about the extent of the new spirit of tolerance:

The redefined notion of tolerance, on the other hand, doesn't merely ask for a respect of differences but often demands acceptance of the beliefs and practices of others.[9]

Against this background, the Islamic revival, which reasserts the role of religion in the Muslim countries, appears to many people in the West to be intolerant.

Can Islamic teachings be 'tolerant' in this current sense? Can Muslims maintain that Islamic teachings could be reinterpreted to sanction campaigns for sexual freedom, for instance? Can Muslims say that these are matters of personal freedom and religion has no say in them? Such a position, if held by a Muslim, would be untenable. Muslims read in the Qur'an that there are things which God has forbidden and even if individuals cannot live up to

226

that standard, no one has the right to determine as lawful that which God has made unlawful (16:116). Those who deviate from religious norms know they are deviating and know that God forgives those who come back to Him but would not accept from them to claim or campaign for their practices to be accepted as a norm.

Limits to the concept of tolerance
Islamic law does not search into the heart or the private behaviour of any person: the Prophet of Islam even recommended that individuals who deviate from religious norms should keep their sins to themselves and ask God for forgiveness but, as Law, Islam protects social order. Thus it ordains enjoining what is good, and forbidding what is wrong. In fact, no religion can be said to be fully 'tolerant' in this respect, nor can any legal system. In this age of political lobbies and campaigns, Islam would not allow campaigning for the decriminalisation of drugs or practices that fundamentally undermine the family system:

> Those who love to see scandal spread about among the believers will have a grievous penalty in this life and the life Hereafter: God knows, and ye know not. (24:19)

Muslims in non-Muslim countries
In Western society, where religion is increasingly marginalised, Muslims, within their own community, are under the obligation to maintain the Qur'anic injunctions of ordering what is good and forbidding what is wrong, and acting within the general rule, 'Call to the way of your Lord with wisdom and kindly exhortation' (16:125). They are under the obligation not to dilute their religious teachings in keeping with whatever practices or campaigns appear in the society around them. In their relations with others, the guiding principles for Muslims are that 'there is no compulsion in religion' (2:256), 'to you is your religion and to me mine' (109:6) and 'whoever will, let him believe and whosoever will not, let him disbelieve' (18:29). Muslims are under a religious obligation not to force their religion or norms on others and they are forbidden to accept norms of 'tolerance' that undermine their religious teachings, which others may at-tempt to force on them. They are under a religious obligation to co-operate with other people who work to maintain what is good, but not to do what is wrong:

> Aid one another in what is good and pious; do not aid one another in what is sinful and aggression. (5:2)

A draft report presented to the European Parliament in 1997, entitled 'Fundamentalism: a challenge to the European Judicial System'[10] asserted that:

> The model of Western society draws its characteristics from the history of Europe. Some key elements of this are democracy, the rule of law, human rights, separation of church and state. It shows evidence of a great tolerance with regard to ideas, convictions and different modes of life...

Democracy, the rule of law and human rights are all cherished by Muslims. 'The history of Europe' with regard to tolerance has already been discussed. As for respect for human rights, the European country that issued a Declaration of the Rights of Man and the Citizen two centuries ago still denies Muslim girls the right to wear headscarves in school.

If, because of their historical background, some in the West feel that in order to become tolerant, they have to 'separate Church and State', and distance themselves from religion, Muslims do not have to abandon their religious teachings in order to become tolerant: true tolerance is enshrined in the teachings of the Qur'an.

Notes

1. *Encyclopaedia of Religion and Ethics*, 1921, vol. 12, p. 360.
2. *Al-Qamus al-muhit* of al-Fayruzabadi.
3. For example 11:118, 18:29-30, and see any concordance of the Qur'an.
4. Friedman,Y. (trs), *The History of Tabari*, vol. 12, (New York, 1992) pp. 191-2.
5. T. Jones and A. Ereira, *Crusades*, BBC Books, (London, 1994) p. 75.
6. See Y. al-Qaradawi, *Ghayr al. muslimin fi'l-mujtami' al. Islami*, (Cairo, 1977) pp. 35-9.
7. In response to the charge that large numbers of Armenians were massacred by Turkish Muslims during the First World War, it should be noted that this genocide was committed by the secularists who brought about an end to the Islamic Caliphate of the Ottoman Empire, and were thus not acting in the name of Islam.
8. See also 17:2-7.
9. *The Redefining of Tolerance* http://www.ezlink.com/~trbr./toleranc.htm.
10. Document ref: PE 223 423/def. 23 October 1997

Human Rights – Islamic and Secular Perspectives

Azzam Tamimi

The concept of human rights in Islam is rooted in the concept of Divinity. Muslims believe that the human being was created by a transcendental God who favours no human over another except in terms of piety and good conduct. In a bid to defend Islam or to promote it, several contemporary Islamic scholars and thinkers have sought to show that Islam has from the outset laid the foundations for human rights by asserting the supremacy of the value of justice and of the principle of human dignity. Some of the effort made in this regard has been aimed at developing an Islamic, as compared to a secular, discourse on human rights.

Both in the Qur'an and the Sunnah, the value of justice is considered the highest of all values, for it derives from one of God's main attributes, The Just. Hence is the emphasis on 'equity' rather than equality in Islamic thought. This is one of the areas where the Islamic conception of human rights differs from the secular conception. The principle of human dignity derives from the belief that al-insan (the human being) is the vicegerent of God on earth. *Al-insan*, who is honoured and preferred to all other creatures, is expected to lead a life guided by God's law, or the Shari'ah. This is another area where disagreement exists. The word al-insan, in the Islamic terminology, refers to the human being irrespective of gender, colour or race.

Three Qur'anic verses, which are crucial to determining a Muslim's identity, summarise the concept of human dignity:

1. Behold, your Sustaining Lord said to the angels: "I will create a vicegerent on earth." (2: 30)

2. We have honoured the children of Adam; provided them with transport on land and sea; given them for sustenance things good and pure; and conferred on them special favours, above a great part of Our Creation. (17:70)

3. O human beings! We created you from a male and a female, and made you into nations and tribes, that you may know each other. Indeed, the most honoured of you in the sight of God is the most God-conscious of you. (49:13)

In spite of Islam's assertion of the value and dignity of human beings, violations of basic human rights in the Muslim countries are very common. Although repression and persecution go back to the colonial era, more subtle methods have been devised by post-independence regimes in the modern territorial states that inherited power from the colonial authorities.

The Muslim world is one of very few remaining regions in the world where local culture is being systematically eroded through the persistent violation of fundamental human rights. Mosques have been placed under direct government control, freedom of the press is non-existent, opponents are silenced or liquidated, women are punished for choosing to be modest, men are persecuted for choosing to follow the sunnah (way of the Prophet), and prisons host more prisoners of conscience than criminals.

In the absence of the rule of law, and in the courts of military 'justice', thousands have lost their lives without being able to defend themselves or appeal against their convictions. Even in countries where some form of democracy was experimented with, when it became apparent that democratisation did not serve the interests of minority ruling elites, the process was immediately interrupted or even reversed. Though not the only one, the Algerian case may be the best example.

Such a miserable situation has prompted many NGO's to dedicate part of their resources to defending human rights in the Muslim world. Most of these NGO's are foreign. Although local human rights groups are not tolerated, some have managed to establish themselves, but regrettably not without stringent conditions, either in response to pressure from local authorities or from funding institutions. As a result, some of the values promoted, defended and universalised by the Western-led international human rights movement have gained local platforms. Since these values clash with some of the basic principles of Islam, the human rights movement does not enjoy a good reputation among the Muslim masses.

The secularist discourse on Human Rights undermines Islam by negating, in the name of universalism, the right of Muslims to cultural specificity. To prove their respect for human rights, Muslims are told they must board the boat of modernity. The price they are expected to pay for this ride is to re-think their religious convictions or re-interpret their sacred texts so as to conform to international standards and universal values.

It is not surprising, thus, that some Muslims regard the human rights movement as a post-colonial tool of cultural imperialism. Regrettably, such a radical view amounts to a denial of the role played by numerous organisations around the globe in defending human rights and in exposing the violations and the violators. The contribution of the international human rights movement is indispensable and should be greatly appreciated.

What is also greatly appreciated, and should in all fairness be recognised, is that the Western human rights tradition, whose roots are founded in the European Enlightenment, has enhanced both the dignity of the human being and the value of human civilisation. Four major contributions are accredited to this tradition. Firstly, it has endowed the individual with certain basic rights such as the right of free speech, the right of association, the right to a fair trial and so on. Secondly, it has strengthened the position of ordinary citizens against the arbitrariness of power. Thirdly, it has expanded the space and scope of individual participation in public decision-making. And fourthly, it has forced the State and authority in general to be accountable to the public.[1]

However, in spite of the positive contributions, there are serious misgivings. Some of these misgivings relate to the attitude of the West, both past and present, toward the issue of human rights. Historically, the 'human' the Europeans referred to when they spoke of human rights was none but their own citizen; the French human, the English human or the Western human in general.[2]

This probably explains why Europe, which - as a fruit of the renaissance - engaged in the process of building the edifice of the individual within its own borders, destroyed the human person without.

While human rights expanded among 'whites', European empires inflicted horrendous human wrongs upon the coloured inhabitants of the planet. Native populations in the Americas and Australia were eliminated and millions of Africans were enslaved. Millions of humans throughout the world were suppressed. Western colonialism in Asia, Australia, Africa and Latin America represented the most massive systematic violation of human rights ever known in history.[3] Much of this violation involved undermining other people's cultural and religious identities.

Though formal colonial rule has ended, Western domination and control continues to impact upon the human rights of the vast majority of the people of the non-Western world in ways which are more subtle and sophisticated but no less destructive and devastating.[4] On the one hand, the colonial ruling elite has been replaced, in many cases, by Westernised local elites, very often authoritarian and corrupt, who serve their Western masters and help to perpetuate this unequal and unjust relationship.[5] On the other hand the dominant West controls global politics through the United Nations Security Council. If the Western powers so desire, they can get the Security Council to starve a million people to death to force them to submit to their will. The dominant West controls global economics through the IMF, the World Bank, GATT and the G7 or the G8. The dominant West also controls global news and information and it has the powerful means to dictate to the rest of the world styles of life through means such as music, cinema and fashions.

Some misgivings concern the way human rights organisations conduct their business. The overwhelming majority of human rights organisations have a radical secularist vision of the human being and the world. For the secularists, human rights are based on the idea of natural rights. This means that God is left little or no place in human life. While this supposes that nothing sacred remains, in reality the Divine sacred is replaced by a secular sacred.

Inevitably, some of what Muslims may hold to be unquestionable, or immutable, may be considered a violation of human rights. Questions such as the roles of men and women in family life, the Islamic law of inheritance, the Islamic code of penalties and the Islamic code of moral conduct are some of the issues constantly targeted by the secularist human rights movement.

I have, over the past few years, participated in debates over these issues with representatives of international as well as regional human rights organisations. Insisting on the universality of their vision, the secularist human rights defenders refuse to entertain the mere suggestion that a common ground can be reached not by re-interpreting Muslim sacred texts, but rather by revising, re-examining, rethinking or re-writing the Universal Declaration of human rights. After all, this declaration, whose articles I would say are acceptable save for few exceptions, was born out of the global conditions that prevailed in the aftermath of the Second World War. I would like to share with you some of the experiences I have had. For I believe they illustrate the magnitude of the problem.

One of these experiences was in the form of a live TV debate between me and the assistant to the secretary general of Amnesty International. The

Amnesty official insisted that the Universal Declaration was binding upon all and that it was Islam which needed to be re-interpreted in a manner conducive to reconciling it with the declaration. It could clearly be seen throughout the debate that the spokesman for Amnesty found it more outrageous to cast doubt on the universality of the Universal Declaration than to cast doubt on the validity of Divine revelation.

Another experience occurred when I was invited to participate in a symposium organised in Helsinki by yet another American foundation called 'Search for Common Ground'. On the eve of the first session, which was supposed to be exclusively for the Arab participants to discuss the promotion of human rights in the Arab region, delegates were invited to have dinner in a nearby Chinese restaurant. As part of the informal discussion over dinner, a Palestinian secularist colleague of Christian origin expressed the opinion that only secularisation could bring about an improvement to the standard of human rights in the Arab region.

Together with an Islamist colleague from Lebanon, I argued against the secularist thesis and sought to prove that, contrary to the claim made, secularisation has been accompanied by a marked deterioration in the respect for human rights in the Arab region. The discussion shifted to an analysis of international standards and the universal declaration of human rights and as to whether cultural specificity should be taken into consideration.

The following morning as I headed for breakfast, the organiser's secretary whispered into my ear that the organiser wished to speak to me. I waited for her and we had breakfast together. She said that she was told I had a very interesting discussion the previous night. I thought she was impressed. I briefed her on the main points raised in the discussion and reiterated that if common ground is indeed what we are searching for we needed to assert the right to cultural specificity and to question the assumption that the universal declaration of human rights was universal.

She turned to me and said: "Azzam, I don't know how to say this to you, but I would like you not to speak at today's session." She explained to me that my ideas would disrupt the harmony of the series of meetings her institution had held so far. In other words, it was not recommended at this stage to question what had already become an absolute.

I understood from her, and later on from other key persons involved in the organisation of the function, and who were put in charge of steering the discussions, that this forum had a well-defined, previously agreed on, agenda and that it would not be acceptable to throw in new proposals. This experience confirmed my suspicion that the whole project was designed to bolster the peace process in the Middle East through the enforcement of secular notions of human rights.

One of the ways of doing this is to assert universality and deny specificity; to come up with ideas as to how to change the perceptions of people in the Middle East to make Israel more acceptable to them. The assumption was that the values that make Israel unacceptable are those derived from Islam, and for this reason Islam had to be re-questioned.

One of the main objectives of this project was to suggest plans aimed at effecting changes in school curricula. It was suggested for instance that values that are not conducive to respecting the human rights of the Israelis or to the establishment of peace in the region should be removed from teaching curricula. The Islamic value of jihad was a prime target.

Muslim intellectuals have been critical of the position adopted by the Western human rights movement in support of Salman Rushdie and later on in support of Taslima Nasreen. It is not support for Salman against the fatwa, which concerns me. In my assessment, the fatwa was issued for purely political reasons and had benefited the author of Satanic Verses – whom it brought fame and prosperity – more than it benefited Islam and the Muslims.

What is of concern is the support for Salman's, and later on Taslima's, alleged right to free expression without any consideration for the fact that their writings insulted the entire Muslim community that constitutes no less than one fifth of the world's population. While secular human rights activists talk about freedom of expression as a very important civil liberty, they forget that there is also a right to honour and to dignity for whole communities.

It has been suggested that the Western civilisation, by virtue of the way it has developed, seems unable to empathise with the notion of the sacred, which is very important in other societies. What about the rights of the people who consider the sacred and the transcendent important values? Should they not be entitled to be respected? Should not their right to honour be observed?[6] It has also been suggested, as Richard Webster once remarked, that the unconditional Western support for writers Rushdie and Nisreen is not a support for the freedom of thought, but for the European secular tradition of blasphemy.[7]

There is a need today for the establishment of an Islamic human rights movement to defend human rights without compromising Islam. One of the objectives of such a movement would be to introduce Islam's compassionate image to the world through the defence and promotion of human rights. At the same time, the movement would be expected to search for a common ground on which all the defendants of human rights, irrespective of their ideological convictions, may stand. The value of Human Rights is indeed a universal value and the cause of defending these rights is a universal cause.

For both the value and the cause to remain universal and in order to prevent their monopoly by one particular culture, cultural specificity has to be recognised and respected. In fact, cultural specificity is an indispensable feature of universality.

Notes

1. Dr. Chandra Muzaffar, From Human Rights to Human Dignity, p.1,International Conference on Human Rights 6-7 December 1994, Kuala Lumpur, Malaysia.

2. Ibid.

3. Dr. Chandra Muzaffar, see ref. above.

4. Ibid

5. Hj. S. M. Hohd. Idris, International Conference on Human Rights 6-7 December 1994, Kuala Lumpur, Malaysia.

6. Chandra Muzaffar, from a talk at the Islam and Equality Symposium, organised by the Lawyers Committee for Human Rights, London 14-16 October 1997.

7. Richard Webster, Paper entitled: Free Speech, History and the Christian Tradition of Blasphemy, The Collapse of Secularism Symposium, Centre for the Study of Democracy, London, June 10, 1995.

Hope for a Troubled World
A reflection on the Qur'an
ABDULWAHID HAMID

Life with all its fluctuations, necessarily and logically, must have meaning and purpose. Otherwise, nothing makes sense and everything is chaos. The Qur'an is a call to the human being to observe, reflect and ponder on the vast, intricate and steadily expanding universe and our place in it and to realise what this meaning and purpose is. This purpose must be positive and generate optimism, well-founded optimism. It must sustain, enhance and elevate life. It must lead to, and be firmly rooted in, the recognition of the Source of all life.

At the same time, the Qur'an intellectually challenges us to be aware of and to examine all that runs counter to this positive purpose: deficient systems, false ideas and beliefs, and destructive habits and practices. Systems such as corrupted religion involving false worship or earth-bound, dead-end ideologies; false trends and attitudes such as nihilism and arrogance; and destructive habits and behaviour such as hedonism or the reckless pursuit of sensual pleasure.

The Qur'an is not just a challenge. It is a plea to the human being to remain morally responsive to all truth, goodness and beauty and morally alert in avoiding all that is false, unjust, evil, ugly and destructive.

The core of our being is our minds and our hearts. God has given the human being a mind or an intellect and has also provided him with guidance – in various forms – to distinguish between what is true and what is false. When the mind is alert and clear, it recognises truth and goodness for what it is. However, the mind can become muddled and warped or simply enfeebled, not just by the natural processes of ageing, but, for example, by the blind acceptance and following of tradition. When the mind is corrupted, there is no hope of engaging the heart in moral choices. He who has no mind has no true religion.

'Won't you use your minds?' is a frequent plea in the Qur'an to all human beings.

There is the possibility that the mind may remain quite clear. A person may intellectually realise the truth for what it is but negative feelings or narrow self-interest often prevent him from responding with his heart, from identifying with what he knows to be right and sound. Such negative qualities as arrogance and malice, greed and cowardice can so overwhelm the heart that it is unable either to respond positively to truth and goodness or avoid falsehood and evil.

Such a person becomes incapable of making sound moral choices. In the process, he forgets his origin and His Creator and persistently rejects any form of right guidance. He becomes wayward and delinquent. It is only then that God entrenches him in his delinquency and causes him to forget himself. He becomes corrupt and sinks to the depths of depravity (see 59: 19).

There is nothing whimsical or arbitrary on the part of God in this process as some – including academics – hastily conclude after a superficial reading of Qur'anic verses like 'So God causes to go astray whom He wills and He guides whom He wills' (14: 4).

It is important to stress that those whom God 'causes to go astray' are only those who, in the first place, refuse to use their God-given faculties to observe and reflect upon the wondrous signs within their own selves and all around them, signs that are eloquent arguments for the existence and creative power of God. They refuse to listen to and consider the message of truth and wilfully decide to follow their own whims and emotions rather than reason and sound argument. They are not true to or honest with themselves. These are the ones who are led or left to go astray (see 8: 22-23 and 10: 99-101). Only those who show a willingness to follow the path of truth and goodness can be guided aright: right-doing then becomes easy and natural for them.

It is the human being who first deviates and then only when he persists in sin and wrong-doing and consciously rejects the ultimate good that the path of deviance becomes easy and indeed attractive for him. This is what is meant by the statement that God 'facilitates for him the way to hardship' (92: 10).

Even so, God's grace and mercy – the Qur'an tells us – is so great that He always holds out, barring desperate pleas at the point of death, the possibility of the acceptance of true repentance and of redemption.

God says: 'O My servants who have wasted their lives against their own self-interest, do not ever despair of God's grace and mercy' (39: 53) and

'My grace and mercy extends over every thing' (7: 156).

Such comforting and reassuring words from the Creator and Sustainer of all is like life-giving rain to a barren, lifeless human heart, even one that has been buried in heedlessness, or hardened by conscious, flagrant rebellion against God and what is right. We can retreat from the brink of self-destruction and turn back to what is pure and wholesome ways of thinking and living.

> Is it not time
> for those who (still) have faith
> that their hearts should be humble
> at the remembrance of God
> and all the truth that has been revealed,
> and that they should not be
> like those to whom the scriptures were given before
> and their hearts became hardened with the passage of time
> so that many of them are now depraved?
> Know that God gives life to the earth after it has been dead.
> We have indeed made Our messages clear to you
> that you may use your minds.
> (Surah al-Hadiid, 57: 16-17)

The first critical fact: the Source of all creation

The Qur'an is a sustained argument establishing the critical fact, to begin with, that human beings and all creation owe their existence to a Creator who must be One and who is, above all, good and gracious in the extreme.

An indication of this is that every surah or chapter of the Qur'an (except the ninth which is said to be a continuation of the eighth) begins with the beautiful, elevating and sustaining words – *Bismillaahi-r Rahmaani-r Rahiim* – In the name of God, the Most Gracious, the Ever Merciful. God not only creates, owns and governs but He provides for, guides and sustains all that exists in a manner that befits each entity.

So far as human beings are concerned, God provides for our physical well-being as well as our psychological balance and moral direction. Over and over again, the Qur'an insists that it is natural and logical for the human being to acknowledge, and then place faith and trust in, the One Creator and Sustainer of all. Such faith is not a blind faith. It is based on knowledge and awareness. Those who bizarrely deny the existence of God are asked:

238

'Were they created out of nothing?
Or were they their own creators?
Or have they created the heavens and the earth?'
(Surah at-Tuur, 52: 35-36)

Three rapid-fire questions. And the crystal clear manner in which they are put leaves us in no doubt, each time, about the inescapable response.

Since it is inconceivable for something that has a beginning in time to come out of, or be made by, nothing at all – by 'some spontaneous generation' as it were, and since it is also inconceivable that it should bring itself into being, then the only conclusion is that it must have a creator outside itself.

It is inconceivable then that there could be more than One Creator, or that there could be associates or partners with this One God. A sentence of four short Arabic words expresses this succinctly and powerfully: *Laa ilaaha illa Allah* – no god but the One God. There is absolutely no-one or nothing that is worthy of worship or adoration but the One Creator of everything. *Ilaahukum ilaahun waahid* - Your God is One God (2: 163). True worship is to express – in thought, word and deed – our overwhelming sense of gratitude and thanks to our Creator and Sustainer; it is to order and live our lives in obedience to and in harmony with His laws and thus to seek His pleasure.

False worship
All created beings and things – heavenly bodies, people, prophets, so-called saints, idols and other images fashioned by their own hands – that people have taken as gods and objects of worship are nothing more than parts of God's creation. To worship them is an insult to the human mind and 'a terrible injustice' to God – *zulmun 'aziim* is the Qur'anic phrase (31: 13). Worship, it should be said, does not necessarily involve bowing down before another. Worship also involves following a particular life-style, or adopting laws and codes of behaviour that others have set for you, or indeed that you have set for yourself. When we follow such life-styles or adopt codes of behaviour that conflict with the natural and just laws of God, we are in effect worshipping them instead of God.

A liberating force
To realise that there can only be and that there is only One God liberates the human mind from all sorts of superstition and possible manipulation and exploitation by others. God does not need human worship but it is the

human being who stands in need of his Sustainer and needs to show gratitude to Him.

A conscious and rational belief in the Creator and an awareness of the creature-status of human beings will liberate a person from negative and noxious feelings and character traits such as selfishness and arrogance, assumptions of total self-sufficiency on the one hand, or vain hopes, despair and frustration on the other. More importantly, it will generate positive qualities like optimism, strength and determination, humility and a befitting concern for the welfare of others. A man-centred universe can be and is a dangerous and terrible place. This is true even or especially when some people justify their subjugation of others 'in the name of God' and in the exercise of the so-called 'Divine right of kings and rulers', for example. A truly God-centred universe, however, where every being functions as it was meant to, holds no perils. The message of *laa ilaaha illa Allah* – nothing deserves to be worshipped but God – diverts people's preoccupations and lives from greed and other vices, crime and transgression to the pursuit of virtue and God-consciousness wherin lies true beauty.

God has honoured and blessed human beings in so many ways including the bestowal of the power of reason to observe, study, ponder, analyse and come to conclusions about what is true and what is false, what is beneficial and harmful to us and others in creation. He has placed the resources of the earth, the seas and the heavens at our disposal, as a trust or *amaanah*. Such a trust requires that we should be questioned about whether and how we discharged it.

The second critical fact: the Hereafter
The other major critical 'fact' or aspect of Reality which the Qur'an then constantly seeks to impress on the human mind is the logical necessity for believing in the existence of a life beyond this life. The world we live in cannot be the only world, where everything comes to an end with our death. If this were so, life would be terribly unjust and unfair. It would be inescapably cruel.

'I can accept the idea of a God,' said a devoted reader of the existentialist writer Albert Camus, 'but I see no necessity to believe in the existence of anything beyond this world. I see no need to believe in a hereafter or the idea of judgement and reward and punishment associated with it.'

He was not of course saying anything new or profound. Such has been the careless utterances of morally myopic human beings since ages past.

We really need to appreciate that there must be an important part of

Reality beyond our life in this world. And we need to keep this whole, larger picture constantly in focus if we are to make any sense of life on earth and if indeed we are to lead truly fulfilling, happy and successful lives, in tune with what we were meant to be.

For the one who ungratefully rejects his Creator and Sustainer and does not have the liberating belief in the life hereafter, his is a life that clings heavily and stultifyingly to the earth. It is a narrow and ultimately fruitless life – like a stunted and uprooted tree in contrast to a flourishing tree that is firmly rooted with its branches yielding fruit and reaching up to the heavens (see 14: 24-26).

A belief in the Hereafter, it should be patently obvious, is an essential corollary to the belief in God who is all-Knowing and absolutely Wise, Merciful, and Just. The belief in the Hereafter recognizes the inescapable need for judgement and just recompense – in the need for reward for good done and especially for punishment of crime and injustices committed on this earth whether secretly or openly.

The alternative would be to accept the notion that God is totally callous and oblivious to injustice, oppression and all sorts of tyranny. 'Where is God or where was God?' ask some survivors of gruesome genocide, sometimes out of incomprehension and ignorance, or even disgust and anger. If there is a just and merciful God, why does He not intervene to stop cold-blooded and indiscriminate slaughter, pillage and devastation, mutilation and rape?

Freedom and responsibility

The answer to such questions lies not in the nature of God. It lies in the fact that human beings have been blessed with intellects and a moral sense. They have been provided with an inbuilt knowledge of what is naturally right and what is wrong. And, they have been given choice and freedom, the freedom to do what is right – what they ought to do, as well as the freedom to do what they want to do, which can be and often is far, far removed from what is right and just. With this freedom comes responsibility and accountability for their actions and intentions. Crucially, actions will be judged only according to intentions.

We have the choice and the capacity to do what is right and good, or to commit wrong and evil; and human history continues to show that we can do so on a grotesque scale and with chilling premeditation. We also have the choice to resist and combat evil or allow it to spread by being 'neutral' and doing nothing. Nor can we dissimulate and make out that we are doing good and setting things right when in fact we know that we are committing or compounding injustice and corruption of all kinds. Nor should we sink to such levels that the evil we do and the injustice we perpetrate to satisfy our greed and lust for excitement or domination actually and perversely seem fair and beautiful in our eyes (35: 8).

Clearly, for example, it is not enough to be free and brave with no moral direction or constraints; it is more important to be morally alert, and scrupulously fair and just, even if it is against our own selves (see 4: 135) and even if we are dealing with people whom we dislike (see 5: 8). Each one of us bears the responsibility for the choices we make.

The killing of innocents – by any individual or group whoever they may be or whatever religion they may profess, terrorist outrages and such terrible and indiscriminate slaughter that we continue to witness in many parts of the world, whether it is done by alleged 'precision' bombing or carpet bombing, or with the use of other weapons of mass destruction like the imposition of poverty, should further strengthen our belief in the necessity of a hereafter, of judgement, and of just recompense. It is often the case that the real instigators of such devastation and slaughter sit comfortably in lands far away counting their profits from arms sales or assessing their worldly economic, political or strategic gains for their tribal nations, their power blocs or their corporations. Such motives cannot be laid completely bare by conducting interviews or delving into archives. Journalism and the study of history have their uses but they also have their limits. And too often they are diverted from the scent by what the Qur'an calls 'the hiding and suppression or the dressing up of truth with falsehood'. Such motives will ultimately be exposed by the awesome knowledge of God who knows 'every leaf that falls' and 'the innermost secrets hidden in the breasts of human beings'. Unfailing justice is bound to follow if there is any real meaning and purpose in life.

> 'Whoever does an atom's weight of good shall see it then (on the day of Judgement) and whoever does an atom's weight of evil shall see it then' (99: 7-8).

Chilling words. A promise and a threat from the One who has given us freedom.

It is inconceivable that life in this world could carry on and end as it is, with all sorts of criminals and vicious people - either on their own or as parts of groups and governments and coalitions - committing mayhem and destabilization, exploitation and injustice and wholesale genocide and that they would be allowed not only to continue enjoying the fruits of their

242

crimes and sins but to escape judgement and go unpunished.

There are other reasons why we need to maintain a focus on the bigger picture of Reality as a whole, especially on the judgement and just recompense to come.

A *spur to righteous action*

Such a necessary and logical focus on the life Hereafter provides a spur to righteous action in this world. Contend with one another in the doing of good deeds, to get 'forgiveness from your Sustainer and a Paradise the vastness of which is as the vastness of the heavens and the earth' (57: 21), urges the Qur'an. It is full of God's promises to reward those who remain conscious of Him and who strive with their human and material resources to do good and fill the world with goodness. The Qur'anic verse defining what is not and what is righteousness (2: 177) shows the link between true faith in God and the Hereafter, attending to a range of active social concerns, and demonstrating remarkable human qualities like endurance in the face of adversity.

The belief in the life Hereafter is not just pie in the sky but has enormous, immediate and positive impact on life on earth. It is not only a spur to correct action. The inevitability of the day of Judgement also acts as a warning to people as individuals to keep away from crime and sin, however small, however secretly done. It is the most potent instrument – more potent than any man-made laws and regulations – for reducing vice, self-inflicted harm, crime and suffering in this world and bringing about positive social reform.

As an indication of how this works in practice, A'ishah, the wife of Prophet Muhammad, peace be on him, said that the Prophet did not start (to bring about moral and social transformation) by telling people not to drink wine or not to commit fornication and adultery. Instead, he started by telling them about God and the Hereafter (the reality of the eternal life, the bliss of Paradise and the pain and humiliation of Hell) until they had firm belief in them. It is only then that he told them not to consume intoxicants or commit adultery and they happily and unconditionally obeyed him. And, significantly, she added: 'Had he started by telling them not to drink wine or not to commit adultery, they would have said, 'We will never abandon them.'

People not only have the obligation to do good or themselves keep away from obnoxious and destructive acts. They also have the obligation to promote what is right and discourage what is wrong in society and to be mentally, physically and materially prepared for this.

'Corruption does appear on land and sea because of what the hands of human beings have wrought,' says the Qur'an (30: 41). 'And, if God had not enabled people to defend themselves against one another corruption would surely overwhelm the earth' (2: 251).

'Do people think that they will be left alone if they say we believe and they will not be tested?' (29: 2)

'Not equal are those among the believers – other than those who have a disability – who sit idly by and those who struggle for good against evil, in the path of God' (4: 95).

Solace and comfort

The logical belief in the Hereafter provides solace and comfort to victims of crime and injustice with the assurance that absolute justice in the end will be done. Moreover, the certainty of the judgement to come promises the ultimate vindication for those who remain steadfast and stand up for what is right in the face of all types of corruption and tyranny.

Belief in the absolute wisdom and power of God should also provide strong emotional and psychological support to people in times of acute sorrow and distress. When earthquakes, floods and hurricanes strike and there is destruction and death, there should be no question of blaming God whose sole prerogative it is to give and take life. These occurrences may be taken as reminders – albeit awesome reminders – to people to constantly take stock of their lives and their balance of good deeds in this world before the inevitable Day of Accounting. When calamities such as these strike, believers respond with the words of the Qur'an: *Innaa lilaahi wa innaa ilayhi raaji'uun* – To God indeed we belong and to Him indeed we shall all return (2: 156).

There is also incomprehension and anger at times when innocent children die young of natural causes. An attorney-general of the state of Oregon said at the death of his twenty-year old daughter: 'It's an occasion of deep anger that this thing should be visited upon our child. If there is a God, why should this happen?' He forbade the name of God to be mentioned in a memorial service for her. What desolation! While it is natural to weep and be saddened at the passing away of a loved one, it is fitting to remember that eternal life on earth is not an option for anyone. All the children of the Prophet Muhammad, except one, died before him, three males as infants and three as young married ladies. And he wept publicly. He did not forsake God and the rest of humanity, and God did not forsake him.

Life-death-life: one continuum

Our fleeting moments of life on this earth must be spent in preparation for the inevitable and eternal afterlife. Salvation in the life Hereafter is only through sincere faith in God and good works in this life and this is constantly stressed in the Qur'an. Sincere faith comes from 'a sound heart', one that is transparent, without rust, purified from pride, ostentation and hypocrisy, and responsive to and humble before God.

This life is our only chance to work for a good life and avoid humiliation in the next world, And there should be an urgency about it (see 63: 10-11). We need to realise that good deeds here are good for the individual, the society, humanity, all living things, the environment as a whole, and our long-term future. The Prophet Muhammad famously said: 'If the hour comes while one of you is holding a palm shoot, if he can plant it before the hour overtakes him, he should plant it. And he shall have a reward for that.'

One might have expected the noble Prophet to have said that when the hour or the cataclysmic end of this world comes, at such a time of panic and terror, people should leave whatever they are doing and hasten to seek forgiveness and God's help. Instead, he emphasised the doing and completion of a good deed in this world, and thus showed the inseparability of faith, true worship and good works and the seamless transition from this world to the next. One leads inevitably to the other and the quality of life in the other is solely dependent on our sincere faith and good works here.

Life after death – necessary, desirable and possible

The Qur'an shows that the existence of life after death and the reality of judgement and just recompense is not only desirable and necessary but that it is also possible and indeed easy for the One who has created everything 'in the first instance'. In response to the skeptical questioning of short-sighted human beings, 'After we will have become bones and dust, shall we be raised from the dead as a new creation?' – the Qur'an answers: 'Are they not aware that God who has created the heavens and the earth, has the power to create them anew in their own likeness?' (17: 98-99). And to a similar question, 'Who will give life to bones that have crumbled into dust?' – the Qur'an answers: 'He will give life to them Who brought them into being in the first instance' (36: 79).

> 'For (in the life to come) all shall have their degrees, according to whatever (good or evil) they did, and so, He will repay them

in full for their doings and they shall not be wronged.'

The Hereafter is real; it is no figment of human imagination. The reality of the Hereafter compels an awareness of our long-term future and the need to work for it, with others, here on earth. In the Hereafter, we will have no opportunity to change anything, to offer a new performance, to repent or seek forgiveness for our failings. The only opportunity for that is here and now, in this life, which is given only once – for the Qur'an does not speak, for example, of cycles of rebirths and deaths.

This one life, then, is the only life where we can work and earn and sow those seeds that will bear fruit 'in the end'. And we need constantly to take stock of ourselves, to judge ourselves before we face the final judgement. 'Judge yourelves before you are judged,' is advice from the noble Prophet that we ignore at our peril.

The third critical fact: God's guidance

i. Original goodness and natural guidance
To enable him or her to respond positively to what is true and good and beautiful and to react with unease and rejection to all that is false, evil and morally ugly, God has created the human being in a naturally good state that is free from sin. This state in the Qur'an is called the *fitrah*.

There is thus no such thing as original sin and no person bears the sinful burden of another. The human heart or conscience is part of this natural state which, kept clean and pure and burnished by the constant remembrance of God, acts as a sort of moral weather vane. It provides orientation and minutely registers what it does and what it does not feel comfortable with. But dangerously, the human being has been given choice and the capacity to corrupt this original good state. The Qur'an says:

> 'Consider the human self and the One Who has fashioned it
> (in accordance with what it was meant to be).
> And He inspired it both with the capacity to corrupt itself
> and to grow in God-consciousness.
> Successful is the one who keeps it pure,
> and ruined is the one who corrupts it' (91: 7-10).

A person's conscience or heart is thus an inbuilt source of guidance. In defining virtue and sin, the noble Prophet said that 'virtue is that which your soul and heart feel satisfied about. Sin is that which troubles the soul and about which the heart is uneasy and confused, even though people may give their legal opinions in its favour'. A person's conscience or heart can lose its sensitivity when he becomes so steeped in sin that he no longer responds to truth and goodness.

More than that, persons in this morally torpid state even bizarrely seek to portray truth and goodness as warped, self-righteous prattle on the part of those who are concerned about decency and morality and people's long-term fate.

In addition to intellect, therefore, God has given us a moral conscience that makes us recognise good as good and evil as evil, and a will to pursue either. But this is not all.

ii. Guidance through Prophets and Messengers

In addition to the sensitive conscience or the pure heart with which every person is blessed at birth, God in His grace has – especially in times of moral crisis, gross ignorance and rebellion – sent chosen individuals to remind people of their origins and their purpose in life and to reorient them to their naturally good and God-conscious selves. These messengers were bringers of good news for all those who responded positively to truth and goodness and worked hard to make them flourish. They were also warners to all those who persisted in falsehood and evil, misled others and caused corruption on earth, reminding them that ultimate and just recompense – including Divine wrath and punishment for deliberate and persistent wrong-doing – is inescapable.

These chosen individuals are called prophets or messengers of God. They lived exemplary lives and nothing immoral, obscene or unjust can be attributed to them.

The true Prophets of God did not require people to believe in anything outrageous nor did they ask for or expect any reward or favours. Many of them may have performed extraordinary acts called miracles but they never claimed any credit for these themselves. And while these miracles would have provided evidence of support from God, Prophets as the Qur'anic accounts show appealed to people's reason, to their consciences and their better judgement in calling them to acknowledge and worship their Creator alone, to lead the good life and shun all evil.

The messages or revelations from God to the chosen Prophets were themselves events in the category of the extraordinary but they are consistent with the abundant and continuous manifestations of the grace and mercy of God. The role of these messengers and prophets is a third major theme of the Qur'an together with the belief in the One God and the certainty of the Hereafter.

The message of these guides or prophets was essentially the same – to call people to acknowledge and submit to the knowledge, wisdom and justice of the One Creator of all being – for their own good. The message varied only on points of emphasis, such as the need to highlight honesty in economic dealings in one society, or the need to call for gentleness, kindness and justice in the face of oppression and tyranny in another, the need to shun sexual perversion in one, or the need to abandon idolatry and false worship in others.

Some of messengers of God were also blessed with revelations that were preserved in writing and known as Divine scriptures. Among these were the Tawrah, the Zabuur (Psalms), the Injiil (Gospel) and the Qur'an. The ones before the Qur'an have either been lost or have not survived in their original form. Some have been tampered with in ways that make it impossible to get a clear, consistent or credible picture of the nature of God, the status and role of the prophets and the true nature of reality. Only the Qur'an has survived exactly as it was revealed. Muhammad was the last messenger and the Qur'an, revealed to him over a period of twenty three years from 610 to 632 CE, is the final Divine scripture.

One of the purposes of the Qur'an in fact is to set the record of Divine revelation straight. It confirms the residual truth of earlier revelations, restores the good name of the Prophets and gives us a consistent view of Reality as a whole.

The Prophet Muhammad, known as the Truthful and the Trustworthy, a person of impeccable honesty and integrity – even before his call to prophethood – was sent to perfect the light of God's guidance for the benefit of all people, for all time to come. This last revelation – the Qur'an – has been preserved intact both in the hearts and minds of people and in writing. If all the copies of the Qur'an were to be destroyed, there are thousands of people who today will be able to reproduce it exactly as it was revealed in the early seventh century CE.

Muhammad and the Qur'an

The Qur'an was not from but through Muhammad. He is described as having been sent 'as a mercy to all beings'. His life-example and the Message he brought are not limited to any tribe, ethnic or racial group, geographical place or time. He is also described as 'a beautiful example for whoever hopes for God and the Last Day, and remembers God unceasingly' (33: 21). His character mirrored the teachings of the Qur'an..

While the Qur'an is the message of God, Muhammad exemplified this

248

message in practice. Islam is both a message and a method. The example of the Prophet Muhammad is crucial as having shown in a very detailed and practical way how God's message was and can be and should be implemented in the world. 'If you love God, then follow me. God will then love you,' the Prophet is instructed in the Qur'an (3: 31) to say to all people.

Engaging with the Qur'an

True belief or faith is based on knowledge, sound evidence and proofs, and on honest reflection and contemplation. It is not based on miracles and the mysterious. It is not based on obscurantism and dogmatism. We do not of course know or understand everything and do not automatically dismiss whatever appears out of the ordinary. 'Of knowledge you have been given little,' says God in the Qur'an (17: 85) addressing the human being.

Even so, what we often regard as ordinary and take for granted is full of wonderment and awe. The breath you take, the word you speak, a smile, a gentle touch, your wondrous eyes – these are all precious gifts that we often take for granted as being ordinary and commonplace, but they actually belong – as do the processes of thinking, reflection and contemplation – to the category of the miraculous.

> 'Have We not made for the human being
> two eyes, a tongue and two lips
> and showed him the two ways (of right and of wrong)?' (90: 8-10)

True belief acts as a powerful light dispelling all darkness which is a metaphor for disbelief, doubt and despair. Light is really guidance from God illuminating the path of righteousness.

Human happiness and success

The Qur'an is concerned pre-eminently with human happiness and success. It provides reasons for thinking and acting rightly. It does not simply command people to shun evil. It sets out the results and consequences of actions. Everything that it forbids is forbidden because it is harmful or dangerous for the individual human being, for the rest of society or for other creation.

Over and over again, the Qur'an admonishes people for putting their faith and trust in silly ideas, in accepting notions and practices uncritically. It uses historical data and recalls the fate of individuals and communities that considered themselves secure and self-sufficient without any need for moral guidance.

249

The Qur'an is for people who think, and act sensibly. It constantly puts direct and searching questions to the human being:

> Why do you worship idols and false gods, when you know that they are useless and can neither harm you nor help you in any way?
>
> Why do you continue to believe in what is false and deny God's favours? Why do you dress up the truth with empty falsehood?
>
> Have We not given you two eyes, a tongue and two lips? What would you, or what could you do without these tiny organs?
>
> Are you the biggest thing or the greatest thing in creation? What are you in relation to the vastness of the entire universe, a universe that We are steadily expanding and will ultimately cause to disintegrate in a mighty cataclysm?
>
> Can you create life? How does life come about? Do you know the future? What's going to happen to you tomorrow?
>
> Do you think about the water you drink? Is it you who send it down from the rain clouds? Won't you give thanks?
>
> What will you do if your sources of water – indispensable for life itself disappear? Do you not realise that you were created from a single drop? Why do you cling heavily to the earth? Are you content with the comforts of this life in preference to the life to come?

The Qur'an pleads with people to come to their senses and to give up their delusions for much of the life of this world is but 'an enjoyment of delusion' (57: 20). We are more than ever preoccupied with things and images, with fantasy and virtual reality and with ever changing fashions and fads. In our pre-occupation with these, we fail to see the whole picture, and miss out on the real show in which we must use our talents and resources for improving ourselves and adding value to the world about us.

The Qur'an sets valid and satisfying goals for us to pursue and is the only certain way to human success. It puts everything in its proper place. Confusion and alienation, tyranny and injustice – to others and to our own selves – occur only when things are not located in their proper place.

(Extracted from *Burnishing the Heart* to be published, God willing, in Autumn 2002.)

From the Farewell Sermon of the Noble Prophet

❝ All praise and gratitude is for God. We praise Him. We seek His help and forgiveness and we turn to Him in repentance. We take refuge with God from the evils of ourselves and the bad consequences of our actions. There is none to lead him astray whom God guides aright and there is none to guide him aright whom He misguides. I bear witness that there is none worthy of worship but God alone - no partner has He. I bear witness that Muhammad is His servant and His messenger.

I admonish you, servants of God, to be conscious of God and I urge you to obey Him.."

O people, indeed your lives, your properties and your honour are sacred and inviolable to you till you appear before your Lord, like the sacredness of this day of yours, in this month of yours, in this city of yours. You will certainly meet your Lord and He will ask you about your actions. Have I conveyed the message? O Lord, be witness!

So he who has any trust to discharge, he should restore it to the person who deposited it with him.

Be aware, no one committing a crime is responsible for it but himself. Neither is a son responsible for the crime of his father nor is a father responsible for the crime of his son.
O people, listen to my words and understand them...

Verily, I have left among you something clear which if you hold fast to, you will never go astray after that - the Book of God (the Qur'an) and the Example (Sunnah) of His messenger...

O people, verily your Lord and Sustainer is One and your ancestor is one. All of you descend from Adam and Adam was made of earth. There is no superiority for an Arab over a non-Arab nor for a non-Arab over an Arab; neither for a white man over a black man nor a black man over a white man except the superiority gained through God-consciousness. Indeed the noblest among you is the one who is most deeply conscious of God..."

(From the Farewell Sermon of the noble Prophet, delivered in Arafat and Mina in the month of Dhu-l Hijjah, 10 AH/630 CE.)

Beyond blindness

KAAMILEH HAMID

His metal walker clattered slightly as he let go, reaching out one hand at a time for the reclining chair behind him. He sat down with a thud, unable to lower himself with control, his body spreading as liquid, moulding to the chair. His prosthetic leg stood out crookedly, a healthy tanned colour against the pallor of this wrinkled white flesh. I straightened it and placed some pillows behind Mr. Neuville.

After laying a towel across his upper body, I began to cut and arrange his dinner. Mashed potatoes 12 o'clock. Cubed roast beef 6 o'clock. Peas 3 o'clock. Mr. Neuville, you must understand, was legally blind.

For all his physical ailments, however, he was totally cognitive. He told me tales of his youth, of how his career as an engineer was fruitful, where he had worked and with whom. He related long stories of his wife, children, and grandchildren with pride between bites of food which I either fed or directed him to using the layout of a clock as a guideline.

His television was fixed to a news channel all day long. We would listen and discuss the hot topics of the day as they were broadcast.

"So, where are you from?" says he.
"By nationality, Sir?"
"That's right"
"I'm British." I reply – it was the easier answer.
"Ahh, I could tell from your accent."
"Oh really? I think I'm losing it."

It was common enough banter which I engaged in with many of my patients.

"Ahh no, I can pick up on it. What side are you from?"
"London, Sir."
"I'm very familiar with London. My wife and I used to visit there frequently – to watch the shows only – nothing more. This was before I had lost my sight of course, and my wife has passed now."
"I'm sorry to hear that...."

A brief pause.

"Yeah, she loved the theatre."
"Which shows have you watched?"
"She loved The Phantom of the Opera...and the one on skates... what was that again? Ummm..."
"Starlight Express?"
"Yeah, that's the one – I didn't really like it."
"I've..."

The blaring television spliced through our banal conversation with a 'new' headline. We listened momentarily about the updates on 'The War on Terror'. Mr. Neuville decided instead to continue our own conversation.

"Yeah, we travelled frequently, my wife and I."
"Where would you say is the place you love best?"
"Oh, I'm not sure but one area we never went to was China. I've always wanted to see that place."
"China? Ah! Me too. China and Africa – Tunisia and Morocco and Sudan. I would love to go to those places."
"I'm not sure about that." Mr. Neuville replied.
"How so? I've heard they're really beautiful."
"They may be beautiful – but the people? Yeah, I would check with your embassy first. You can never been too careful."
"I'm not sure what you mean exactly." I had an idea and my heart sank, hoping that my idea would be farthest from the truth.

"Well, these Moslems. Very violent they are. I would think twice about going. They might make you wear those things on your head. They might attack you."

254

"Muslims?"

"Yeah, very uncivilised they are." He drawled.

Continuing – "No class at all. I had a neighbour who was
one of them. Palestinian. Very crude man." Mr. Neuville spoke
as he gouged some beef bristle out of his teeth and wiped it on the
table before him. "Very crude. He would butcher his own chickens."

"Well, someone has to do it." Says I.

"Yeah well, not in his backyard. Not in the suburbs."

I wondered what the difference was between the country and the suburbs.
Perhaps it was the just the 'out of sight, out of mind' scenario. It wasn't as if
he was a vegetarian.

"Very uncivilised." He repeated.

The television cut through again… "Differentiating between mainstream
Moslems and those who committed the acts of September 11th….is like
differentiating between borderline Nazis and fully fledged Nazis…."

Disgusted, I blurted out "How can someone make such a comparison?"

Mr. Neuville evidently hadn't heard the statement and so I paraphrased for
him. He considered it momentarily. "Yeah, that's right. It's true."

"Oh really? To me, there are people this world over who are good, and
people who are bad. Regardless of race or religion, regardless of your
beliefs, there will always be people who are supposedly part of your group
but do not adhere to the same standards as you do. To me, this whole
situation is just as that of the Ku Klux Klan. They're violent. They perform
acts which they justify according to Christianity but people don't generalise
and say that all Christians are peace loving. Why? Because it just isn't true.
Why make such a sweeping statement about Muslims then? There are over
one billion Muslims in this world. If all were religiously obliged to be
violent, well then where would this world be?"

Irritation started to peek through in my voice. "A person can't generalise, it
just doesn't work."

Mr. Neuville slumped forward, chewed noisily on his cherry pie and said, "I
guess you're right."

I lifted the spoon to his lips once more and wondered if he thought me a savage. It seemed not – he spoke to me as 'an equal'.

Would he have said all this if his sight had not been taken away? Would he have said this if my blurred face was sharply focused in his view? I looked at my dark brown skin and adjusted my headscarf, my hijab.

I may be British born and raised. I may have a London accent but those things were merely given to me through circumstance.

I am a Muslim born and raised. Now as an adult I choose to be Muslim.

I stood there looking down at him and felt a deep sadness as I remembered his words and insinuations – 'uncivilised, uncouth, and violent'. Appearances can be deceiving, so the saying goes. I suppose that is true, even if you can't see a person.

Some recommended books

ISLAM

Abdul Wahid Hamid, *Islam the Natural Way*, MELS, London & Miami
Recognised as a standard, contemporary introduction. It provides an understanding of the main concerns of Islam and the foundations on which it is built.

THE QUR'AN
GENERAL INTRODUCTIONS

Muhammad Abdel Haleem, *Understanding the Qur'an – Themes & Styles*, I B Tauris, London & New York
A refreshing and in many respects unique contribution to Qur'anic studies in English. The book has a good general introduction to the Qur'an and includes chapters on life and eternity, marriage and divorce, peace and war, water and nourishment. It also deals with misinterpretation of the Qur'an perpetuated by recent scholars among others.

Fazlur Rahman, *Major Themes of the Qur'an*, Kazi Publications, Chicago
This is a ground-breaking work in English in using thematic studies to achieve an in-depth understanding of what the Qur'an says on specific topics. Themes treated are God, Prophethood and Revelation, Man as an individual and Man in society.

Khurram Murad, *Way to the Qur'an*, Islamic Foundation, Leicester
Suggests ways in which the Qur'an may be studied for self-development. By an author whose life reflected the beauty of its message.

TRANSLATIONS AND COMMENTARIES

Readers will benefit from comparing available translations and commentaries especially to clarify verses requiring elaboration.

Arthur J Arberry, *The Koran*, Oxford University Press
An elegant, though closely literal, translation of the Qur'an which attempts to convey – apart from the message itself – some of 'the sublime rhetoric of the original'.

Muhammad Asad, *The Message of the Qur'an*, Dar al-Andalus, Gibraltar
This is a work of monumental scholarship with copious and well-researched notes and commentary that also relate the message of the Qur'an to the contemporary world. The dedicated reader will feel amply rewarded, and challenged, by close study and scrutiny of this translation and commentary.

Abdullah Yusuf Ali. *The Holy Qur'an*, Text, Translation, and Commentary
A work of impressive scholarship and one of the most widely used translations of the Qur'an. An inexpensive edition of the translated text only is published by Wordsworth Classics of World Literature, Ware, Herts.

SIRAH OR BIOGRAPHY OF THE PROPHET

Abdur Rahman Azzam, *The Eternal Message of Muhammad*, Islamic Texts Society, Cambridge, UK

Zakaria Bashier, *The Makkan Crucible*, Islamic Foundation, Leicester

Akram Diya al Umari, *Madinan Society at the Time of the Prophet*, Vol. 1, IIIT, Herndon, USA

Martin Lings, *Muhammad - his life based on the earliest sources*, second revised edition, Islamic Texts Society, Cambridge, UK.

Tahia al-Ismail, *The Life of the Prophet Muhammad*. Taha Publishers, London

HADITH

Fatima M D'Oyen and Abdelkader Chachi, *In the Prophet's Garden*, Islamic Foundation, Leicester
A thematically arranged anthology of sayings of the noble Prophet.

Ahmad von Denffer, *A Day with the Prophet*, Islamic Foundation, Leicester
Sayings and practices of the noble Prophet on various aspects of daily living.

MUSLIM CULTURE AND CIVILIZATION

Ismail R al-Faruqi and Lois Lamya al-Faruqi, *The Cultural Atlas of Islam*, Macmillan.

For the convenience of readers, the contact details of publishers are given below:

The Islamic Foundation, Ratby Lane, Markfield, Leicester LE67 9SY. Tel: 01530 244944 Email: i.foundation@islamic-foundation.org.uk

The Islamic Texts Society, 22a Brooklands Avenue, Cambridge, CB2 2DQ Tel: 01223 314 387 Email: mail@its.org.uk

MELS, 61 Alexandra Road, London NW4 2RX. Tel: 020 8202 1799 Email: mels@webstar.co.uk

Taha Publishers, 1 Wynne Road, London SW9 0BD. Tel: 020 7737 7266 Email: sales@taha.co.uk

Notes on contributors
(in order of appearance in the text)

Iqbal Sacranie is an accountant and currently serves as secretary general of The Muslim Council of Britain.

AbdulWahid Hamid, an editor of this book, is a writer and publisher.

Kaamileh Hamid is studying, and working as a nurse in Chicago.

Natasha Rafi is a freelance journalist in the US who writes for The Friday Times, Lahore.

Sarah Joseph is a writer and lecturer and is doing doctoral research on British Muslims.

Inayat Bunglawala is secretary of the MCB's Media Committee.

Brian Whitaker is Middle East editor of *The Guardian* and manages the non-commercial web site www.al-bab.com for better understanding of the Arab world.

Mohammed Elmasry, professor of engineering at the University of Waterloo, is national president of the Canadian Islamic Congress.

Mahmud Al Rashid is a barrister. He has served as deputy secretary general of The Muslim Council of Britain and is a founding member of the Association of Muslim Lawyers.

Lorraine Sheridan, Ph.D, is a lecturer in psychology at the University of Leicester.

Khurshid Ahmad is the founder and chairman of the Institute of Policy Studies, Islamabad and The Islamic Foundation, Leicester. He has served as a member of the Senate of Pakistan from 1985 to 1997.

Chandra Muzaffar is president, International Movement for a Just World, Malaysia and professor, Centre for Civilisational Dialogue, Universiti Malaya, Kuala Lumpur.

Tariq Modood is professor of sociology, politics and public policy and director of the University Research Centre for the Study of Ethnicity and Citizenship at the University of Bristol.

Jeremy Henzell-Thomas is chair of the Board of FAIR - Forum Against Islamophobia and Racism, and executive director of curriculum development for The Book Foundation.

Fakhry Davids is a member of the British Psychoanalytical Society and the Tavistock Society of Psychotherapists.

Daud Abdullah is senior researcher at the Palestinian Return Centre and editor of its Return Review. He is a regular contributor to The Palestine Times.

259

Christopher Allen is co-author with Dr Jorgen Nielson of the recent EUMC document on Islamophobia. He is a research office at FAIR.

Zahra Williams is a media officer at The Muslim Council of Britain.

Professor Ali A. Mazrui is the director, Institute of Global Cultural Studies and professor in the humanities at the State University of New York at Binghamton.

Tavis Adibuddeen is a library media specialist in Illinois and a member of The Muslim Writers Society.

Tokunbo Ojo is a sports writer from Montreal, Canada.

Jamil Sherif, an editor of this book, is secretary of the MCB's Research and Documentation Committee.

M Abdul Bari is the deputy secretary general of The Muslim Council of Britain. He is an educationalist and writer on social issues.

Mrs Wahida Valiante is a family counsellor and national vice president of The Canadian Islamic Congress.

Shiban Akbar is a writer and lecturer at the University of Oxford. She is chair of the MCB's Social Affairs Committee.

Kauser Ahmed is a solicitor. She is the education liaison officer of the Mosque and Cultural Centre, Exeter.

Zakaria Bashier is vice chancellor of the University of Juba in Sudan. He is a writer on Muslim history, philosophy and politics.

Muhammad Abdel Haleem is professor of Islamic Studies at the School of Oriental & African Studies (SOAS), University of London, and director of its Centre of Islamic Studies.

Azzam Tamimi is director of the London-based Institute of Islamic Political Thought.

THE MUSLIM COUNCIL OF BRITAIN

The Muslim Council of Britain (MCB) is an inclusive body that represents the interests of all Muslims in Britain and is pledged to work for the common good of society as a whole. It was founded in November 1997.

The MCB is a body that is made up of major national, regional and local organisations and institutions. It includes mosques, education and charitable bodies, cultural and professional bodies, relief agencies and women and youth groups. It encompasses the diverse range of linguistic and geographical cultures that make up the mosaic of the British Muslim community. It also thrives on the special skills, talents and resources of individuals throughout the country.

The MCB is a body that has been built on consultation, co-operation and co-ordination among Muslim institutions and concerned Muslims throughout Britain over a long period of time. In the few years since its inception, it has achieved much at many levels of society and government for the benefit of the Muslim community at a critical time in its development. It has done so through the grace of God and the goodwill, the enthusiasm and the voluntary work of many.

The MCB seeks to meet the growing needs and expectations of the Muslim community. These are in such areas as: policy research and strategic planning, the needs of youth and families, identifying major social problems and campaigning, upgrading facilities in the community, encouraging participation in local and national affairs, the media, and outreach to the wider society.

The MCB has a structure that makes for full participation and accountability. It functions through the work of several committees. (For a list of affiliates, committees, contacts and other MCB information, visit the MCB website - http://www.mcb.org.uk.)